SHARED FOUNDATIONS

Include

SHARED FOUNDATIONS SERIES

I. **INQUIRE,** by Lori Donovan

II. **INCLUDE,** by Julie Stivers

III. **COLLABORATE,** by Mary Catherine Coleman

IV. **CURATE,** by Len Bryan and Daniella Smith

V. **EXPLORE,** by Sarah Culp Searles

VI. **ENGAGE,** by Kathryn Roots Lewis and Marcia Mardis

SHARED FOUNDATIONS

Include

JULIE STIVERS

ALA Editions

CHICAGO | 2022

AASL American Association of School Librarians
TRANSFORMING LEARNING

ISBNs
978-0-8389-1917-0 (paper)
978-0-8389-9400-9 (PDF)
978-0-8389-9646-1 (ePub)

Library of Congress Cataloging-in-Publication Data

Names: Stivers, Julie, author.
Title: Include / Julie Stivers.
Description: Chicago : ALA Editions, 2022. | Series: Shared foundations series ; II | I ncludes bibliographical references and index. | Summary: "Part of the Shared Foundations series, this book examines effective implementation of the Shared Foundation Include from AASL's National School Library Standards"—Provided by publisher.
Identifiers: LCCN 2020053394 | ISBN 9780838919170 (paperback) | ISBN 9780838994009 (pdf) | ISBN 9780838996461 (epub)
Subjects: LCSH: School libraries—Aims and objectives—United States. | School librarian participation in curriculum planning—United States. | Libraries and schools—United States. | Libraries and minorities—United States.
Classification: LCC Z675.S3 S79 2021 | DDC 027.8—dc23
LC record available at https://lccn.loc.gov/2020053394

∞ This paper meets the requirements of ANSI/NISO Z39.48-1992 (Permanence of Paper).

Printed in the United States of America

26 25 24 23 22 5 4 3 2

Purchases of AASL publications and products fund advocacy, leadership, professional development, and standards initiatives for school librarians nationally.

ALA Editions purchases fund advocacy, awareness, and accreditation programs for library professionals worldwide.

SHARED FOUNDATION II

Include

KEY COMMITMENT

Demonstrate an understanding of and commitment to inclusiveness and respect for diversity in the learning community.

Contents

Acknowledgments

Thank you to the powerful, incredible, and generous librarians, scholars, and learners who contributed their expertise, experiences, and ideas to this Include guide.

- Rachel Altobelli
- Allie Jane Bruce
- Anita Celluci
- Kathryn Cole
- Cesar Falcon
- Jose Gomez
- Kimberly Hirsch
- Sandra Hughes-Hassell
- Cicely Lewis
- Jaida Morris
- Liz Porter
- Casey Rawson
- Debbie Reese
- Juan Rivera
- Ness Shortley
- Jennifer Sturge
- Julia E. Torres
- Chiquita Toure

Series Introduction

The Shared Foundations series from the American Association of School Librarians (AASL) examines the six Shared Foundations that anchor the comprehensive approach to teaching and learning in the *National School Library Standards for Learners, School Librarians, and School Libraries*. The Shared Foundations—Inquire, Include, Collaborate, Curate, Explore, and Engage—represent the core concepts that all learners, school librarians, and school libraries develop and promote in their K–12 learning environment.

Each of the six books in this series is dedicated to the deep exploration of a single Shared Foundation. Although each of the Shared Foundations supports its own inherent priorities, it cannot be implemented in isolation. The writing process used by the authors created a series of books that, like the AASL Standards Frameworks, are unique and yet parallel each other. Common elements are found throughout the series:

- A balance between theoretical discussion, practical strategies, and implementation examples, promoting reflection and creativity
- Development of the Competencies and Alignments for the Learner, School Librarian, and School Library in all four Domains—Think, Create, Share, and Grow
- Differences in application and assessment across grades K–12, promoting a growth mindset and envisioning outcomes for all learners, whether student learners, school librarians, or other educators
- An emphasis on personalized learning experiences, project-based learning, and authenticity of learning and projects
- Challenges addressed, illustrating ways to implement the Shared Foundations in various environments and levels of support

Questions for the Reflective Practitioner conclude each chapter, allowing readers to consider the application of concepts specific to their own learning communities and stimulate nuanced professional conversations. For ease of reference, readers also will find the AASL Standards Integrated Framework for the relevant Shared Foundation included in this work.

AASL and its series authors hope that this immersive and dedicated examination of the Shared Foundations will help school library professionals deepen their understandings, broaden their perspectives, make connections for personal relevance, and innovate and reflect on their practice with a professional community.

For more information about the *National School Library Standards,* and to access the latest implementation assistance resources, visit standards.aasl.org.

SHARED FOUNDATION II.

Include

Domain	LEARNER DOMAINS AND COMPETENCIES	SCHOOL LIBRARIAN DOMAINS AND COMPETENCIES
A. Think	**Learners contribute a balanced perspective when participating in a learning community by:** 1. Articulating an awareness of the contributions of a range of learners. 2. Adopting a discerning stance toward points of view and opinions expressed in information resources and learning products. 3. Describing their understanding of cultural relevancy and placement within the global learning community.	**School librarians direct learners to contribute a balanced perspective when participating in a learning community by:** 1. Engaging learners to articulate an awareness of the contributions of a range of learners. 2. Guiding learners as they adopt a discerning stance toward points of view and opinions expressed in information resources and learning products. 3. Differentiating instruction to support learners' understanding of cultural relevancy and placement within the global learning community.
B. Create	**Learners adjust their awareness of the global learning community by:** 1. Interacting with learners who reflect a range of perspectives. 2. Evaluating a variety of perspectives during learning activities. 3. Representing diverse perspectives during learning activities.	**School librarians establish opportunities for learners to adjust their awareness of the global learning community by:** 1. Providing opportunities for learners to interact with others who reflect a range of perspectives. 2. Devising learning activities that require learners to evaluate a variety of perspectives. 3. Designing opportunities that help learners to illustrate diverse viewpoints.
C. Share	**Learners exhibit empathy with and tolerance for diverse ideas by:** 1. Engaging in informed conversation and active debate. 2. Contributing to discussions in which multiple viewpoints on a topic are expressed.	**School librarians facilitate experiences in which learners exhibit empathy and tolerance for diverse ideas by:** 1. Giving learners opportunities to engage in informed conversation and active debate. 2. Guiding learners to contribute to discussions in which multiple viewpoints on a topic are expressed.
D. Grow	**Learners demonstrate empathy and equity in knowledge building within the global learning community by:** 1. Seeking interactions with a range of learners. 2. Demonstrating interest in other perspectives during learning activities. 3. Reflecting on their own place within the global learning community.	**School librarians explicitly lead learners to demonstrate empathy and equity in knowledge building within the global learning community by:** 1. Creating an atmosphere in which learners feel empowered and interactions are learner-initiated. 2. Initiating opportunities that allow learners to demonstrate interest in other perspectives. 3. Showcasing learners' reflections on their place within the global learning community.

KEY COMMITMENT

Demonstrate an understanding of and commitment to inclusiveness and respect for diversity in the learning community.

SCHOOL LIBRARY DOMAINS AND ALIGNMENTS — The school library facilitates the Key Commitment to and Competencies of INCLUDE	Domain
The school library supports balanced perspectives through resources and learning opportunities by: 1. Providing challenging and authentic opportunities that address the needs of the broad range of learners. 2. Offering diverse learning experiences that allow for individual differences in learners. 3. Providing a comprehensive variety of resources.	**A. Think**
The school library represents all members and their place in a global learning community by: 1. Establishing and maintaining a collection of reading and information materials in formats that support the diverse developmental, cultural, social, and linguistic needs of the range of learners and their communities. 2. Organizing facilities to enhance the use of and ensure equitable access to information resources and services for all learners. 3. Featuring learning opportunities that include diverse viewpoints.	**B. Create**
The school library facilitates opportunities to experience diverse ideas by: 1. Implementing solutions that address physical, social, cultural, linguistic, and intellectual barriers to equitable access to resources and services. 2. Promoting the use of high-quality and high-interest literature in formats that reflect the diverse developmental, cultural, social, and linguistic needs of all learners and their communities. 3. Constructing a learning environment that fosters the sharing of a wide range of viewpoints and ideas.	**C. Share**
The school library builds empathy and equity within the global learning community by: 1. Ensuring that all learning needs are met through access to information and ideas located in a diverse collection of sufficient size for the learner population and supported by reliable hardware and software. 2. Enabling equitable access to learning opportunities, academic and social support, and other resources necessary for learners' success. 3. Clearly and frequently articulating the school library's impact when communicating with administration, faculty, staff, learners, parents, and the community.	**D. Grow**

Introduction: School Libraries as Driving Force for Equity and Inclusion

The Shared Foundation Include is at the heart of an effective school library practice. Not as a buzzword or feel-good mantra, but as the driving force—the muscle—that builds an inclusive school space and community. Its Key Commitment—"Demonstrate an understanding of and commitment to inclusiveness and respect for diversity in the learning community"—further supports the idea of Include as a muscle powering the *National School Library Standards* and the AASL Standards Frameworks in our school libraries. School librarians can be bastions of equity, inclusion, and access because we are uniquely situated to interact with every learner. Decisions school librarians make or do not make—by default—have tremendous impact on our learners, their families, our colleagues, and our communities.

What Are the Goals for This Guide?

My goal every time I read a professional book is—simply put—to learn and become better for our learners. Thus, the overarching goal for this book is that we all become better and do better so that we can create anti-racist, inclusive spaces. To work toward that goal, this guide will

Show how the Include standards live in real school libraries. The programs, initiatives, activities, and lessons you'll read about in this guide are not exercises in theory. They are *real*. They've been born in actual school libraries with actual learners and highlight Competencies and Alignments from the Include framework.

Showcase a tapestry of school librarian voices. A strength of this book is that it is not written by one person. Instead, it's a chorus of school librarian stories that represent a range of identities across the school library world. This tapestry of librarian expertise and experience benefits us for the very reasons that the Include Shared Foundation is so crucial for our school libraries and learners.

Serve as both inspiration and roadmap. Do I want these chapters to inspire readers to meet the Competencies and Alignments of Include by building inclusive school libraries and practices? Of course. Inspiration is meaningless, however, if it only lives in the pages of a guide. Inspiration translates to action when it partners with a roadmap. Each chapter concludes with action steps and takeaway ideas.

Help us relearn. To have a "commitment to inclusiveness and respect for diversity in the learning community" (AASL 2018, 76) is to commit to unlearning false narratives that are rooted in ignorance and bias. Our continued learning of anti-racist, anti-sexist, anti-cishet supremacy ideologies must be based in our learners' humanity. We'll name white supremacy, institutionalized racism, and school inequities as we unpack ways in which to build inclusive school libraries that align with the AASL Standards.

Call out barriers. We cannot celebrate diversity and ignore the barriers—yes, in our own schools and libraries—that are harming our learners. To truly Include, we have to undo systems that disadvantage and exclude some learners. If we don't, we're reinforcing those systems—there is no neutral. The AASL Standards Framework for Include will help!

Stress an asset-driven perspective. A key thread running through all the Competencies and Alignments under Include is that diverse learner identities are strengths and assets that advance learning for all of us, not challenges to overcome or address.

Amplify learner voice. One of the guide's chapters is co-written by three eighth graders, and learner ideas, work, experiences, and wisdom are embedded throughout this guide. To truly Include means to include our learners at every stage of our school library practice and to make sure that we remember to provide our learners with the microphone!

What Myths Stand in the Way?

Two dangerous myths can poison Include. As school librarians, we need to expose and push back against these myths.

Myth 1. Include is the self-affirming foundation—the foundation that allows us to pat ourselves on the back in a spirit of "multiculturalism." Although this may be an access point, just stressing diversity or multiculturalism is not enough to build an inclusive practice. After all, we cannot talk about how to

Include if we do not also identify who historically has been—and continues to be—excluded from school spaces and school libraries. To commit ourselves to *include* means committing ourselves to identifying—and disrupting—who is being *excluded* and in what ways. Meeting the Competencies and Alignments of Include with fidelity will help us quell this myth.

Myth 2. Include can be driven primarily through curation. Are the Shared Foundations of Curate and Include natural partners? Of course. Yet Include also works beautifully with—and is a necessary partner to—Inquire, Collaborate, Explore, and Engage. Curating an inclusive collection is just one facet of Include. Dropping diverse books onto a school library shelf without any accompanying work is hollow and harmful. Meaningfully meeting the wide range of AASL Standards Competencies and Alignments under Include will expose this myth as false.

What Will We Discover Along the Way?

I'm in the arena with you.[1] I am a full-time, working middle school librarian who completely understands the joys and challenges that come with our positions. I want this guide to be casual, as though we are sitting down together at a table—all of us bringing experiences and perspectives and sharing ideas. That's not to say this guide is not research-based, equity-framed, and guided by our AASL Standards Framework. It is. But a stiff, dry book is not what I enjoy reading, and it's not what I can share with you in good conscience. I'm aiming for relaxed, professional, inspiring, conversational, engaging, and challenging—with our precious learners always at the forefront as we journey through the AASL Standards Frameworks and the Include Shared Foundation.

As we explore the **Think** Domain, we'll meet a school library district supervisor who is rewriting the school library curriculum to align with the Learning for Justice Social Justice Standards. We'll spend time with #ReadWoke (a powerful librarian-led reading initiative) and meet three learners who worked with their school librarian to create professional development centered on building inclusive school libraries.

Through the **Create** Domain, we'll learn from a school librarian who is developing engaging literacy programs, be introduced to an equitable writer-in-residence model, and journey with a school librarian who reopened a closed school library and reestablished a reading culture in her school.

The **Share** Domain will guide us as we explore restorative practices in a school library setting, gain strategies from a school librarian who developed a mental wellness curriculum, and discuss how to build LGBTQ+-inclusive school libraries.

Using the **Grow** Domain, we'll hear from sixth graders who critically examined book covers, unpack a new anti-racist professional curriculum for youth librarians, and see how a summer library program transformed a school into a community space.

The Domains, Competencies, and Alignments under Include do not work in isolation and neither do school librarians. We'll explore **Across Include** and discuss how to build inclusive spaces for our disabled learners and their families, see how the four Domains can be combined with an inquiry framework to include comic books and manga, learn about Critical Indigenous Literacies, and examine an equitable model for school book fairs.

How to Use This Guide

The chapters in this guide are structured to parallel the Domains of the AASL Standards Frameworks and are presented within four parts—"Learner Competencies," "School Librarian Competencies," "School Library Alignments," and "Across Include." Each section will introduce not only the accompanying chapters but also ways in which the Competencies and Alignments are the key ingredients for the Include Shared Foundation.

Common elements are found in each chapter:

- An introduction explains how the program or initiative that anchors the chapter aligns with the Shared Foundation Include—either Competencies or Alignments—under the specific Domain.
- A school library program or model is presented by the librarian or librarians who lived it. These accounts have been written by an array of school librarians and school library professors doing powerful work with learners, families, and fellow librarians. I'm humbled by the amazing school librarians—and student learners—who contributed to this guide.
- A wrap-up details the ways in which the powerful work illuminated in the chapter connects to specific Competencies and Alignments under Include.
- "Questions for the Reflective Practitioner" connect to the *National School Library Standards,* the Include Shared Foundation, and the chapter's specific school library program or initiative.
- A "Moving Forward" section details action steps and takeaway ideas for each chapter. The school libraries and programs this guide will introduce are *big*. They represent incredible work and effort on the part of school librarians. But they are doable! To not overwhelm, I break down each chapter into quick yet meaningful steps that can be taken today—"What Can I Do Today?"—and tomorrow—"How Can I Build on It Tomorrow?" Then "Action Steps" are listed to scaffold suggestions for implementing the programs and ideas from the chapter.

Additionally, this guide incorporates a "Conclusion" connecting Include across and through the other five Shared Foundations in the *National School Library Standards*. Finally, a key element of Include is utilizing and leveraging resources from an inclusive array of scholars, authors, and educational partners. Appendix A provides an annotated bibliography of foundational scholars and resources for Include. I wanted this guide to be written by—and for—real, working school librarians. School librarians are unique in the library world and in the education world, and a strength of this guide is that its content is written by us, about us, and for us. It is, of course, also important for school librarians to access learning from across the education and library worlds, and Appendix A is crucial for continuing this learning. Scholars highlighted include Dr. Gloria Ladson-Billings, Dr. Beverly Tatum, and Dr. Edith Campbell as well as classroom educators Tricia Ebarvia and Cornelius Minor. Resources spotlighted include

- *Muslims in Story: Expanding Multicultural Understanding through Children's and Young Adult Literature* (Manglik and Siddique 2019),
- *LGBTQAI+ Books for Children and Teens: Providing a Window for All* (Dorr and Deskins 2018),
- *Cultivating Genius: An Equity Framework for Culturally and Historically Responsive Literacy* (Muhammad 2020), and
- *An Indigenous Peoples' History of the United States for Young People* (Dunbar-Ortiz, Mendoza, and Reese 2019).

Key Terms

We are almost ready to get started! An inclusive conversation helps everyone get on the same page. There are key terms that will be woven into our discussions unpacking the Competencies and Alignments under Include, and it's necessary that we have a shared understanding of what those terms mean.

BIPOC/BIYOC. BIPOC stands for Black, Indigenous, People of Color, and BIYOC stands for Black, Indigenous, Youth of Color. The umbrella term *people of color* has been criticized for erasing the unique experiences that Black and Indigenous people in the United States have had historically and that still impact their present realities—namely, the ongoing legacy of slavery that continues to impact Black Americans, and the legacy of Native colonization and genocide. Black Americans who have recently immigrated to the United States have a different relationship with our country's racial history, and the term *BIPOC* acknowledges the diversity of experience within the Black community. (*Note:* This definition is from Project READY, which is highlighted in chapter 8, "Grow with Project READY.")

#OwnVoices. This term refers to books written by authors who share a marginalized identity with their protagonist. Originated by Young Adult (YA) author and *Disability in Kidlit* reviewer Corinne Duyvis, the hashtag and concept center marginalized voices from across identities including race, language, LGBTQ+, mental health, disability, religion, and immigration status. #OwnVoices titles have another layer of credibility as being a part of a community gives the author knowledge and experiences that cannot be duplicated. The foregrounding of #OwnVoices literature is threaded throughout this guide as a way to build inclusive collections, support learners, and meet key Include Competencies. Please note that centering #OwnVoices literature is not a call for prying into authors' lives but is instead a way to celebrate what authors have freely shared. There is growing disagreement surrounding the use of the #OwnVoices marker. It is *always* best to use the identity descriptions that authors use for themselves and their characters.

Racism. Racism equals social and institutional power plus racial prejudice (Tatum 2017; Wellman 1977): racism = power + prejudice. There is a harmful idea that racism is driven by a small group of individuals who actively and loudly hate. Racism is bigger than individuals. It is about systems of advantage and oppression based on race and is widespread, deeply entrenched, and insidious in societal institutions—including education. Racism will not be eradicated by individuals treating each other with respect but by identifying structural inequities and disrupting systems.

Getting Started!

The AASL Standards remind us that "competence is not developed as an all-or-nothing phenomenon; gaining competence is both progressive and personalizable" (AASL 2018, 125). My hope is that this guide shares that sentiment—it represents learning through the Include Shared Foundation that is both progressive and personalizable. It is not all-or-nothing. We can all grow by learning about and through these Include-centered programs, initiatives, and frameworks.

I am ready to get started. You? The Shared Foundation of Include—and our learners—are waiting for us.

NOTE

1. Brené Brown has a great quote about this concept! See B. Brown, "Why Your Critics Aren't the Ones Who Count" (keynote presentation at 99U Conference, 2013). Retrieved from https://99u.adobe.com/videos/20052/brene-brown-stop-focusing-on-your-critics.

PART I

Learner Competencies

A climate of intentional, innovative, and engaging learning. This idea—pulled directly from the *National School Library Standards* in a description of the goal for meeting school librarian Competencies (AASL 2018, 43)—is a knockout description of what can make school libraries so powerful for learners. It's also an accurate representation of the school libraries and programs you'll read about in this section.

Intentional. Strong school libraries that nurture and challenge all learners—including ourselves and our colleagues—do not happen by accident. They are intentionally built with a youth-centered framework. Learner Competencies that demonstrate a respect for diverse perspectives, empathy and equity in knowledge building, and an understanding of cultural relevancy are possible only through the intentionality of the school librarian.

Innovative. It is necessary for school librarians to understand the inequities that are a toxic reality in our schools, most significantly for Black, Indigenous, Youth of Color (BIYOC), learners with disabilities, and English learners (those learning English as a new language). Instead of thinking in terms of achievement gaps, it is more accurate to identify opportunity gaps and our educational debt. Dr. Gloria Ladson-Billings identified *education debt* as encapsulating the historical, economic, and sociopolitical inequities that have accumulated over time (Ladson-Billings 2006). To disrupt these inequities, school librarians must access innovative teaching methods that align with culturally sustaining pedagogies.

Engagement. Engagement is often the key that can unlock learning in our schools. True engagement is built by honoring and amplifying learner voice and leveraging learners' interests to create collections, instruction, and spaces where learners feel valued and seen. Effectively meeting learner Competencies requires a school library curriculum that is welcoming *and* engaging.

There is another necessary characteristic of school libraries that are successful in helping learners meet Competencies: the school librarians themselves are constantly learning. Effective school librarians seek opportunities to learn, especially from the learners in their schools. Our learners have lived experiences that in many contexts make them more knowledgeable than we are—we become the learners and our learners, the teachers. Additionally, strong school librarians learn through professional development and guidance—the chapters in part I all feature school librarians who access additional learning to build strong school libraries.

The chapters in this section are guided by and structured according to the four Domains under the Shared Foundation Include—Think, Create, Share, and Grow. We'll **Think** with a Maryland library and digital learning supervisor who is using the Social Justice Standards from Teaching Tolerance (now Learning for Justice) to rewrite her district's library curriculum. By **Creating** a spoken word program and learner literary magazine, an Ohio school librarian shows how creative writing experiences can build literacy capacity in learners. A North Carolina school librarian shows how integrating restorative practices into a school library can foster inclusion and allow for meaningful **Sharing** among learners. A New York school librarian offers insights about how she worked with sixth graders to **Grow** a discussion-based curriculum on social issues through the lens of book covers.

1

Think with the Learning for Justice Social Justice Standards

A **key tenet of the Think Domain is the gaining of knowledge.** This principle is especially critical for us as school librarians—as learners—because we are uniquely, and often solely, situated in educational contexts with their own sets of structures, standards, and pedagogical practices. This position adds challenging layers to our school library practice but also opens us to a world of scholars and thinking in the K–12 environment.

To align with Include and be able to guide and engage our learners, we must intentionally prioritize learning from equity-focused educators and organizations. Learners are called to "contribute a balanced perspective when participating in a learning community by describing their understanding of cultural relevancy" (AASL 2018, Learner II.A.3.). The ability to direct learners in this way requires us to build capacity in our own learning about cultural relevancy and culturally sustaining pedagogy.

For support in this learning, school librarians can look to Learning for Justice, a project of the Southern Poverty Law Center, which provides educators with free, innovative resources that are framed in social justice and antibias principles. Learning for Justice resources can help put the learner Competencies under the Think Domain into action.

Jennifer Sturge, a teacher specialist for school libraries and digital learning for Calvert County (Maryland) Public Schools, worked with school librarians in her district to build an inclusive school library curriculum that realizes Competencies under Include by leveraging the powerful resources from Learning for Justice.

Integrating Social Justice Standards into a Library Curriculum

Jennifer Sturge

School librarians are collaborators. We work with other educators across content areas and with many different perspectives and experiences. In addition to living our library practice through the AASL Standards, it is only natural that we would collaborate with other sets of educational standards.

Social Justice Standards: The Teaching Tolerance Anti-Bias Framework was developed by Learning for Justice (formerly Teaching Tolerance) with the intent that it be integrated with all subject areas. The standards are anchored by four domains—identity, diversity, justice, and action—and learners of any age can enter the standards at a level that is developmentally appropriate. These standards provide a common language and an organizational structure that can assist with building curriculum and provide educators with a powerful tool to encourage antibias education, ensuring that all learners feel welcome and supported in a school community.

The Shared Foundation of Include is a natural partner to these Social Justice Standards. Our school district, Calvert County Public Schools, integrated the standards from Learning for Justice into our K–12 school library curriculum through an intentional process. Although this is a story about curriculum, it is also a story about change. This has been a journey that is continuing to unfold. As I share our experiences, I'll detail how we utilized a growth mindset to understand why we were undertaking this task, the process that we took, and the trajectory we are hoping to be on for the future.

Finding the Why

As I was planning how to kick off the 2017–18 school year with our first face-to-face professional development for school librarians in our district, I was struggling to define the direction in which I felt our school libraries should go.

Earlier in the summer, I had attended a professional development event with the Lilead Project at Old Dominion University. I had the opportunity to develop my "why" as part of participating in the fellowship and was thinking about how powerful it was to self-discover the reasons that I believe in strong school libraries. After wrestling with my why for quite a long time, I finalized what—for me—is my reason to go to work each day:

> To make personal connections so that all students can experience an excellent school library program in order to explore, learn, and ignite their passion for learning.

How does my why translate to the Include Shared Foundation? Embedded in my why is the importance of making personal connections, exploring, and having a passion for learning. Every learner deserves a space to be included, seen, and heard. The Include Key Commitment is clear: "Demonstrate an understanding of and commitment to inclusiveness and respect for diversity in the learning community" (AASL 2018, 76).

As the district specialist for school libraries, I work with many different departments within our district. Sandy Walker, the supervisor of equity and diversity for our district, and I had offices next to each other during his first year. As colleagues often do, we were chatting one day about diversity and equity and I happened to mention that I wanted to take a deep dive into our collection development process, our curriculum, and who we are as school librarians. It was clear that we needed to look at the learners we served with an eye that would allow us to include every member of the school community in the school library. A partnership was formed.

Sandy participated in our first school librarian professional development day and led participants through a series of exercises to assist them with crafting their "why." It was a day full of honest conversations about ourselves, our backgrounds, and our motivations. I curated the school librarians' why statements into a word cloud to guide us, and it's clearly centered on our learners—filled with words like *believe, create, joy, love,* and *stories.*

At our next district professional development session that fall, we returned as a group and unpacked who our school library community encompassed—we went beyond the obvious groups in our schools such as grade level and thought about who our learners really were.

Only after thinking deeply about our learners did we move to concentrating on our collection habits. What is it we like to purchase? What do we shy away from? Why? (Figure 1.1 shows the tool we used to frame these reflections and discussions.) Are we self-censoring at an unconscious level or even at a conscious level? At the conclusion of our second day of professional development, each school librarian was challenged to come to our next meeting with a new title or resource, or both, that was outside their normal collection development routine. We wanted all our school librarians to purchase more titles that reflected their learners who were not currently well represented in the collection.

Over our next several meetings, each of us continued to revisit our why and share our strides in more reflective collection development. When the *National School Library Standards for Learners, School Librarians, and School Libraries* were released at the AASL National Conference in November 2017, I was among the many who were excited to see what changes to our framework would be in store. The new standards did not disappoint. I was giddy to see the Shared Foundation of Include in the finished product. It was clear that this Shared Foundation directly related to the work our district was doing in our collection development processes.

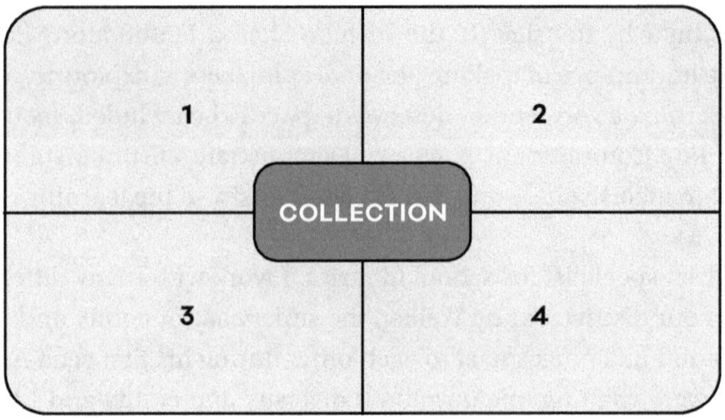

Box 1 (individual): Think about how you develop your collection for your library. How do you put your collection together? What do you look for in books as you are building your collection? What do you gravitate to? What do you stay away from?

Box 2 (group): Who are you students? Jot down who the students are in your building. Don't just think grade level, go deeper.

Box 3 (group): Thinking about the students and the demographics you listed, what do you think these students would want in a book collection? What types of books would these groups of students be interested in?

Box 4 (individual): Go back to thinking about your library collection. What types of books might be missing from your collection? List three types of books that you may not have in your collection. What plan will you put in place to be sure you order some this year?

FIGURE 1.1 **The collection reflection tool**

As I was thinking about incorporating the AASL Standards, my equity colleague Sandy popped into my office one day and asked whether I wanted to go to a Learning for Justice workshop in Philadelphia. I had been reading the *Teaching Tolerance* magazine for years and using the website as well, but this would be something new.

Remember when I said that this initiative was a journey? The Learning for Justice workshop in Philadelphia began critical learning for me. It was humbling and empowering at the same time. What I learned about the Social Justice Standards intrigued me. What I learned about bias, especially our unconscious bias, scared me, yet empowered me to return home stronger. I felt ready to move forward with creating spaces, lessons, and curriculum that would truly *Include*. It was time to move beyond looking only at collection development. It was time to start revising, rebuilding, and rethinking our curriculum.

Taking Action

The AASL Standards Frameworks and the Social Justice Standards challenge us to identify and embrace the concepts of inclusion and diversity. The school library is the largest classroom in the school. What better place than the school library to ensure that everyone feels—and is—welcome?

I knew that our school librarians could fully realize the Include Shared Foundation by digging into the Social Justice Standards. Learning for Justice developed these standards—grouped in the four domains of identity, diversity, justice, and action—to be integrated into any subject area. Grade-level outcomes and scenarios enable educators to guide learners through the Social Justice Standards at a level appropriate to their learning at that age. The common language and organizational structure provided by those standards assist educators with collaboratively building curriculum and provide a powerful tool to incorporate antibias frameworks. In our district we realized that in order to fully accomplish the ideals behind the AASL Standards and the Shared Foundation of Include, we needed to rewrite our curriculum—and that the Social Justice Standards could be our guide.

After applying on the Learning for Justice website, I was awarded grant funding to write curriculum for grades K–12. I am profoundly grateful to the Southern Poverty Law Center for making this undertaking possible. The funding enabled me to provide substitute teachers, thereby allowing a group of school librarians to work with me to revise our curriculum during the school year and the summer.

With a team of school librarians dedicated to issues of inclusion and social justice, we moved forward. We decided to develop four overarching ideas found in our curriculum in grades K–12:

- Creation and Design
- Media, Information Literacy, and Digital Citizenship
- Inquiry, Exploration, and Research
- Reading, Literature, and Community

Writing Curriculum

We started writing curriculum with our elementary school librarians for grades K–5. Because we wanted to use the Learning for Justice resources to fully realize the AASL Standards, we felt the best place to begin would be the overarching area of Reading, Literature, and Community. Throughout our curriculum building, we continually reflected on our whys to ground our work.

> The school library is the perfect place to help students develop pride and confidence. The "Include" Shared Foundation and the Teaching Tolerance Social Justice Standards are important to me as a librarian because they promote

diversity and they challenge my students to examine the perspectives of all people. (Lauren Lynn, school librarian, Huntingtown Elementary School)

Our work in the Reading, Literature, and Community curriculum for grades K–5 is displayed in table 1.1. Our starting point was the Key Commitment for Include, complemented by the Key Commitment for Explore. From there, we created an essential question and identified the Anchor Standards from the Social Justice Standards that illuminated these Key Commitments and met the needs of our school library curriculum. The "students will" statements that make up the domains of the Social Justice Standards represented our learning outcomes.

TABLE 1.1 / **K–5 curriculum: Reading, Literature, and Community**

Essential Question: How do we build a respectful, kind, and caring school library community?
National School Library Standards: Shared Foundations and Key Commitments (AASL 2018) • **II. Include:** Learners will demonstrate an understanding of and commitment to inclusiveness and respect for diversity in the learning community. • **V. Explore:** Learners will discover and innovate in a growth mindset developed through experience and reflection.
Learning Outcomes Using the Social Justice Standards: Anchor Standards and Domains (Teaching Tolerance 2018) **Anchor Standard: Identity** 3. Students will recognize that people's multiple identities interact and create unique and complex individuals. 4. Students will express pride, confidence and healthy self-esteem without denying the value and dignity of other people. **Anchor Standard: Diversity** 6. Students will express comfort with people who are both similar to and different from them and engage respectfully with all people. 9. Students will respond to diversity by building empathy, respect, understanding and connection.

Kindergarten

- **Read-Aloud:** *All Are Welcome* by Alexandra Penfold and Suzanne Kaufman
- **Lesson Seed:**
  - Discuss: What is your favorite page in the story? Why?
  - Discuss: What could you teach others?
  - Draw and Share: What is your special talent?
  - Draw and Share: Draw a picture of what you could do to make a new student feel welcome.

Grade 1

- **Read-Aloud:** *Shades of People* by Shelley Rotner and Sheila M. Kelly
- **Lesson Seed:** Use the online resources from the publisher.

Grade 2

- **Read-Aloud:** *What I Like About Me!* by Allia Zobel Nolan and Miki Sakamoto
- **Lesson Seed:** Have learners use Wixie to draw/illustrate/write what they like about themselves.

Grade 3

- **Read-Aloud:** *The Juice Box Bully* by Bob Sornson and Maria Dismondy
- **Lesson Seed:** Use the Juice Box template in Schoology: Learning Management System. Have learners write what they can do to be a positive bystander in the school library.

Grade 4

- **Lesson Seed:** "Developing Empathy" lesson from Learning for Justice

Grade 5

- **Lesson Seed:** "Discovering My Identity" grades 3–5 lesson from Learning for Justice

As a curriculum writing team, we understood the power of using literature as a teaching tool. Each grade level was assigned a required read-aloud along with a lesson seed that helped our school librarians and learners dive into the Include Shared Foundation using the Social Justice Standards as a guide. Recognizing that all school librarians have their own teaching styles, we purposefully decided to use lesson seeds rather than require full lesson plans.

Included as a separate document in the curriculum were author studies for our youngest learners profiling Donald Crews, Ann Jonas, and Nina Crews. We loved sharing with our learners the fact that these authors are a family!

Finally, we created a picture book list that could be used for enhancing the curriculum in order to promote an inclusive environment and social justice. A representative sample of our list is depicted in figure 1.2—look at those beautiful covers!

Example book covers from the picture books suggested for use in enhancing the K–5 curriculum.

FIGURE 1.2 / **Supplemental picture book list**

Media and Information Literacy + Digital Citizenship = Digital Literacy

An essential component of school librarianship is information and media literacy combined with digital citizenship—or digital literacy. The Learning for Justice website includes an entire framework for digital literacy and citizenship whereby learners gain an understanding of how to appropriately harness the power of the internet.

As we were working on revising our digital literacy curriculum, we knew that Include could again guide and frame our work if we used the Social Justice Standards as a foundational piece. Incorporating Include into digital literacy enables school librarians to work with learners in becoming global citizens who understand the value of utilizing the web for information. In addition, by focusing on the Social Justice Standards, the digital literacy framework, and the Shared Foundations, learners are able to develop soft skills, such as empathy, as well as a better understanding of the critical thinking and evaluative skills necessary to navigate the information landscape.

Table 1.2 shows an example of a fifth-grade essential question and learning outcomes for the overarching curriculum area of Media, Information Literacy, and Digital Citizenship.

TABLE 1.2 /

Fifth-grade curriculum: Media, Information Literacy, and Digital Citizenship

Essential Question: How do we use digital tools and resources to work with others respectfully while doing so in an ethical manner?

National School Library Standards: Shared Foundations and Key Commitments (AASL 2018)

- II. Include: Learners will demonstrate an understanding of and commitment to inclusiveness and respect for diversity in the learning community.
- III. Collaborate: Learners will work effectively with others to broaden perspectives and work toward common goals.
- VI. Engage: Learners will demonstrate safe, legal, and ethical creating and sharing of knowledge products independently while engaging in a community of practice and an interconnected world.

Learning Outcomes Using the Social Justice Standards: Anchor Standards and Domains (Teaching Tolerance 2018)

Anchor Standard: Identity

4. Students will express pride, confidence and healthy self-esteem without denying the value and dignity of other people.

Anchor Standard: Diversity

9. Students will respond to diversity by building empathy, respect, understanding and connection.

Anchor Standard: Action

18. Students will speak up with courage and respect when they or someone else has been hurt or wronged by bias.

Grade 5 Discussion Example

What should you do when someone uses mean or scary language on the Internet?

- Empathize with those who received mean and hurtful messages.
- Identify what it means to cross the line from harmless to harmful communication online.
- Generate solutions for dealing with cyberbullying.

As we work through this process, we are beginning to tackle the middle and high school curricula. As of this writing, we are in the initial stages of developing curriculum frameworks for sixth through eighth grades and ninth through twelfth grades using the Include Shared Foundation as a guide with an emphasis on the Social Justice Standards. Because our middle and high school libraries have flexible schedules, these curriculum frameworks will be structured differently than our elementary plans, providing more of a guide than an actual curriculum. Tables 1.3 (middle school) and 1.4 (high school) show some of our initial efforts to create these new curriculum frameworks. We also continue to develop curriculum frameworks to address the remaining overarching frameworks—Creation and Design as well as Inquiry, Exploration, and Research.

TABLE 1.3 / **Middle school curriculum framework**

Media and Information Literacy
AASL Standards Framework for Learners **Include** • II.A.2. Learners contribute a balanced perspective when participating in a learning community by adopting a discerning stance toward points of view and opinions expressed in information resources and learning products. **Collaborate** • III.D.2. Learners actively participate with others in learning situations by recognizing learning as a social responsibility. **Engage** • VI.A.2. Learners follow ethical and legal guidelines for gathering and using information by understanding the ethical use of information, technology, and media. • VI.D.3. Learners engage with information to extend personal learning by inspiring others to engage in safe, responsible, ethical, and legal information behaviors. **Learning for Justice Social Justice Standards** • Identity: 4. Students will express pride, confidence and healthy self-esteem without denying the value and dignity of other people. • Diversity: 9. Students will respond to diversity by building empathy, respect, understanding and connection. • Action: 18. Students will speak up with courage and respect when they or someone else has been hurt or wronged by bias.

For each grade (6–8), school librarians will choose two lessons from a buffet of options to teach during the school year.

- 6: Digital Footprint and Privacy/Security
- 7: Media Balance and Cyberbullying
- 8: Relationships, News Media, and Literacy

Reading, Literature, and Community

AASL Standards Framework for Learners

Include

- II.A.3. Learners contribute a balanced perspective when participating in a learning community by describing their understanding of cultural relevancy and placement within the global learning community.
- II.C.2. Learners exhibit empathy with and tolerance for diverse ideas by contributing to discussions in which multiple viewpoints on a topic are expressed.

Learning for Justice Social Justice Standards

- Identity: 1. Students will develop positive social identities based on their membership in multiple groups in society.
- Identity: 3. Students will recognize that people's multiple identities interact and create unique and complex individuals.
- Diversity: 9. Students will respond to diversity by building empathy, respect, understanding and connection.
- Justice: 11. Students will recognize stereotypes and relate to people as individuals rather than representatives of groups.

For each grade (6–8), school librarians will choose two lessons from a buffet of options to teach during the school year.

TABLE 1.4 / **High school curriculum framework**

Relationships and Communication; Digital Communication
AASL Standards Framework for Learners **Include** • II.C.1. Learners exhibit empathy with and tolerance for diverse ideas by engaging in informed conversation and active debate. • II.D.2. Learners demonstrate empathy and equity in knowledge building within the global learning community by demonstrating interest in other perspectives during learning activities. **Explore** • V.C.3. Learners engage with the learning community by collaboratively identifying innovative solutions to a challenge or problem. **Engage** • VI.D.3. Learners engage with information to extend personal learning by inspiring others to engage in safe, responsible, ethical, and legal information behaviors. **Learning for Justice Social Justice Standards** • Identity: 4. Students will express pride, confidence and healthy self-esteem without denying the value and dignity of other people. • Diversity: 9. Students will respond to diversity by building empathy, respect, understanding and connection. • Action: 18. Students will speak up with courage and respect when they or someone else has been hurt or wronged by bias.
Collaborate with English/language arts to incorporate real-world applications of e-mail communications with various writing prompts (for example, tenth-grade editorial project).

Digital Footprint and Identity
AASL Standards Framework for Learners **Include** • II.D.3. Learners demonstrate empathy and equity in knowledge building within the global learning community by reflecting on their own place within the global learning community. **Collaborate** • III.D.2. Learners actively participate with others in learning situations by recognizing learning as a social responsibility. **Engage** • VI.D.3. Learners engage with information to extend personal learning by inspiring others to engage in safe, responsible, ethical, and legal information behaviors. **Learning for Justice Social Justice Standards** • Identity: 4. Students will express pride, confidence and healthy self-esteem without denying the value and dignity of other people. • Diversity: 9. Students will respond to diversity by building empathy, respect, understanding and connection.
Essential Question: What is my digital footprint and how does it impact my future?

(cont.)

TABLE 1.4 (cont.)

News and Media Literacy
AASL Standards Framework for Learners **Include** • II.A.2. Learners contribute a balanced perspective when participating in a learning community by adopting a discerning stance toward points of view and opinions expressed in information resources and learning products. **Curate** • IV.A.3. Learners will act on an information need by making critical choices about information sources to use. • IV.B. Learners gather information appropriate to the task by: 1. Seeking a variety of sources. 2. Collecting information representing diverse perspectives. 3. Systematically questioning and assessing the validity and accuracy of information. **Explore** • V.A. Learners develop and satisfy personal curiosity by: 2. Reflecting and questioning assumptions and possible misconceptions. 3. Engaging in inquiry-based processes for personal growth. **Engage** • VI.A. Learners follow ethical and legal guidelines for gathering and using information by: 1. Responsibly applying information, technology, and media to learning. 2. Understanding the ethical use of information, technology, and media. 3. Evaluating information for accuracy, validity, social and cultural context, and appropriateness for need. **Learning for Justice Social Justice Standards** • Identity: 3. Students will recognize that people's multiple identities interact and create unique and complex individuals. • Diversity: 10. Students will examine diversity in social, cultural, political and historical contexts rather than in ways that are superficial or oversimplified.
Essential Question: How do I become a responsible consumer of news and information?

Our school libraries are places where social justice, diversity, and inclusion matter. School librarians and learners can work together using the Shared Foundation of Include and the Learning for Justice Social Justice Standards to make new meaning, forge new friendships, and create opportunities for inclusive learning.

Social Justice Standards and Include

Jennifer's work in her district is so powerful because the team is using the AASL Standards to rewrite their school library curriculum across grades, and this work can guide librarians at the school or district (or even state) level. It's the Include Shared Foundation in action in ways that are both immediate and sustainable.

The six Shared Foundations are designed to partner and are interconnected across the four Domains of Think, Create, Share, and Grow. We are weakening Include when we connect it only through Curate. Are they natural partners? Of course, but Include must go beyond inclusive resources. It was meaningful when Jennifer came to that realization in her journey—"It was time to move beyond looking only at collection development. It was time to start revising, rebuilding, and rethinking our curriculum." Yes!

Through the AASL Standards Frameworks, we know that "learners who include other perspectives in their understanding exhibit tolerance for differing viewpoints" (AASL 2018, 29). When we unpack *tolerance* we can see that the Teaching Tolerance website offered a powerful—and beautiful—definition: "We view tolerance as a way of thinking and feeling—but most importantly, of acting—that gives us peace in our individuality, respect for those unlike us, the wisdom to discern humane values and the courage to act upon them" (Teaching Tolerance, n.d.). These words can help us weave Include throughout our libraries.

I too attended a Learning for Justice workshop on the Social Justice Standards, and the learning was so powerful that I attended the same workshop again the following year. These standards are now interwoven into our school library lessons and classroom collaborations. When preparing formal lesson plans to meet necessary state standards, I include the Learning for Justice Social Justice Standards as a complementary foundational piece.

A direct correlation between the Competencies under Include and the Learning for Justice Social Justice Standards is evident:

- We can engage learners to articulate "an awareness of the contributions of a range of learners" (AASL 2018, Learner II.A.1.) by connecting to Anchor Standard 6 in the Diversity domain of the Learning for Justice Social Justice Standards (SJ.D.6): "Students will express comfort with people who are both similar to and different from them and engage respectfully with all people."
- We can help learners adopt a "discerning stance toward points of view and opinions" (AASL 2018, Learner II.A.2.) through SJ.D.8: "Students will respectfully express curiosity about the history and lived experiences of others and will exchange ideas and beliefs in an open-minded way."
- We can support learners as they describe their understanding of their "placement within the global learning community" (AASL 2018, Learner II.A.3.)

by accessing the lessons under SJ.D.7: "Students will develop language and knowledge to accurately and respectfully describe how people (including themselves) are both similar to and different from each other and others in their identity groups."

Questions for the Reflective Practitioner

1. Jennifer's entry into this work started with identifying her why. How can I use the AASL Standards to develop a why for myself and the school library?
2. How can Jennifer's work with the Learning for Justice Social Justice Standards inspire work in my own school library and programs?
3. How can I use the AASL Standards to truly exhibit justice through my programs and instruction?

Moving Forward

WHAT CAN I DO TODAY?

Visit the Learning for Justice website and read the "About Learning for Justice" page.

HOW CAN I BUILD ON IT TOMORROW?

On the Learning for Justice website, under Classroom Resources, access the "Lessons" page. Filter lessons by grade level and subject or topic, or browse the range of lessons available for your grade level. Find at least one lesson to add to your school library curriculum this year.

ACTION STEPS

- Learning for Justice workshops are incredibly affordable—think about attending one in your area. If in-person attendance is not feasible, utilize their free, online professional development to gain this crucial learning in antibias education.

- Browse the free publications that Learning for Justice has available and choose one to download. Examples include *Reading for Social Justice, Teaching Hard History: American Slavery, Serving ELL Students and Families,* and *Learning the Landscape of Digital Literacy.*
- Explore the activity guide developed by a 2019 American Library Association (ALA) Emerging Leaders team that includes reflection activities, scenarios, and resources to support school librarians in developing inclusive learning communities: *Developing Inclusive Learners and Citizens* (https://standards.aasl.org/project/inclusive). The Shared Foundation Include is the centerpiece of this guide!
- Does your school district have a department that is focused on equity, diversity, and inclusion? If so, reach out to access their professional development opportunities or learning resources to strengthen your work on Include in your school library.

2

Create by Slamming in the School Library

In the section "Include Learner Competencies in Depth" in chapter 6 of the *National School Library Standards,* the paragraph for the Create Domain begins, "When learners create in the school library" (AASL 2018, 78). This language represents a powerful shift for our learners and our spaces and in the way school libraries interact with our learners: *Think kitchen, not grocery store.*[1] We cannot be only places where learners come to "shop" from our shelves and access resources. We must also function as kitchens, where learners use our resources—including us—to create, well, anything. From poetry to robotics to art, our learners are creating in the school library.

You may be thinking that everyone knows this. Do they? Do all our teaching colleagues know it? Administrators? Families? Community stakeholders? Schools of education? Part of our advocacy charge is to be transparent about this culture of creation we nurture in our school libraries. Our learners themselves are our best advocates, and showcasing their creative brilliance can be a cornerstone for our school libraries—and schools.

The AASL Standards illuminate this idea: "Learning activities that include participants' expression of diverse perspectives foster deep thinking and relevant results" (AASL 2018, 78). The "expression of diverse perspectives" is key here. We can't have diverse expression without having learners from a wide range of identities participating in the first place. School libraries that center on creating must include culturally sustaining pedagogical practices that engage all learners. This is true for programs embedded in the curriculum and for extracurricular opportunities that are carved out of—and into—the school day.

Columbus, Ohio, school librarian Chiquita Toure builds innovative, culturally sustaining opportunities for high school learners to create in her school library through poetry. These inclusive literary activities demonstrate the power of the Create Domain as learners express themselves as members of the global learning community.

Slamming in the School Library*

Chiquita Toure

Nine years ago, I created the Spoken Word Club. *Spoken word* is a term used to describe the articulation of free verse poetry that might or might not be accompanied by rhythms. Club members and I met in a small, intimate room sharing our interests, hopes, dreams, and anxieties. There were creative expressions from young people who used words, both simple and complex, to find their voices.

I wanted to help learners find their voices in a world where they felt invisible and overlooked. The club was particularly appealing to learners who didn't fit the mold or stereotype of the popular kid, the athlete, or the cheerleader. Their poems often reflected personal, community, or global issues they faced every day. Sometimes participants spoke solely of problems; other times they spoke of innovation and solutions. The most interesting part of our gatherings was introducing learners to the idea that rappers are also considered poets. In fact, many rappers take on the title of spoken word artists because they write and rap about personal experiences and use their writings and performances as a form of therapy to overcome barriers in their lives.

During this time, I was serving as the school librarian at a middle school whose school library was in another building on the other side of the school campus, which was not ideal. Due to the location of the school library, the Spoken Word Club met once a week during lunch in a small classroom in the middle school building. Our meetings inspired me to connect to learners. It was my goal to provide a forum for learners to generate ideas for writing and compare and contrast traditional poets with contemporary writers. Additionally, I knew that learners were required to provide four writing pieces for their portfolio, which meant that the more they practiced writing, the more comfortable and confident they would become.

We shared poetry during lunch periods, in classrooms, and in school literary publications. In 2013, I was hired as the head librarian at a high school, which meant I did not have to travel to several schools; I was in one building five days a week. Imagine my excitement when I learned that I would be working with the English educator who created the district's Poetry Slam competition. Not only was he a huge supporter of student writers, nurturing them to become developed writers and performers, he was also a writer and spoken word artist himself. Our collaborative

*Reprinted and adapted from "Slamming in the Library" (Toure 2019), a blog post on the Knowledge Quest website.

relationship did not unfold immediately, but after some time, I knew I wanted to work with him. Soon I started the Warrior Word Writing Club, and our collaboration was a wonderful fit.

The club produces *Warrior Words,* our school literary publication that learners contribute to and for which I am the advisor. Learners interested in performing their poems can do so through our Poetry Slam competition. That's where my colleague Wyk McGowan serves as a great collaborator. He identifies writers and coaches them on their performances. Each year, about six weeks before the district's annual Poetry Slam, which is held at our school, we showcase learners in the school library in preparation for the competition. Learners can sign up in the school library, the main office, or English classes to perform during one of three lunch periods. On that day learners and educators are invited to listen to the spoken word poets, participate themselves during open mic, or do both.

Each year the event is used to determine who will comprise two teams for the Poetry Slam competition. It is our hope that learners will see the showcase as an opportunity to hone their writing skills and gain confidence in performing. Additionally, we want our writers to feel included in a welcoming community. Over the years, the district's Poetry Slam has become very competitive, engaging judges from the community who may themselves be writers or performers or both. A strict rubric is used to determine winners, and yes, our school's Poetry Slam team has earned first place in several years. Because of increased interest, the annual Poetry Slam was extended to the middle school level. Now we celebrate this event with competitions at both the middle and high school levels, and, with our strong team, we hope to earn the first-place trophy again!

Although I consider myself a writer, one does not need to be a writer in order to support learners who yearn to be a part of a community of writers. Here are some ways you can start a spoken word club in your building.

- Start with a vision statement that includes district goals and AASL Standards.
- Solicit assistance from English educators and visit classes to speak to learners.
- Create exciting flyers and announcements about your meetings.
- If transportation is an issue, hold lunch meetings so everyone interested can attend.
- Post the works of spoken word artists and previous competition winners on www.poetryoutloud.org and YouTube.
- Invite community artists to share their writings and speaking tips with learners.
- Allow learners to use free-writing prompts and share in a safe and judgment-free environment. Jason Reynolds has created a series of short video segments—the "Write. Right. Rite." series—which include creative and open-ended questions and writing prompts that make excellent jumping-off points for learners.

As school librarians, our commitment to the Include and Collaborate Shared Foundations can be best expressed when we advocate for learners and work with our colleagues. I have found that learners will seek out those adults who are willing to listen and who will help them develop their own creative expressions. The rewards of offering these opportunities are tremendous.

Slamming in the School Library and Include

Chiquita has initiated powerful programs through her school libraries and at her schools that connect to Include and the learner Competencies under the Create Domain: "Learners adjust their awareness of the global learning community" by:

- "Interacting with learners who reflect a range of perspectives" (AASL 2018, Learner II.B.1).
  - By supporting spoken word and creative writing programs that are inclusive, Chiquita has built opportunities for learners to interact and create with a range of other learners and hear a variety of lived experiences and perspectives.
- "Evaluating a variety of perspectives during learning activities" (AASL 2018, Learner II.B.2).
  - As part of creating writing activities, learners become accustomed to sharing—as Chiquita explains—"in a safe and judgment-free environment." This sharing happens because the learners in the space are listening to and "evaluating" different perspectives—and appreciating them.
- "Representing diverse perspectives during learning activities" (AASL 2018, Learner II.B.3.).
  - Creative writing—including spoken word—is often deeply personal and is a powerful way for learners to represent diverse perspectives—*their own*. Again, we put this Competency into practice by building learning opportunities and spaces that are welcoming to learners across a range of identities—including racial, language, disability, and LGBTQ+ identities.

While working on this chapter and learning about Chiquita's library programs, I've made a commitment to start a spoken word club at my school this year. In the past, I've incorporated spoken word into the curriculum (see "Moving Forward"), but I haven't yet created a space and time where spoken word performances were nurtured. That is going to change! Using Chiquita's example—as both inspiration and roadmap—and the AASL Standards Frameworks, I'm excited to grow this opportunity in my school library.

Questions for the Reflective Practitioner

1. How do learners create in my school library? What activities that foster creative expression are happening?
2. How am I being transparent about creative, learner-centered activities (school library as kitchen!) as part of my library advocacy with stakeholders?
3. How do I build a space in which "interacting with learners who reflect a range of perspectives" (AASL 2018, Learner II.B.1.) is encouraged and commonplace?

Moving Forward

WHAT CAN I DO TODAY?

Visit the Poetry Out Loud website. Created by the National Endowment for the Arts and the Poetry Foundation in 2005, Poetry Out Loud provides free teacher resources and a large anthology of classic and contemporary poems.

HOW CAN I BUILD ON IT TOMORROW?

Watch at least one youth-performed spoken word poem. The Poetry Out Loud, Youth Speaks, and Global Writes websites are powerful starting points.

ACTION STEPS

If you have an existing poetry, slam, or creative writing club, consider how you could incorporate Chiquita's ideas into your group. If you do not yet have such a club, investigate starting one at your school. Identify a collaborator!

- For optional clubs that offer literacy enrichment, we must ensure that we are attracting and including learners with a range of experiences. Writing opportunities are necessary and valuable for learners who do not (yet) self-identify as writers! Invite learners from across a spectrum of classes, clubs, and interests to participate. Include learners who have been identified for reading intervention services. Let the anime club know that the writing club could be a great space to write fan faction about their favorite series, character, or ship. Work with special education and English learner educators to be intentional in your invites. (And then, of course, build a writing club that is welcoming to all members!)

In addition to optional clubs, literary brilliance and shared activities with learners cannot begin and end with the written word. Incorporate spoken word into classroom collaborations!

- Identify an upcoming lesson, unit, or circulation visit that could be enhanced by watching a spoken word performance. When I worked with seventh-grade learners on the power of names as we were reading *The House on Mango Street* by Sandra Cisneros, we watched *Unforgettable* by Pages Matam, Elizabeth Acevedo,[2] and George Yamazawa as a complementary text. Spoken word is a literary art form, and its value for learners goes beyond performance. Listening to, reflecting on, and discussing spoken word adds great literacy value to core classes.
- Allowing for multiple modes of expression is a culturally sustaining practice. Build opportunities for spoken word into project choice! Identify a project that could be enhanced with a wide range of choices available for learners. For example, if you collaborated on a World War II research project for which learners presented information in a traditional Google Slides presentation, choices could be added so learners could demonstrate what they've learned by developing a podcast, creating video content, or writing a poem they perform as spoken word—either live or on video. We have to think beyond the five-paragraph essay—and a presentation of slides!

NOTES

1. Way back in 2008, Joyce Valenza wrote a blog post about this idea: "Library as Domestic Metaphor." It was Joan Frye Williams who said, "We need to stop being the grocery store or candy store and become the kitchen." Joyce carried the metaphor farther by writing, "But, for me, library space is definitely *kitchen*, but not just a *kitchen*. It is also dining room, family [room], and perhaps entertainment room." Read the original blog post (Valenza 2008)! Still relevant more than thirteen years late.

2. When I started this lesson, it was pre-*Poet X*. Now, when learners watch *Unforgettable,* they love learning more about Elizabeth Acevedo, and it's a wonderful opportunity to booktalk *The Poet X, With the Fire on High,* and *Clap When You Land.*

3

Share with Restorative Practices and Circ[2]

Among the definitions of *restorative* is this one—having the ability to restore a feeling of well-being. Does that impact you as being particularly meaningful for school libraries? How often do we do this? In the myriad small ways throughout each day that we know are anything *but* small for our learners?

We can be restorative in macro ways, as well, by dismantling inequities and building truly inclusive, equity-driven spaces that honor the multiple identities of our learners. When we carry these actions to the school level, this restoration is serving to disrupt inequities at a larger systems level. This work builds an ideal foundation for intentionally including restorative practices in our school library curriculum—and throughout our schools.

When we look to the AASL Standards, the Share Domain centers on "guiding learners to contribute to discussions with diverse partners while respecting diverse perspectives" (AASL 2018, 150). A cornerstone of restorative practices involves "circles," which offer an ideal way to guide learners in these rich discussions. Additionally, the AASL Standards include Best Practices for each Shared Foundation. For Include, a key Best Practice calls for school librarians to "model discussion techniques and strategies to engage all participants" (AASL 2018, 82).

I'm a bit nervous about sharing my journey into using Socratic Seminars, restorative practices, and circles in my school library because I am not an expert. But what better way to model using the AASL Standards Frameworks to build the Competencies of Include in learners? I am a learner, just like all our learners. This is my learning journey.

Circ²: Restorative Practices in the School Library

Julie Stivers

Tomorrow is the first day of school. Like most educators I know, I still get those first day of school jitters. You? I'm glad I still do, because I never want to forget how hard it is to walk into a new school, a new hallway, a new classroom. Much of my intentionality about our school library centers on my wish for it to be the easiest space to step into throughout the day—like coming home.

In a class discussion, we were unpacking the differences between equality and equity. A learner, William, said, "*Equity means home.*" He unpacked that definition further, saying that equity in schools means that you can be yourself and that someone is always on your side. Boom. Middle schoolers are brilliant. William, you are brilliant.

Equity means home. That doesn't just mean that we love our learners—which we should. It doesn't just mean that we truly welcome our learners—which we must. It means that we have to identify the inequities that are keeping our learners from being their full, brilliant selves and work to disrupt those inequities in our school spaces—starting with our own school space, the library.

It's not possible to disrupt inequities without building our instruction on the principles of culturally sustaining pedagogy. As Django Paris and H. Samy Alim have explained, culturally sustaining pedagogy "positions dynamic cultural dexterity as a necessary good, and sees the outcome of learning as additive, rather than subtractive, as remaining whole rather than framed as broken, as critically enriching strengths rather than replacing deficits" (Paris and Alim 2017).

As school librarians, how is our instruction—from co-teaching content lessons to booktalking to leading clubs—honoring and enriching the strengths of our learners? We have to go beyond accepting learners' cultures and move toward supporting and affirming languages, literacies, and cultural traditions. Culturally sustaining practices in the school library can include the following:

- Welcoming multiple languages, including world languages and authentic variations of English outside "standard" English
- Seeking out nontraditional texts to use during instruction such as videos, spoken word, learner writing, and contemporary poetry including rap lyrics
- Welcoming physical movement during instruction
- Having an asset-driven perspective (as opposed to a deficit model way of thinking) for parents, families, and communities
- Centering learners in instruction, where the educator/librarian serves as a facilitator and co-learner
- Foregrounding collaborative activities, as opposed to competitions

- Recognizing a range of literacy gifts, from rhyming to drawing to creative writing to improv to debate
- Providing choice—as often as possible—for texts, summative assessments, and activities
- Engaging learners in setting norms for the library space

In her blog post "A New Vision of School," Tala Manassah proposed that we must shift from a scarcity mentality to an abundance mentality: "Scarcity mentality is a paradigm of the world that says that there are limited resources and we are in a zero-sum game to compete for them. We have an education system that is largely based on competition rather than cooperation." An abundance paradigm "proposes the opposite: there is enough to go around and that everyone benefits when justice, resources, visibility, and love are shared" (Manassah 2019).

Think about this shift in relation to our school libraries. Are we operating with an abundance paradigm? A library that has fines, limits checkouts, and uses detectors is reflecting a scarcity mentality. What could all our libraries be if we switched to an abundance paradigm? More collaborative projects, fewer tests. More books in learners' hands, fewer barriers. More love, less shushing.

As my school library journeys toward being more culturally sustaining and striving to operate within an abundance paradigm, I keep learning. I keep making mistakes and recognizing how much I don't know and fighting against the barriers of my own privilege, ignorance, and implicit biases. I keep learning.

Shifting to a Circle: Socratic Seminars in the School Library

Effective librarianship means putting scholarship and research into action for the benefit of learners throughout our school. I knew I wanted to help shift classroom instruction to be more culturally sustaining, so I collaborated with core teachers to build Socratic Seminars into multiple units. The organization Facing History and Ourselves explains that in a Socratic Seminar activity,

> students help one another understand the ideas, issues, and values reflected in a text through a group discussion format. . . .Through this type of discussion, students practice how to listen to one another, make meaning, and find common ground while participating in a conversation. (Facing History and Ourselves 2020)

Another key resource for us in planning was the National Paideia Center, which defines a Paideia Seminar "as a collaborative intellectual dialogue facilitated with open-ended questions about a text" (National Paideia Center, n.d.).

Seventh-grade science educator Beth Campbell and I built a unit on genetic engineering and genetically modified organisms (GMOs) that culminated in a Socratic Seminar. In the days leading up to our seminar, learners conducted research and read texts showcasing both sides of the GMO debate. Because this was the first time many of our learners had participated in a facilitated classroom discussion in which they were the prime speakers, we heavily scaffolded the unit.

On the day before our GMO Socratic Seminar, learners participated in a practice seminar on a topic of their choosing. Classes brainstormed and chose topics such as Best NBA Player, Why the School Dress Code Must Change, and Most Important Apps on a Teen Phone. For the practice seminar, Beth created table tents with learner names on the outfacing side along with question or statement stems, and, on the side facing the learner, a checklist of clear expectations for what participation in a seminar would look like (for example, "I'll share at least one thought about an article we've read"; "I'll ask a clarifying question of a classmate"). Again, we provided question and statement stems to help (for example, "I agree with you because . . ."; "I see your point, but have you considered . . ."). Our learners liked the table tents so much that we adapted them—with learner input—for the content GMO seminar. Learners asked for a bubble to be added next to each expectation so it could be easily marked off when completed!

The learner-led GMO seminars were powerful. Beth and I were merely observers of the facilitated discussion that was happening in the school library. It was an opportunity for learners to shine based on their auditory gifts, and we were impressed by the care that our learners showed for each other—helping quiet learners by asking direct questions and using affirming language to boost confidence. We found that the seminars allowed for individual learner excellence without being competitive. For the seminars to be successful, learners needed to collaborate with each other.

The opportunities for collaborating on Socratic Seminars are infinite! Soon after the GMO unit, I collaborated with seventh-grade social studies educator Rachel Carter during her World War I unit. To help learners understand the intricacies of that war and to honor many of our learners' love and appreciation for the graphic format, we used Nathan Hale's *Treaties, Trenches, Mud, and Blood* (2014) as a class text. Again, the culminating activity after reading the novel together was not a project or a test—it was a Socratic Seminar during which learners discussed historical elements from the novel. We scaffolded by creating table tents and bookmarks with question and statement stems. Additionally, learners had a graphic organizer to refer to that they had completed while reading the novel. The resulting learner-centered discussions were rich—and creative!

Megan Grandmont (2017) offered the following strategies in "Crafting and Conducting a Successful Socratic Seminar":[1]

- Prepare students with expectations for participation.
- Provide students with seminar questions in advance.
- Offer a mix of required and optional seminar questions.
- Open with a round robin. Opening with a round-robin question—where we go around the circle and each student shares their response—means that I hear every student's voice at least once. Again, students who are introverts or who have social anxiety are never taken by surprise. This strategy works particularly well as a warm-up when the question connects to students' personal experiences or asks them to bring in a piece of outside media.
- Get comfortable with the uncomfortable.
- Facilitate, don't dominate.
- After the seminar, allow time for reflection.

Each time, after the Socratic Seminars were finished in the "classroom" area of our school library, I left in place the circle layout of tables. I liked how the arrangement impacted a range of activities in the school library—from lunchtime to independent reading to classroom instruction to our library electives. I loved the circle!

Remember awesome science educator Beth Campbell? She had been advocating for restorative practices to be formally implemented in our school, and I eagerly joined that push.

Restorative Practices

Restorative practices can be broadly defined as "processes that proactively build healthy relationships and a sense of community to prevent and address conflict and wrongdoing" (International Institute for Restorative Practices, n.d.). Restorative justice—through which many people come to learn about restorative practices—focuses on mediation and restitution as opposed to punishment and is just one piece of building a restorative school community. Restorative practices are built to be proactive, centering active listening, and ultimately seek to prevent the need for reactive discipline.

Restorative practices are not new. Indigenous communities across the world and Native nations and peoples on this continent were using restorative justice and restorative concepts long before North America was colonized. It's key to realize that these "new" educational practices being used today in schools were originated by Indigenous and Native communities hundreds of years ago and are still practiced as a means to resolve conflict, repair harm, and build community.

Many schools are turning to restorative practices to address racial inequities and disparities in school discipline. There are many resources for bringing restorative practices to your school. I've listed some of these resources to drive home the point that I am not an expert—I am a learner who is accessing scholarship and strategies from other practitioners to weave restorative practices into my school library.

- *Better Than Carrots or Sticks: Restorative Practices for Positive Classroom Management* by Dominique Smith, Douglas Fisher, and Nancy Frey
- *Restorative Practices: Fostering Healthy Relationships and Promoting Positive Discipline in Schools,* developed by the Schott Foundation, the Advancement Project, the American Federation of Teachers, and the National Education Association with the help of a working group of educators and school personnel
- National Educators for Restorative Practices (https://nedrp.com/)
- "Toolkit for Restoring Justice" from *Teaching Tolerance* (https://www.learningforjustice.org/magazine/summer-2014/toolkit-for-restoring-justice)
- Resources written by Kay Pranis

Some of my deepest learning regarding restorative circles took place when I had the opportunity to participate in several circles during sessions at the National Summit for Courageous Conversation. It was there that I learned from Skye Howell (@RestorativeEDUC) and Becky McCammon (@MsMcCammon) how truly restorative a circle can be and how its very structure can facilitate conversations about deep topics. We must infuse equitable and anti-racist practices into our adoption of restorative practices—otherwise, we are simply scattering community practices onto our pedagogy instead of truly embedding a culture of community in our schools.

There is a common misconception that restorative practices are strategies put in place to react to instances of bullying in schools. This view is limiting and aligns more closely with restorative justice, a subset of restorative practices. Restorative practices are a foundational shift in mindset for a school setting. The concept means putting strategies in place to build community so that issues like bullying are reduced. School activities like morning meetings, community circles, and Socratic Seminars can all be part of a shift to restorative practices in a school setting.

Restorative Circles in the School Library

Community circles are a cornerstone of restorative practices and have become an essential part of my school library—from instruction to circulation visits to the actual setup of the space. At the beginning of a recent school year, I reorganized the school library to accommodate a permanent circle of chairs that is never removed. The number of chairs fluctuates between six and eighteen, but a physical circle is always present. Having a permanent and visible circle in the school library is powerful. The NCTE Committee Against Racism and Bias in the Teaching of English noted the value of constructing your space to honor learners: "A student-centered moment within a shifted physical space communicates that this is their room and that you want to hear their voices" (NCTE 2018). This shift in school library layout is key—it lets learners intuitively know that communication and community are foregrounded.

If you're wondering about the size of my school library's circles, let's talk about those numbers! I am a librarian at an alternative middle school, and our class sizes are small, ranging from about six to fifteen, but most of my core classes have eight or nine learners. Circles still work with bigger class sizes! I've seen successful circles with more than twenty learners. Also, as secondary school librarians, we are often co-teaching. You and the collaborating educator could split the class and each conduct a circle. Or, if you are having classes come for circulation, half the class could visit at a time. I realize that this arrangement can be trickier for elementary school librarians, especially if you're operating on a fixed schedule. With librarian creativity, school libraries can start building in time for circles.

In her Learning for Justice article "Talking Circles: For Restorative Justice and Beyond," middle school educator Amy Bintliff (2014) noted three main benefits and purposes for circles in addition to building community: creating safe spaces, building connections, and offering educators a unique method of formative assessment. Of course, those benefits mesh beautifully with our *National School Library Standards*.

Almost every time a class is in the school library, we start with a circle. If the bulk of our lesson is focused on research or if we're using the library's large screen and devices to write, watch, or learn, we'll simply begin with a community circle and then transition to the classroom space in the school library. Our community circles are just that—a time and space for us to connect and for me to check in with learners. All our circles follow guidelines that we establish together at the beginning of the year during learners' first visits. The wording may change from year to year, but four basic concepts are always included:

- *Honor the talking piece or speaking object.* The talking piece is anything that can be held and passed around the circle. When someone has the talking piece, that person (adult or youth) has the attention of the circle.
- *No one is required to speak, but every voice is valued.* If the talking piece comes to someone in the circle who does not wish to speak or has nothing to add, that individual can simply pass it to the next person. I've found, though, that even my quietest learners will contribute to circle conversations, especially when they have time to process and think as the speaking object travels to them.
- *Learning and lessons can leave the circle, but stories cannot.* Learners will sometimes share personal stories in circles. Those stories stay in the circle. The learning that we do and the understandings and lessons that we come to

can be carried throughout our day. But personal stories never leave the circle.

- *Listen to understand, not respond.* Active listening is key. As your learners get used to circles, they will realize that everyone will get a chance to speak; this knowledge can be a comfort and allows learners to relax and listen to their classmates.

Additionally, it's important to have a focus object in the center of the circle so circle members have something for their eyes to focus on if they do not want to make eye contact.

Community circles can be guided by what's happening in the school, our communities, or the larger world. Circles provide an opportunity for learners to discuss events that are affecting them. And, of course, circles provide an opportunity to learn more about our learners! Carefully assess your questions ahead of time. Asking learners what they did over the summer or on a vacation can remind learners of trauma or highlight economic inequities in our classes, or do both. Use questions and prompts that are more trauma sensitive: What do you most look forward to this year? What is one thing you'd like your classmates and teachers to know about you? What is a skill you have that you could teach me how to do? What is a subject you wish were going to be taught this year? What does success look like to you? How do you like to be celebrated? Tell me about someone you know who really gets you. Tell me about your favorite teacher and why that person is your favorite.

Again, I'm learning. Before my first circle with learners, I talked to experienced circle facilitators, read their books and articles, and participated in circles myself. I attended a multiday circle keeper training. Circles can be a truly restorative part of the school day, but if facilitated irresponsibly or without an equity lens, they can be harmful to the very learners we are trying to reach. Work collaboratively with trained student support staff in your building—counselors, social workers, psychologists—who have deep knowledge about social-emotional learning and trauma-sensitive practices.

In addition to building community to jump-start a lesson, circles can be used to enhance content learning. They are a powerful formative assessment tool for gauging learners' understanding of either background knowledge or new learning. Any content-related question that you could ask at the front of a class can be adapted to ask in a circle. Allowing each learner time to share their understandings is a useful way to assess the future direction for learning and any need for differentiation.

In addition to formative assessments, circles can be used for content-related discussions. This approach blends especially well with history units. For example, seventh-grade social studies educator Abra Rearte and I facilitated circle discussions as a way to discuss the Holocaust, learn key historical concepts, and welcome survivor Abe Piasek to our school. Soon after, as I was working with eighth-grade social studies learners on creating podcasts based on a self-selected social justice issue, we started with circles in which we discussed current events and youth activism.

*Cir*culation Visits through *Cir*cles = Circ^2

I operate a hybrid model in our school library whereby I collaborate with other educators to build focused, literature-rich lessons that span multiple days or weeks, but I also have a fixed schedule for classes to come to the school library for circulation. When I started intentionally incorporating circles into the school library, I honestly wasn't sure how this method would work for circulation visits—or even *if* circles would work for circulation visits.

They worked. They worked! I created a structure for my Circulation + Circles that follows the same general flow each visit. (Classes visit for circulation every two weeks.)

- Circle
  - Check-in + greeting
  - Introduce sharing object
  - Literature/text: Quote, story, image, novel excerpt, poem
  - Group sharing
  - Tie-in to library books + resources with booktalks, video resources/trailers, activity, or any combination of these
  - Parting thoughts or question
- Circulation
  - Readers' advisory, self-selection, individual booktalks, checkouts, sustained silent reading

I found that circles added value to our circulation visits and that using circulation visits to discuss reflective literature added value to our circles. Thus, I began to think of these visits as Circ^2, because their value wasn't just additive, the benefits were exponential. I have many favorite Circ^2 days—here are just a few.

- In the fall, we talked about how our reading lives were going to change during the year. (One of my goals as a school librarian is to heal the reading trauma that has been inflicted on our learners who have not seen themselves in enough books—or have been othered for the reading material they love.) I asked, "Who do you want me to reach out to with good news about how well you're doing in the school library?" Learners wrote down names and contact information, and I used those cards to make calls all year. During the calls with family members, I shared good news about engaged reading, great comments made during discussions, kind behavior toward fellow learners, or engagement during electives, or simply said, "Your kid is great. I'm so glad they are with us this year."[2]
- Often, when booktalking a group of books connected by genre or a theme, I would start by placing the books in the center of the circle and asking learners to choose one to hold. (I'd have enough for everyone to have a book

in their hands.) When I got to a learner's book, they could decide whether they just wanted to hold it up while I talked about it, or they could choose to speak about the book if they'd read it, or they could simply read the back or the first few lines or even make comments about the cover. This approach made booktalking feel more interactive and organically invited learner voice and input.

- In our library, a very clear point is made about "history" months. The learning and celebrations should happen throughout the year, not just over the course of a few weeks. During Black History Month (which, again, lasts all year in our library), we started Circ^2 by celebrating Black YA and middle grade authors. Eighth-grade learners then wrote down what they *really* wanted to make sure we studied during Black History Month (and beyond). The answers—from Black Lives Matter to Malcolm X to Colin Kaepernick to *Black Panther* to the Black Panthers to Jason Reynolds—were put on a poster in the school library, and that is how we built many of our collaborated English and social studies lessons throughout the year.

Equity Means Home

It's the first day of school tomorrow. My jitters are lessened because the circles I'll be welcoming learners to will, I hope, help calm *their* jitters. I hope I can build a space that every learner feels comfortable stepping into. A space that becomes a kind of home. A space in which learners know that their whole selves are seen, welcomed, valued, and nurtured.

Socratic Seminars, Restorative Practices, Circ^2, and Include

Socratic Seminars and circles align beautifully with Include and the Learner Competencies for the Share Domain. "Learners exhibit empathy with and tolerance for diverse ideas by:

- "Engaging in informed conversation and active debate" (AASL 2018, Learner II.C.1.).
    - This is an apt definition for Socratic Seminars! Their very structure calls for learners to engage in background research and reading so that they are informed while they converse with their classmates. Strategies for active debate are taught, practiced, and scaffolded. Adding seminars to your school library instruction is an excellent way to meet this Competency.

- "Contributing to discussions in which multiple viewpoints on a topic are expressed" (AASL 2018, Learner II.C.2.).
    - Socratic Seminars are built to allow for multiple viewpoints to be shared and discussed. Additionally, circles allow learners to engage with this crucial skill because they are using the restorative structure of the circle to contribute to discussions on deep and personal topics.

The AASL Standards establish that "assessment should be a meaningful and positive learning experience for learners" and that "traditional assessments, such as those with multiple-choice questions that focus on recall, are not sufficient to measure a competency" (AASL 2018, 130–131). Their potential to be used for both formative (circles) and summative (seminars) assessments is another powerful benefit of these discussion-based school library activities.

Questions for the Reflective Practitioner

1. How can I use the AASL Standards to support learners in contributing to class discussions and seminars?
2. How does my school library actively center and honor diverse ideas to model Include and the Share Domain for learners?
3. How can I use my school library curriculum to help learners meet the Competency for "engaging in informed conversation and active debate" (AASL 2018, Learner II.C.1.)?

Moving Forward

WHAT CAN I DO TODAY?

Visit facinghistory.org to access resources across a variety of topics. The Socratic Seminar page has a wealth of strategies, including a ready-to-print PDF of Socratic Seminar Stems.

HOW CAN I BUILD ON IT TOMORROW?

Does your school intentionally engage in restorative practices? If yes, great! Consider sharing your experiences with your professional network and the greater school library world. If not, speak to the counselor or social worker (or with administration) at your school to see if you could partner in learning more about restorative practices and accessing resources and training.

ACTION STEPS

- Identify a unit in which you could embed a Socratic Seminar and search out a collaborator to co-teach or co-facilitate.
- If you've never participated in a restorative or community circle as part of professional development, identify a training to participate in—starting with district or state resources.
- Identify multiple culturally sustaining practices to build into your school library programming and commit to sustaining those practices. For each new year, engage your learners in setting norms for their school library space.

NOTES

1. Visit Megan Grandmont's article at https://www2.ncte.org/blog/2017/12/crafting-conducting-successful-socratic-seminar/ for the full text and valuable resources.
2. I don't betray learners' confidentiality about their specific reading material during these calls.

4

Grow with Loudness in the School Library

The Grow Domain centers the skills necessary to guide learners to reflect on "products as part of a collaborative learning culture locally and globally" (AASL 2018, 150). Books are, of course, the true meta-"products" in our school libraries. They are the visual foundation of learners' literacy and our currency that connects with learners' interests and experiences. Books also powerfully—and often harmfully—form and drive the narrative of people, communities, and nations. This capability can result in what Chimamanda Adichie refers to as the "single story" in her seminal TED Talk—and required watching for every school librarian—"The Danger of a Single Story" (Adichie 2009).

Pushing back against a single story is reflected in Include's Key Commitment because to have "respect for diversity in the learning community" means we are representing learners and their families as whole individuals with a wide and infinite potential for stories. As we actively show multiple stories through our collections, we can also extend our disruption of the single story by intentionally building engaging experiences through which our learners reflect on and think critically about books as "products."

Learner Competencies for the Grow Domain are based on demonstrating "empathy and equity in knowledge building" (AASL 2018, Learner II.D.). Bank Street School librarian Allie Jane Bruce worked with fellow educators Anshu Wahi and Jamie Steinfeld to create a curriculum that guides learners in critically examining book cover images, building knowledge about the power of imagery, and opening up wide conversations about stereotypes, race, and gender. Presented here is a condensed and adapted version of blog posts that Allie published over several years about Bank Street's innovative Loudness in the Library curriculum.

Loudness in the Library

Allie Jane Bruce

Several years ago, as I was booktalking realistic fiction titles to a sixth-grade class, a girl asked a seemingly simple question: "Why is there a bird on that cover?" This question launched a lesson that turned into a yearlong curriculum that used book covers as a starting point for examining biases and stereotypes in children's literature and the wider world. Collaborating with Jamie Steinfeld's sixth-grade humanities class and Anshu Wahi, our diversity director, we began that first lesson by initiating a class discussion about the ways in which people of color are portrayed on book covers.

The sixth graders' comments were insightful.

- "What I learned today really changed how I look at book covers. After we finished the conversation in the library, I had so many questions to ask."
- "I learned a lot from the library session about covers, and how they affect people's first impressions of the book."
- "I learned that book covers are a lot more important than they seem."
- "I feel like all books have a huge impact on our society."

We learned that some covers "hide" the fact that characters in the book are dark-skinned.

- "Why do the people who make covers sometimes make the people of color not have the spotlight? Like *Locomotion*, why couldn't we see the African American face?"
- "I think the cover could be hurtful because there is a light shining on the boy's face, who is from Vermont, and the girl, who is from Mexico, has her back turned."
- "Society is almost afraid of putting a dark-skinned or Asian character on the cover of a book. I feel like these are minor forms of segregation."
- "Do illustrators think that if a person of color is fully shown, it won't sell as many copies?"
- "The skin of dark-skinned characters is not always allowed to look dark on book covers."

Content for this contribution was adapted from the Bank Street College of Education's *Center for Children's Literature* blog, "Part 1: Are All Covers Created Equal? Bank Street 6th-Graders Weigh In on RACE" (March 18, 2013); "Rewriting History: American Indians, Europeans, and an Oak Tree (Loudness in the Library Year Three, Part 3)" (August 12, 2015); and "Allie's Reflections (Loudness in the Library Year Three, Part 4)" (August 13, 2015).

We learned that silhouettes can disguise a character's race or hide their features.

- "One thing I didn't like about the cover [of *Chains*] was how they didn't show the features of the girl on the cover."
- "I felt a little uncomfortable looking at the covers of *Same Sun Here, Bird in a Box,* and *Chains.* I wouldn't go to extremes and say I was mad at the publishers, but I was definitely a little shocked when I first saw the books and then later realized that all of the characters in the books were people of color. I didn't really understand why they thought it was OK to do that, like people wouldn't notice. I mean, I guess you wouldn't really notice unless you read the books, and by that time, you would have already bought the books."

This discussion quickly expanded to include conversations about portrayals of girls, boys, Queer characters, overweight characters, and more as we built our yearlong curriculum. The curriculum was so successful that we've repeated it every year since. Jamie, Anshu, the sixth graders, and I look forward to the time we spend together, talking and learning about identity. The program has evolved over the years, and I'm constantly delighted by the new discoveries that kids make and by the wisdom and insight already present in 11- and 12-year-olds. This year, in addition to our discussions about race, gender, and sexual orientation, and our annual field trip to Barnes and Noble, we discussed censorship, hair, and American Indian history and stereotypes.

I had done a doubletake when I cracked open *As an Oak Tree Grows,* a 2014 book by G. Brian Karas that inaccurately reflects the history of European and Native American interactions. In the story, which traces the life of an oak tree (planted as an acorn by a young Native boy), the Native character simply disappears as the Europeans move in. Bank Street scholars, who participate in extensive curricula on unlearning Native stereotypes, immediately recognized this portrayal as problematic, because it erases the conflicts and violence that arose when Native people fought to defend their homes and land from colonial invasion. As one sixth grader noted, "Because it's a children's book, they wanted to make it 'nicer.'"

Working together, we identified three primary areas of concern with *As an Oak Tree Grows:*

1. The pictures show a lot of empty land, as if it was uninhabited; one wigwam appears in the first two pages, alongside a vast wilderness. Where is the Native child's community? The pictures send the message that the land was largely empty and there for the taking. Sixth graders said,
    - "If you don't give kids the right images, they get the wrong ideas."
    - "If kids don't see other stories, they might think this is the truth."
    - "These books shape a child's mind."
    - "The illustrations should show more of the truth."

2. Then, there's this text: "The boy grew up and moved away." My sixth graders were puzzled because they knew that the larger story of Native and European interaction is one in which Europeans forcibly removed or killed huge portions of Native populations.

    - "'The boy grew up and moved away'? That didn't happen."
    - "They were there first. It is very unlikely that the boy just moved away."

    An educator asked, "Keeping in mind that this book is meant for young kids, how could we rewrite this so that it would tell the truth?"

    - "They could have said 'Europeans took his home' instead of 'The boy grew up and moved away.'"
    - "It could say 'Different people came and forced the boy's people out.'"
    - "It could say 'Sadly, they were forced away.'"

3. The next sentence reads: "Farmers now lived here." The picture shows people, identifiably European by their clothing, houses, and skin tone, now occupying the land. Together, we revisited what we know about American history: that Native people in fact taught Europeans how to farm in North America and that Europeans depended on Native populations to provide food. If someone didn't know these facts, they could get an incorrect message from this book. Sixth graders said,

    - "It shows that people don't think of Native Americans as farmers."
    - "Instead of 'Farmers now lived here' it could say 'Different farmers now lived here.'"

The sixth graders were deeply troubled by these few pages in an otherwise beautiful book. Our conversation turned to other examples of rewritten history in books, movies, and TV shows. Examples included *Peter Pan* and the Little House on the Prairie series. One young person mused,

- "A lot of times kids' books have the most stereotypical things, when in fact they should be the most honest."

It was a sober conversation, and many of these sixth graders left the room angry. When this happened—because it was not uncommon during the course of this curriculum—we always named that anger and respected it. This acknowledgment helped give learners an avenue to write about what they were thinking and feeling, to help process their reactions. We also channeled a lot of emotions into their end-of-year projects, which varied from year to year but always involved their choosing a topic that meant a lot to them during the course of the curriculum, and sublimating that anger and energy into something creative.

When the Loudness in the Library curriculum emerged, my fellow educators and I realized that it is both possible and necessary to have developmentally appropriate conversations with youth about the hard truth that whiteness is vastly overrepresented in children's literature. We discovered that book covers can be a remarkably accessible entry point into this conversation.

We continue to discuss many of the same points that we have in previous years: how book covers can "disguise" a character's race with a symbol, a blurry photograph, or a silhouette. But one pattern—how often tightly curly hair is disguised, obscured, or altered on book covers—particularly resonated with our most recent sixth-grade class.

For example, compare the covers in figure 4.1A (all of which feature Black main characters) with the covers in figure 4.1B, which feature East Asian, Middle Eastern, white, and South Asian characters. Here's what our sixth graders had to say:

- "You couldn't see the hair on the African American people, but you could on the others."
- "Certain types of hair is what you are supposed to have."
- "People could think they have to change their hair to fit in."
- "You could say, 'My hair isn't liked. I should straighten it.'"
- "If people read the same types of books a lot, they can have a stereotype in their head."
- "People might think, 'I need to change. I need to be that way.'"
- "People might change their hair because of what someone else—not them—thinks."
- "Because of the media certain people are excluded from being considered beautiful. Because of this, people's self-esteem lowers and they are made to feel insignificant."

FIGURE 4.1A / **Book covers used for sixth-grade class discussion featuring Black main characters**

FIGURE 4.1B / **Book covers used for sixth-grade class discussion featuring East Asian, Middle Eastern, white, and South Asian characters**

- "Why are there barely any books featuring minorities in the plot, let alone with minorities being featured on the covers? This sends the message to people that they are not worthy enough to be shown on book covers."

I've learned a lot from my years of teaching Loudness in the Library. Here are some of my oft-recurring thoughts.

Conversations about present-day inequities and injustices are all complicated, but some subjects are more difficult to talk about than others.
Our conversations about sexism flow beautifully. After looking at images of covers, observations about gender and sexism pour out of our sixth graders, sometimes so fast I can't record all the wonderful things they say.

By contrast, conversations about race consistently feature silence, at least initially. The sixth graders struggle to find language to express their ideas. They preface their thoughts with "I really hope I won't offend anyone." They start to say something, then shake their heads and say, "Never mind." This hesitancy doesn't happen with sixth graders as often as it does in adult conversations about race—but there is more silence than occurs in race-related conversations I've had with first graders.

Eventually, a brave soul—usually a kid of color—gets it going. And once it gets going, it's great. But there are often one, two, or three kids who say nothing, deciding that it is safer to stay quiet.

As a white educator, I find that leading race-related conversations is both more invigorating and more draining than leading conversations on any other topic.

Several years in, I still find myself tossing and turning the night before these lessons—partly from eager anticipation, partly from nervous anxiety. I worry that I will burden kids of color with the task of educating white children, or that I myself will unwittingly commit microaggressions against children of color. I worry that rather than engendering a sense of responsibility in white kids, leaving them energized and active, I will merely make them feel shame and guilt, which are paralyzing.

The fact that race-related conversations are so very fraught is a huge part of the problem. We must be able to communicate in order to solve problems that exist at interpersonal, institutional, and societal levels. If kids in sixth grade already have the inclination to stay silent in conversations about race, how much stronger will that inclination be in adults? And if we can't talk about race and racism, how will things ever get better?

Having said all that, I've also concluded that . . .

Sixth grade is a great age for kids to have race-related conversations.

Of course, parents and educators should start talking about race with toddlers,[1] but I have a special fondness for holding these conversations with 11- and 12-year-olds. Sixth graders can think abstractly and love to grapple with big ideas (such as problems that exist on societal levels), but they haven't developed as many of the cautionary filters that prevent adults from having honest and productive conversations. I've been amazed at how quickly and smoothly these kids identify their own prejudices, name them, and resolve to do better. In that respect, they are role models for me.

Every school should have a qualified diversity director who takes the (enormous) job seriously.

As I've stated, conversations about prejudices, injustices, and inequities that exist today are hard to navigate. Educators need training, practice, and professional guidance in these areas. I am so lucky and so grateful to work with Anshu Wahi, Bank Street's director of diversity and community, on this and other projects.

I cannot wait to do Loudness in the Library with next year's incoming sixth graders and to see where the kids take it, how they grow, what they learn, and how they teach me.

Loudness in the Library and Include

The Loudness in the Library curriculum from Allie, Anshu, and Jamie powerfully demonstrates Include and its learner Competencies through the Grow Domain. "Learners demonstrate empathy and equity in knowledge building within the global learning community by:

- "Seeking interactions with a range of learners" (AASL 2018, Learner II.D.1.).
  - This curriculum calls for the entire class to join in discussions after observing and reflecting on book cover imagery. Multiple viewpoints are shared and respected.
- "Demonstrating interest in other perspectives during learning activities" (AASL 2018, Learner II.D.2.).
  - The intentional way in which Allie creates her classroom community fosters listening between and among her learners.
- "Reflecting on their own place within the global learning community" (AASL 2018, Learner II.D.3.).
  - It was clear from the sixth graders' comments that this learning was causing them to reexamine their prior conceptions and experiences.

Allie's work has inspired me to invite discussions with learners that unpack imagery, messages, and stereotypes related to book covers. It's dynamic learning, and her example can guide us—as both inspiration and roadmap—in developing our own experiences for learners.

Moving Forward

WHAT CAN I DO TODAY?

Look at the book covers in your school library, starting with those on posters and in displays. After hearing the thoughts of the sixth graders involved with the book cover curriculum, what do you notice?

HOW CAN I BUILD ON IT TOMORROW?

Building on what you noticed about the book covers, reflect critically on which books are currently face-out in your space. Do you notice any trends? Can any changes be made to push back on a single story and feature more books with representative covers?

Questions for the Reflective Practitioner

1. The Grow Domain for Include calls for learners to "demonstrate empathy and equity in knowledge building" (AASL 2018, 76). How can I foster this ability in my own school library practice?

2. Discomfort with critical conversations is expected and normal but cannot be a barrier to facilitating them with learners. Have I ever avoided a conversation with learners because I was uncomfortable with or scared about how it would go? What could support me in treating that situation differently in the future?

3. The *AASL Standards Frameworks for Learners* is also appropriate for school librarians to build competencies as learners. How can I demonstrate—and model—"interest in other perspectives during learning activities" (AASL 2018, Learner II.D.2.)?

ACTION STEPS

- A key partner for Allie's work with book covers was Anshu Wahi, her school's director of diversity and community. Identify potential partners in your school or district who are focused on equity, diversity, or inclusion. If there isn't such a position in your district, ask why not! In the meantime, search out other supports for your equity journey. The resources from Learning for Justice (chapter 1) and Project READY (chapter 8) are excellent places to start.
- Being able to have conversations about race with our learners and colleagues is essential. As Allie points out, educators need "training, practice, and professional guidance in these areas." Again, start by identifying supports at the school and district levels but search beyond if necessary. Learning for Justice has an excellent, free publication available for download—*Let's Talk! Facilitating Critical Conversations with Students*.
- Identify a class, grade level, or both to work with on developing a lesson in which learners take a critical look at book covers. In addition to using Allie's

work for inspiration, you can find takeaway ideas in fifth-grade educator Jess Lifshitz's powerful post—"Helping Students Confront and Examine Their Own Biases Using the Images on Covers of Picture Books"—on her blog *Crawling Out of the Classroom.*

NOTE

1. See "Children Are Not Colorblind: How Young Children Learn Race" by Erin Winkler (2009).

PART II

School Librarian Competencies

"The language of the *AASL Standards Integrated Framework* is empathetic, inclusive, and active" (AASL 2018, 271). This line from appendix I, "Useful Verbs," in the *National School Library Standards* hit me like a lightning bolt. Why did this sentence strike me as particularly meaningful? Those three words—*empathetic, inclusive, active*—are at the beating heart of effective school librarianship, and they accurately identify the programs you'll read about in this section and the school librarian Competencies under the Shared Foundation of Include.

Empathetic. Empathy is explicitly named in the Competencies under Share and Grow, and it's a foundational concept in the four chapters in this section. Psychological researcher Tyler Colasante defines *empathy* as "the intrapersonal realization of another's plight that illuminates the potential consequences of one's own actions on the lives of others" (Hollingsworth, Didelot, and Smith 2003, 146). For school librarians, this illumination must drive our practice—from selecting books to removing barriers to building instruction. The work is only surface-level, however, unless there is an empathetic school librarian at the helm.

Inclusive. *Inclusive* is the adjectival form of the Include Shared Foundation and is a nonnegotiable for every Competency and Alignment across the Domains. This is not just a feel-good word about welcoming, however. Being inclusive is being aware of who is being excluded and then disrupting those inequities in every aspect of our school libraries, including collections, spaces, instruction, and professional development. As with empathy, being inclusive starts with us. As school librarians, we need to model inclusivity through joyfully including and appreciating all our learners—there is no shortcut or half measure to inclusivity. We are, or we aren't—and our learners always know.

Active. *Active* is the school librarian bringing Include to life. The first two adjectives—*empathetic* and *inclusive*—are mobilized only through action into effective school librarianship. Being active is to consistently and meaningfully create opportunities that are framed in equity for all our learners. School librarians cannot effectively lead without being empathetic and inclusive, but they must also act on those ideals to have a whole practice. Action is the keystone piece!

The AASL Standards Frameworks provide guidance on the school librarian role, naming us as "master educators who provide leadership for a vision of learning centered on learner voice and choice" (AASL 2018, 44). This emphasis on learner agency is key to realizing the school librarian Competencies and is a foundational piece of culturally sustaining pedagogy.

It can sometimes be difficult to tease out what is us as school librarians and what is our library. Because we should also be learner-centered and learning ourselves in a continual loop, it can be hard to see where our student learners end and we begin. And still. And still. *We are school librarians.* We are the architects of our programs and our libraries, of our learner-centered instruction, of our inclusive spaces.

Our Competencies are interconnected with both the learner Competencies and the school library Alignments, but they are unique. Using them, we must "catalyze change that creates . . . life-ready learners as well as passionate, innovative, and engaged citizens" (AASL 2018, 44). Our ultimate goals as school librarians are not improved test scores or higher reading levels. We are in the wonderful business of improving life outcomes through multiple literacies.

The four chapters in this section mirror and are organized by the four school librarian Domains under Include: Think, Create, Share, and Grow. We'll **Think** with a Georgia school librarian who initiated a reading program to empower her learners—and ended up rewriting her school culture. By **Creating** an equitable writer-in-residence model, three North Carolina school librarians show how author experiences can build inclusive school libraries. A Massachusetts school librarian **Shares** how developing a mental wellness curriculum transformed her library—and school. To help all school librarians **Grow,** an anti-racism curriculum from Project READY is highlighted.

5

Think with Read Woke

A **key theme of the Think Domain for school librarians is to** provide "learners access to a diverse collection of resources," which implements a "foundational step toward helping learners respect and appreciate the contributions of others" (AASL 2018, 79). The phrase *diverse collection of resources* sounds simple, but this Competency must be approached with an active and empathetic stance. It is not enough to only build a collection that celebrates multiculturalism. To truly Include, we must identify who has been—or is being—excluded. Our collections must be anti-racist, anti-ableist, anti-cishet supremacy, and anti-sexist in order to reflect true inclusion.

Author Daniel José Older beautifully frames diverse books as honest books:

> When we fight for diverse books, we're really just fighting for a more honest literature. Books that tell the truth. Because when we say, "We Need Diverse Books," we're really saying "We Need Books That Don't Lie To Us About Who We Are Or Whether We Exist." (Older 2015)

Bringing this honest collecting to our school libraries is essential to the Shared Foundation of Include.

Cicely Lewis, librarian at Meadowcreek High School in Norcross, Georgia, found an active, engaging, and powerful way to provide this foundational step of a *diverse collection of resources* by creating Read Woke. Her story—and her Read Woke movement—champion reading and #OwnVoices* titles through challenging the status quo and centering issues of social justice.

**OwnVoices* refers to books that are written by a member of a marginalized community that is centered in the novel. The hashtag #OwnVoices was originated by Corinne Duyvis and is inclusive of all kinds of diversity, including disability, religion, race, and LGBTQ+ status. When the main character and author share a marginalized identity, the book is considered #OwnVoices.

My Call to Action: Leading from the Middle

Cicely Lewis

In the fall of 2017, when I returned to school, I knew I had to do something differently.

DACA had been repealed—a program that had protected from deportation nearly 800,000 young undocumented immigrants brought to the United States as children. Stories of unarmed Black male teens being shot by police dominated our world. My learners had negative perceptions of public safety and didn't trust the police. There was a feeling of unrest in the air. In January of that year, an executive order had been enacted that targeted foreign nationals from seven predominantly Muslim countries along with other refugees. At the same time there was a huge debate about who could use which bathrooms.

I remember that on the day DACA was repealed, my learners were crying. Many thought they couldn't go to college and were unsure of their rights. They didn't know how to protect themselves. Many of my Latinx learners hadn't heard of Michael Brown or Trayvon Martin or Tamir Rice, and my African American learners had no idea what DACA was. I knew that my traditional Harry Potter theme would have to take a backseat. I wanted to make a change, and I wanted my learners to know their rights. I questioned how would I do it?

I saw people marching and shutting down I-285, and I knew that was not my protest. I would scroll through social media and see old friends, coworkers, and family members arguing and torn apart by the issues. That was not for me. What could I do in my role as a school librarian?

The Power of Reading

As a school librarian, I know that I am a leader. School librarians teach learners, educators, and the community. We have an integral position that impacts so many. I decided to do what I did best: read and promote reading. As I was perusing the *Stay Woke* special issue of *Essence* magazine, I saw powerful women on the cover wearing T-shirts emblazoned with the phrase *Stay Woke*. I knew I wanted that shirt, but I wanted to connect it to reading. *Read Woke* was born! I was so excited that I shared my idea with a few colleagues. One said, "The kids won't get it, they don't know what that means, they don't read books anymore, and it won't work." The second colleague said, "I'm sick of that word *woke*." The third colleague said, "Oh my God, I love it! Do it!" Needless to say, I listened to the third colleague.

I had a theme—next I needed books. I started researching. Then I scanned the reviews in *School Library Journal,* and I talked with my learners about what they felt they needed to read more about, and I came up with my Read Woke List. These were my criteria: A Read Woke book must

- challenge a social norm,
- amplify voices not often heard,
- provide information about a group that has been disenfranchised,
- seek to challenge the status quo, and
- have a protagonist from an underrepresented or oppressed group.

The inaugural Read Woke list included *The Hate U Give* by Angie Thomas, *Dear Martin* by Nic Stone, *I Am Not Your Perfect Mexican Daughter* by Erika Sánchez, *All American Boys* by Jason Reynolds and Brendan Kiely, *Being Jazz: My Life as a (Transgender) Teen* by Jazz Jennings, *I Am Malala* by Malala Yousafzai, and more. Our school's Design Lab created the shirts, and the Read Woke Challenge was born! After learners read four books and shared a review, they earned a shirt, free books, and a Read Woke pin. I created a bingo card with a list of the books, which I started booktalking to English/language arts classes, and I used my allocated funds to buy copies of all the books on my list. I was so excited!! Then I came to realize that my first colleague was partially right. My learners had no idea what it meant to be "woke." It was like I was speaking a foreign language.

So I had to back up and teach. I taught the terms *disenfranchised, woke, marginalized,* and *status quo.* I started sharing the stories from the Read Woke list, and the learners were interrupting me and asking, "Miss, can I get that book?" only to be interrupted by another learner saying, "No, I want that book!"

I shared my story with *School Library Journal,* and it went viral. Librarians across the world were reaching out and saying, "Thank You. I have wanted to have these conversations, but I never felt comfortable. Now, with Read Woke, I feel that I can."

I continue to add books to our Read Woke List. In addition to our inaugural titles, some of our most popular books are *Juliet Takes a Breath* by Gabby Rivera, *The Librarian of Auschwitz* by Antonio Iturbe, *The Poet X* by Elizabeth Acevedo, *Turtles All the Way Down* by John Green, *Yaqui Delgado Wants to Kick Your Ass* by Meg Medina, *Dumplin'* by Julie Murphy, *The New Jim Crow* by Michelle Alexander, *Girl Mans Up* by M-E Girard, *Saints and Misfits* by S. K. Ali, and *Sugar* by Deirdre Riordan Hall.

The Power of Stories

I am a school librarian, and we love stories. My Grandma Dorothy instilled my love of stories in me, and this is *her* story. My grandma cried when she was forced to drop out of school in the fourth grade. Her family was poor, and she was needed to take care of her nine siblings. She was the smartest lady I knew. She would have me read her mail for her and help her write her checks. She told everyone I was smart, and she let me read uninterruptedly. I often imagine how her life would have been different if she had received an education. How my life would have been different. I watched her clean white people's houses. I watched her battle to sobriety from alcoholism. I watched her survive domestic violence, and she shared her stories with me. These stories that I treasure. Stories that motivate me.

Next is the story of my college professor, Dr. Genevieve West. I signed up for African American Lit, and I remember sitting in the class along with other learners waiting for the professor. When she arrived, we were shocked to see a young, white woman enter the room. I thought, how is she going to teach us? For so long I had only had white teachers, and we never read diverse texts. I had to seek them out on my own. Was I wrong! She introduced me to a world of literature that I had never known. She treated the works with care and dignity. It changed my life.

I noticed Reynaldo (name changed for confidentiality) had been missing from school for two weeks. Reynaldo was a top learner and a member of the student council. I sent an e-mail to all his classroom educators, and no one knew where he was. I reached out to the counselors, and they made contact. When he returned to school, the counselors told him that he needed to go and see Mrs. Lewis first. He came to me, and I said, "Where were you?" He told me that he had learned he was undocumented and that he felt it was pointless to come to school. He told me he couldn't go to college and he had given up on his future. With tears in my eyes, I told him that he could go to college. I shared with him information about undocumented learner scholarships, and I told him that he needed to get his education because it was a tool, and when the time came, he would need to have the tools ready. He never missed another day again, and I like to think that I had something to do with that. I shared with him Diane Guerrero's *In the Country We Love: My Family Divided,* in which she writes about her family being deported while she was in high school.

> Why am I choosing to reveal so much now? Because on that afternoon when I came home to an empty house, I felt like the only child who'd ever dealt with something so overwhelming. And in the agonizing years that followed, it would've meant everything for me to know that someone, somewhere had survived what I was going through. For the thousands of nameless children who feel as forgotten as I did—this memoir is my gift to you. (Guerrero 2016, 2)

My final story centers on a young girl growing up in a small town. Her father was imprisoned when she was 5, and her mother was a single parent. Every time you would see the girl, she had a book in her hand. Her mother took her to the public library, and she loved to read. She would hide in those books. She escaped into those books while her mother was fighting with her boyfriend. She escaped when there was no food to eat or when her mother couldn't pay the water bill and there was no water. She graduated with honors from high school, went to college on a scholarship, and later became an educator. That girl is me. Reading saved my life. It provided an escape. The stories I read were like a warm embrace on a cold day.

I shared all these stories to illustrate the power of stories. All these people inspired me. They inspired me on each part of my journey. Let your learners inspire you to allow them to have windows and mirrors in their reading. These stories from Starr, Justyce, Dumplin,' Noodles, Xiomara, and more are powerful stories that need to be heard. It is our duty as school librarians, as educators, to make sure our learners are exposed to these stories.

We have to arm our learners with the knowledge that they deserve. Learning about others encourages us to treat people with respect and dignity, no matter their religion, race, creed, or color. Not sure how to start? These steps can help.

1. Find out what your community needs. It doesn't have to be Read Woke.
2. Read Woke yourself! What are you reading? Make sure you are reading diverse books.
3. Join a professional learning network (PLN) via social media or some other means.
4. Share your success story (social media, AASL, your state association, trade publications, news).
5. Read the books aloud. No matter their age, learners love it.
6. Remember, diversity is not just about race.
7. Be a leader, not a preacher.
8. Read Woke is for everyone.

When I started Read Woke, I asked myself how I could make an impact. I never imagined that I could change the school culture on such a level. A quote from *The Librarian of Auschwitz* exemplifies my mission: "The library has now become her first-aid kit, and she's going to give the children a little of the medicine that helped her recover her smile when she thought she'd lost it forever" (Iturbe 2017). I encourage you today to let the healing begin. Read Woke.

Read Woke and Include

It is clear why Read Woke so powerfully impacted both Cicely's school and schools across the country. Read Woke is much more than a catchy hashtag—it is a dynamic, equity-based initiative that promotes literacy, centers issues of social justice, and amplifies marginalized voices.

In Read Woke, we can see clear evidence of the school librarian Competencies under Include in the Think Domain.

- School librarians are called on to "encourage learners to share insights and perspectives" (AASL 2018, 79), and Cicely accomplishes this goal by featuring her learners' Read Woke book reviews on her blog and in library communications. Additionally, Cicely works with her learners to help them "articulate an awareness of the contributions of a range of learners" (AASL 2018, School Librarian II.A.1.) by building spaces in which learner voices and work are honored.
- We can guide learners "as they adopt a discerning stance toward points of view" (AASL 2018, School Librarian II.A.2.) when we are intentionally collecting and promoting reading materials that represent multiple perspectives, especially when we foreground the stories that are not traditionally told and that are written by members of the marginalized communities centered in the novels. We have to look beyond whose story is being told and also consider *who* is getting to tell that story.
- "Differentiating instruction" (AASL 2018, School Librarian II.A.3.) is a key part of Include, and with independent reading programs, it's imperative that we include choices that represent a range of formats and access points—audiobooks, picture books, short stories, graphic novels, and so on.

Common Belief 4 in the *National School Library Standards* states, "Reading is the core of personal and academic competency," specifically outlining that "the school librarian uses story and personal narrative to engage learners" (AASL 2018, 13). This guidance comes to life in Cicely's instruction in her school library and through her engagement with both Read Woke and her learners.

Moving Forward

WHAT CAN I DO TODAY?

Reflect on your own school library collection. Read Woke foregrounds #OwnVoices titles and stories that center social justice. Are the values of Read Woke (challenging the status quo, featuring protagonists from underrepresented and oppressed groups, amplifying voices not often heard) well represented in your school library?

Questions for the Reflective Practitioner

1. Cicely uses the power of story—both personal and from reflective YA literature—to reach her learners. How can I harness the power of story in my own school library?

2. Cicely mentions the importance of windows and mirrors. Using Dr. Rudine Sims Bishop's powerful metaphor as a foundation (Bishop 1990), how am I providing both windows and mirrors to all the learners through my school library and programs?

3. How wide and deep is my own reading? How diverse is my personal TBR pile? What books have I amplified on social media and recommended to learners and staff? How do the answers to these questions directly relate to my own "understanding of cultural relevancy and placement within the global learning community" (AASL 2018, School Librarian II.A.3.)?

HOW CAN I BUILD ON IT TOMORROW?

Access the following resources to identify books to purchase that will strengthen your collection by centering social justice issues and featuring authors who are members of marginalized communities.

- American Indians in Children's Literature
- The Brown Bookshelf
- !Colorín Colorado!
- Disability in Kidlit
- Diverse BookFinder (picture books)
- I'm Here. I'm Queer. What the Hell Do I Read?
- KitaabWorld
- Latinxs in Kid Lit
- Marley Dias's 1000 Black Girl Books
- Reading While White
- Responsive Reads
- Rich in Color
- Social Justice Books (Teaching for Change)
- Vamos a Leer
- We Need Diverse Books

ACTION STEPS

- Cicely used her Read Woke idea to build a program that promoted reading throughout her school. Do you currently have a program in your school library that celebrates reading? Consider beginning a new program or strengthening an existing one to reach the learners in your school.
- Collaborate with another educator at your school to embed a book that centers social justice in the curriculum. Rethinking Schools, Learning for Justice, and Lee & Low Books have resources and lesson plan ideas to help get you started.
- Begin (or strengthen) a staff book club at your school that models #OwnVoices reading by sharing your love of youth literature and foregrounding selections that reflect the diversity and reality of our world—and your learners.

6

Create with an Equitable Writer-in-Residence Model

A **key Common Belief for school librarians outlined in the** *National School Library Standards* is that "reading is the core of personal and academic competency." We are called on to be a literacy advocate who "supports, supplements, and elevates learners' literacy experience by guiding [learners] and involving them in motivational reading initiatives" (AASL 2018, 13). Organizing author visits is a natural way for many school librarians to create motivational literacy experiences. The structuring of these visits is key, however. Not all author visits build inclusive school libraries and experiences. An empathetic librarian recognizes that some common practices associated with visits may actually create barriers and exclude learners.

In the Create Domain, our school librarian Competencies focus on "designing opportunities for learners to create products that illustrate learning and foster collaboration in diverse settings" (AASL 2018, 45). Additionally, "efforts to create an engaging atmosphere that fosters exploration and pursuit of personal interests" live under Create (AASL 2018, 150).

When we unpack the Create Competencies for school librarians under Include, it's clear that creating rich opportunities and learning activities is key, specifically those in which learners can "adjust their awareness of the global learning community" (AASL 2018, School Librarian II.B.).

Using the AASL Standards as a guide, author visits *can* be structured to be inclusive. Doing so requires intentionality, however, and active disruption of the "traditional model" of author visits in which purchasing titles "buys" learners face time with visiting authors or being in a gifted program earns learners a spot in a workshop with an author.

With the support of the University of North Carolina's Susan Steinfirst Artist-in-Residency Program and professors Sandra Hughes-Hassell and Brian Sturm, school librarians Liz Porter, Kathryn Cole, and I partnered with authors Meg Medina, Charles R. Smith Jr., and Matt de la Peña to build inclusive writer-in-residence programs with learners at our respective schools, disrupting the traditional author visit model. Using our experiences, we developed an equitable writer-in-residence model framed by six touchstones that demonstrate the Include Shared Foundation and that can be used as a model for any author or artist visit.

Lift Every Voice: An Equitable Writer-in-Residence Model

Liz Porter, Kathryn Cole, Julie Stivers, and Sandra Hughes-Hassell

An eighth grader bends over a laptop that plays the music he wrote for his poem *Bolted Tombs,* while author Matt de la Peña holds headphones to his ears, listening. Author Charles R. Smith Jr. sits and listens as a fourth-grade learner reads, "I am a tall, handsome, Black boy; I am me," and cheers erupt from the gathered families. Two fifth-grade learners sit in their school library staring intently at their laptop screens. Sitting in between them, also intent on her laptop, is visiting author Meg Medina. What holds their attention so closely? It's their classmate Angelyne's poem "I Call Him Padrino."

When author visits reflect these powerful snapshots within our school communities, they serve as affirmations for our learners and their voices. When visiting authors authentically reflect our learners and their lived experiences, the affirmations increase in power and can help create an inclusive school library practice.

All the reasons we collect and use reflective literature also apply to bringing authors to our schools. What messages are we sending to our learners if the only authors we privilege by inviting them to visit our schools are white and cishet? As school librarians, we must spearhead efforts to ensure that visiting authors reflect the cultures and lived experiences of our learners.

Recognizing this truth and in partnership with the School of Information and Library Science (SILS) at the University of North Carolina at Chapel Hill, three North Carolina school librarians and their learners had the privilege of hosting dynamic authors for weeklong residencies through the Susan Steinfirst Artist-in-Residency Program, funded by the Howard, Steinfirst, and Martin families. Recognizing the inequity that is often inherent in selecting the youth who are invited to participate in writer-in-residence programs, the stakeholders for the Susan Steinfirst initiative focused on creating a program that centered the voices and experiences of youth who often do not get these opportunities in many K–12 schools: youth of color,

English learners, and youth from lower socioeconomic communities. The program had three overarching goals:

- To provide a unique, exciting, intellectual opportunity for learners from marginalized communities
- To allow learners to work with authors who look like them, providing space for BIYOC to express their authentic cultural voices and share their unique perspectives on the world
- To add complexity and depth to the current "single story" most youth encounter in schools

The Susan Steinfirst partnerships of learners, school librarians, and authors took place at three venues:

- Mount Vernon Middle School—an alternative, public, academic recovery 6–8 school with 80 percent male learners. School librarian Julie Stivers partnered with author Matt de la Peña.
- Northside Elementary School—a traditional Pre-K–5 public school and a Historical Rosenwald School for African American Youth. School librarian Kathryn Cole partnered with author Charles R. Smith Jr.
- Carrboro Elementary School—a Pre-K–5 public school that includes both traditional and dual language programs and serves a large population of first-language Spanish speakers. School librarian Liz Porter partnered with author Meg Medina.

We believe these residency experiences illustrate the magic and power of equity-framed and equity-driven writing experiences. Because of the funding provided by SILS and the Steinfirst grants, we were extremely lucky to have these incredible authors at our schools for a full week. However, this model can be used for any author, illustrator, or artist visit, workshop, or virtual session. Even though this model was born out of our weeklong writer-in-residence experiences, it has been refined through additional author experiences we've hosted—both in person and virtually.

Touchstones

In developing these programs, we identified six touchstones (figure 6.1) that we found to be essential in building writing experiences within an equity framework. The touchstones include classroom educator and school librarian language as well as learner-friendly language. We were intentional about building these touchstones to be learner-centered, and viewing them through the lens of our learners was critical for us in identifying and describing each touchstone's central message.

BUILDING WRITING EXPERIENCES WITHIN AN EQUITY FRAMEWORK

1 Builds a learning environment that honors and amplifies student voice.

My voice matters.

2 Collaborates with stakeholders to ensure program resonates, fostering engagement for reading in the classroom and beyond.

Our whole school is celebrating the work of an author who is BIPOC.

3 Selects students with a framework that strives to eliminate sorting based on systemic racially oppressive factors such as behavior or reading levels and prioritizes students from traditionally marginalized communities.

I was chosen!

4 Foregrounds culturally-sustaining instructional strategies.

I enjoy learning this way.

5 Reaffirms positive racial/ethnic identity and infuses entire process with joy.

I'm proud to be ______________.

6 Removes grading or high-pressure assignments. Focus is on welcoming and appreciating authentic voice and workshopping with students.

I'm free to create.

Based on Steinfirst Partnerships + author/educator collaborations: Meg Medina/Liz Porter, Charles R. Smith/Kathryn Cole, Matt de la Peña/Julie Stivers, with Sandra Hughes-Hassell. Visit www.steinfirstartistinresidency.web.unc.edu

FIGURE 6.1 / **Equitable writer-in-resident model**

The model uses these six touchstones for building writing experiences within an equity framework.

To illustrate the power inherent in these touchstones and to explain how they were created, here are examples from our writer-in-residence experiences for each touchstone, including learner artifacts. This learner work not only illuminates the potential of equity-framed author visits but also can serve as inspiration for creative writing opportunities in your own school library.

TOUCHSTONE 1: Builds a learning environment that honors and amplifies learner voice.

—My voice matters.

The heart of this program is giving learners an avenue to share their authentic selves and a platform to amplify their voices. There is power in self-expression, and learners' voices must be heard. "My voice matters. I have things to say." The twenty-two fifth-grade learners who participated in Northside Elementary's Susan Steinfirst Residency are more than just a number. They are twenty-two births, twenty-two stories, with twenty-two futures. They are seeds, they are roots that run deep, and they are dreamers. They are twenty-two voices that matter and deserve to be heard. Learners expressed their voices through numerous poetry exercises that ended in published "I am" poems that celebrated their identities.

When Mekhai shares, "I am a 3D printer building the pieces of my life," we see his voice echoed through the lines of his poetry. Robin wrote, "I am a vase not easily broken." That strength was not something Robin always showed outwardly, and it was beautiful to witness the power in that line.

I AM by Mekhai
I am the BFG tall and towering.
I am the stitched mouth from Coraline.
I am Allen Iverson dribbling skills that impress.
I am the Grinch on Mondays.
I am alpaca hair.
I am Kobe Bryant cross-ups.
I am Jimmy Butler navigating life without love.
I am Devin Booker's fadeaways.
I am rainbow ice cream with swirls.
I am a 3D printer building pieces of my life.
I am me!

I AM by Robin
I am a drizzy queen nothing but myself.
I am the Smith family tree.
I am red leaves in the fall.
I am awake in the ocean breeze.
I am a chapter in a book of Dork Diaries.
I am a vase not easily broken.
I am the creator of my mind.
I am a believer in my mind.
I am the youngest marcher.
I am one of four.
I am the capital of North Carolina.
I am a beautiful box braid queen.
I am the word "powerful" in the dictionary.
I am a blue and white Tar-heel.
I AM ME!

Through the residency, voices were lifted and celebrated. Author Charles R. Smith Jr. made a point of telling our #CRSjrWriters, "You have to share your words. You have to share your story. If not, someone else will write it for you. Who are you? Make sure others get it right. . . . You write it."

At Carrboro Elementary, eighteen fourth-grade learners created multiple pieces of poetry with author Meg Medina—poems they put together into a zine that celebrated their creativity and identity. (Zines—short for *magazines* or *fanzines*—are self-produced and self-published works of original or collated texts and images, often centered on one topic.) Throughout the week, Meg paused the writing to share a learner's work with the group, lifting up their voices at every stage of the writing process. When learners shared their zines with their parents at a Writers' Cafe, each learner chose which poem they wanted to share with their family. This event at the end of the residency was a truly proud moment: all learners received personalized introductions from Meg and loud snaps from the audience in celebration.

TOUCHSTONE 2: Collaborates with school stakeholders to ensure program resonates, fostering engagement for reading in the classroom and beyond.

—Our whole school is celebrating.

We wanted the entire school to benefit from these powerful author experiences. Using Dr. Rudine Sims Bishop's powerful analogy, we wanted all our learners to see the windows and mirrors of the world through the author's craft (Bishop 1990). In many cases, the author visits provided road maps for our youth and a visual, living representation of a possibility for their futures.

At Northside, Kathryn used Charles R. Smith Jr.'s book *I Am America* as the whole-school choice on World Read Aloud Day. After sharing and discussing the book schoolwide, along with video clips from the author, Kathryn asked everyone—learners, educators, and other staff members—to think of the many ways to describe themselves and to select a favorite descriptor to lift up and highlight. Each learner completed this activity individually, but Kathryn also took class pictures so everyone could see that together they are a family, both in the classroom and across the school. Kathryn then created a hallway display featuring every learner, educator, and staff member, thus reflecting a unique part of their identity on the school's walls and halls. And, of course, the hallway display also allowed learners to see each other in new ways.

In the weeks before author Meg Medina arrived at Carrboro Elementary School, each grade participated in a theatrical reading of her picture book *Mango, Abuela, and Me* in the school's auditorium. Liz read the story aloud with the pages projected on a screen, and learners put on costumes and used props to mime the action of each page. In this way, learners inhabited Meg's story and engaged with her writing in an immersive way. Carrboro learners also helped welcome Meg with art: kindergartners made Mango the Parrot drawings with speech bubbles of a word they wanted someone like Abuela to know, and fourth and fifth graders created and decorated their own autobiographical book titles inspired by *Mango, Abuela, and Me.*

The fourth graders also held an author study of Meg's work, diving deeper into both *Mango, Abuela, and Me* and *Tía Isa Wants a Car*. Liz tied the visit into Carrboro's Women's History Month program: "Women change the world and so can you / Las mujeres cambian el mundo y tú también puedes hacerlo." Learners explored female changemakers, read books about Malala Yousafzai and Pura Belpré, and reflected on the changes they wanted to make in the world themselves. After hearing Pura Belpré's story, learners were able to fully appreciate Meg's winning of the Pura Belpré Award, and it was a wonderful way to prepare learners for her visit. At the end of the residency, every learner in the school received a celebratory Meg Medina bookmark bearing quotes from her books. "It's our job to write the stories that invite a deeper look inside of ourselves" (PEN America 2017).

Julie had a two-pronged approach at Mount Vernon for fostering engagement throughout the school. In the weeks and months leading up to Matt's visit, the English/language arts (ELA) teachers and Julie worked together to bring *Last Stop on Market Street, Believing in Brooklyn* (a short story), and *The Living* into the ELA curriculum. All learners also celebrated Matt's work with art projects related to his book covers.

Author visits can also be naturally embedded into classroom and school community routines. For example, at Northside one of the second-grade educators asked this morning question: "If you could write a book like our resident author, Charles R. Smith Jr., what would it be about?" At Mount Vernon, Matt's visit was seamlessly included in the school's Career Day, giving learners the opportunity to engage in discussion circles with Matt about their futures and then reflect on the experience with their classroom educators at the end of the day. Building community that centers the author and their works expands the impact of their visit.

We realize that in many schools, author visits are often tied to selling books, a toxic reality that serves as a sorting mechanism that can determine which learners get to spend time with an author. In that traditional model, only those learners able to purchase a book get face time in the signing line. School librarians can counteract this sorting inequity by devising workarounds, such as allowing learners to bring books purchased by the library to the signing line. We implore you to think beyond those workarounds. Consider identifying grant opportunities or crowd-sourcing funding opportunities such as Donors Choose to allow *every* learner to own one of the visiting author's books. Ensure that a wide, representative group in your school receives time with your visiting authors—regardless of which learners can afford to purchase titles.

TOUCHSTONE 3: **Selects learners with a framework that strives to eliminate sorting based on systemic racially oppressive factors such as behavior or reading levels and prioritizes learners from traditionally marginalized communities.**

—I was chosen!

For learners these are three powerful words: *I was chosen.* Although each of the residencies included opportunities for whole-school interactions with the authors, the purpose of the residencies was to provide a smaller group of learners at each school the opportunity to engage in intensive writing workshops with an author for an entire week. In other words, to be chosen!

In selecting the learners who participated in the small-group workshops, we employed an equity lens, one designed to intentionally counter the problems inherent in traditional writer-in-residence models that rely on selecting, or sorting, learners based on criteria such as reading level, writing ability, grades, or behavior. You may be wondering what is wrong with sorting for selection. Simply put, too often bias finds its way into the processes used to select learners for enrichment activities. For example, learners may be disqualified for behavior reasons. However, identification of behavior problems is rooted in educational inequities and institutional racism in our schools. There are coded words we must push back on that could be used to describe a learner in order to prevent that individual from participating in a residency: *active, troublemaker, talkative, a handful, tough, defiant.*

Likewise, identified reading levels should never be associated with a capacity to think or discuss big ideas. Reading levels have no place in a discussion about opportunities for writing experiences with an author. Instead, an equitable model encourages selection that prioritizes learners from traditionally marginalized communities.

At Mount Vernon, there were fourteen #MdlPwriters—a seventh-grade group and an eighth-grade group. They were the stars of the work: Kevin, Nia, Brian, Hector, Tony, Sharon, Tae, Fredyi, Maurice, Hunter, Leila, LaKeisha, Amy, and Kamdin. Julie looked at only two factors for participation—interest and willingness—intentionally eschewing factors that could have been barriers to participation such as grades, reading level, or arbitrary behavior standards. Both groups participated in a mini-elective with Julie for an entire quarter before Matt came. The seventh graders read and discussed *The Living* while the eighth graders dove into *Mexican WhiteBoy*.

There were twenty-two #CRSJrWriters at Northside Elementary: Didier, Isaiah, Jasiah, Jordan, Josue, LeShaun, Makai, Michael, Michelle, Natalie, Mia, Avery, Brandon, Chanmeeyae, Jayden, Joel, Robin, Sa'chi, Joseph, Kahlei, Lance, and Mieyari. They were selected in coordination with classroom educators. Kathryn and the participating educators established book clubs with the selected learners before Charles's visit.

There were eighteen #MegMedinaWriters at Carrboro Elementary: Azul, Jocelyn, Evelyn, Marilan, Kevin, Gary, Antonio, Allisson, Kelvin, Alex, Daniel, Kalani, Angelyne, Andrea, Jamie, Hermione, Aylin, and Jacqueline. Liz worked with classroom educators and support staff to choose writers who spoke Spanish at home from among the Latinx learners in the school's fourth-grade dual language program. Again, the youth were chosen regardless of their reading or writing levels or their perceived disciplinary status.

Equity in selecting learners was the backbone of the Susan Steinfirst Writer-in-Residence program and should be the backbone of every program like it. It matters. And the benefits last far beyond the time the author is with you. One of Julie's seventh-grade writers, Nia, is now in twelfth grade at one of the early college academies in her school district. When Julie asked her about writing and how her seventh-grade experiences had changed her, she said, "I still really love to write. When I'm bored, get depressed, or when I want to reflect and spill out ideas, I write."

Kevin was another of Julie's seventh-grade writers. He had never written for pleasure before that experience, but the Monday after Matt left, Kevin said, "Ms. Stivers, I wrote eight pages this weekend." Kevin wrote every night for the rest of the year and brought in his notebook each morning. Of course, Julie read that writing every day and left encouraging notes in the margins! Kevin is now a twelfth grader and recently told Julie, "When I'm down, I write. When I need it, I write."

Matt wrote this message for all the Mount Vernon learners on the library wall: "Let 'em know you're here!" When learners are selected using an equity lens, they will do it. They will let the world know that they are here!

TOUCHSTONE 4: Foregrounds culturally sustaining instructional strategies.

—I enjoy learning this way.

As Django Paris and H. Samy Alim (2017) have explained, culturally sustaining pedagogy (CSP)

> seeks to perpetuate and foster—to sustain—linguistic, literate, and cultural pluralism as part of schooling for positive social transformation and revitalization. CSP positions dynamic cultural dexterity as a necessary good, and sees the outcome of learning as additive, rather than subtractive, as remaining whole rather than framed as broken, as critically enriching strengths rather than replacing deficits.

As school librarians, we can work to incorporate culturally sustaining pedagogy into our work in many ways. The writer-in-residence experience and the preparation for it can be both culturally sustaining and affirming.

Communalism is a strength in BIPOC communities, and to honor that strength, that asset, the pre-visit electives at Mount Vernon were discussion-based and collaborative. These pre-visit electives centered on the shared enjoyment of Matt de la Peña's novels and included collaborative projects, not competitions. Matt also wove community throughout his instruction. On the first day he said, "We have to continue to support each other. We need to respect each other's voices and our bravery, because writing is brave."

Having high expectations is another key tenet of culturally sustaining pedagogy. At Mount Vernon, Julie and Matt communicated high expectations to the writers as they engaged with the texts and had critical conversations about issues of race and power. Matt used writing exercises with the #MdlPwriters—all middle school learners—that he previously had only used with college and high school learners.

Using reflective, inclusive titles and foregrounding #OwnVoices texts are also foundational for culturally sustaining literacy programs. Figure 6.2 shows the texts we used in the classroom and with our writing groups across the three residencies. Of course, having those outstanding, reflective texts and even reading them is not enough: How are we using them? How are we situating them into an antibias, anti-racist curriculum? Across our preparation and residencies, we used those inclusive texts to discuss identity, race, power, racism, microaggressions, countries of origin, history (outside the white normative), family, immigration justice, and the meaning of *home*.

FIGURE 6.2 / **Writer-in-residence texts**

Picture books, novels, and short stories such as these can be used in classroom collaborations and writing groups.

Expanding our expectations of what learners create to include multiple forms of expression is also essential to equitable and inclusive practice. Art was critically important for the lead-up to Matt de la Peña's visit. Mount Vernon does not have an art educator or art program, so Julie works to marry art with literacy. All the seventh- and eighth-grade learners in the school painted alternate book covers for *The Living,* pulling out elements of setting or plot to highlight. The sixth graders created a large collaborative art piece based on the cover of *Last Stop on Market Street.*

To attempt to measure any changes in writers' confidence and comfort levels related to a variety of literacy factors, Julie created a twelve-question writing and reading self-efficacy assessment instrument to administer to the writers both before and after their reading elective and writer-in-residence experiences. All the writers, across both grades, chose a higher value to describe their writing ability *after* Matt's visit. Eighth-grade learner Maurice shared this poem with many educators throughout the school after Matt's residency, and it was published in *Libraries, Literacy, and African American Youth* (Hughes-Hassell et al., 2016):

The Bolted Tombs by Maurice

U Know
Secrets
Darkness hidden

from
the
light
Nowhere
to go.

A
Fighter
hidden

from
the
fight.

I wonder what's

N
E
X
T

Where
will
I
go?

Still smiling.
No emotion to show.

The #MegMedinaWriters met in the school library once a week in the two months before the residency to explore Meg Medina's writing by examining *Tía Isa Wants a Car* and *Sol Painting, Inc.* (a short story). In our exploration of *Tía Isa Wants a Car,* in which a little girl's tía has a dream and accomplishes it, we encouraged learners to connect with their future selves. Learners explored their own dreams for the future and considered the steps they would need to take to achieve those dreams. We created glittery cardstock keys with a dream on one side and the steps on the other. It was beautiful for learners to share their dreams with each other:

- *My dream is to be a doctor*
- *learn 3 other languages*
- *robotics engineer and get a mustang*
- *get a lambo, get a mansion, get a monster truck*
- *my dream is that I want to make the whole world peaceful*
- *my sueños: un caro, es cantar, jugar, corer*
- *Finish College: I will need to learn new things, try hard in school, save money.*

It was important that learners were not only reading Meg Medina's work but connecting that written experience to their future.

In using the works of Charles R. Smith Jr. at Northside Elementary, Kathryn wanted to examine traditionally lesser known historical figures and events. Leading up to the author's visit, she used his book *Black Jack: The Ballad of Jack Johnson* to lead learners in using a critical lens to examine American history, specifically hidden figures. Why haven't we heard of this sports icon before? What was his impact? What barriers did he overcome? The class looked at primary sources such as photographs and video clips. Throughout their exploration, learners captured in words or sketches what they were learning about each historical figure. Together, the learners created a list of words that captured what they had discovered. The learners then used those words to create word poems that described Jack Johnson. Some of the learners created word clouds, while others created poetry that took the shape of a symbol that represented Jack Johnson, like boxing gloves.

Northside fifth graders also explored Smith's book *Brick by Brick* and used various texts to explore this example of *missing history*—history that is not included in most traditional history curricula. Learners asked, "How was enslaved labor used in the construction of the White House?" Comparing two online resources in which the construction is discussed, learners determined what was missing from each resource and then asked *why*. Learners also orally performed the book, setting it to a background beat.

"Music I Like + Writing = Engagement." Powerful learner words, demonstrating how music was one of the many ways Charles R. Smith Jr. connected with Northside learners. He asked the learners what music they liked and then used some of that same music to generate poetry exercises. Learners were able to listen to music that held meaning for them while they crafted their own identity poems. In the school library, they always sat where they worked best, in places of comfort. It was a necessary, learner-centered approach to their writing process.

TOUCHSTONE 5: Reaffirms positive racial and ethnic identities and infuses the entire process with joy.

—I'm proud to be _______________________.

Most of the paragraphs in this section begin with a powerful learner proclamation that highlights the importance of Touchstone 5. As a learner said after Meg's visit, **"I feel good about myself. I am proud to be a writer."** As Meg and Liz planned the Carrboro residency and zine project, they knew they wanted to be explicit about empowering learners as writers and identifying them as writers. Meg designed many of the writing activities to reinforce these goals. She began by inviting learners to finish the sentence, "When I am writing, I . . ." Learners wrote varied responses to this prompt, sharing their diverse writing processes:

- *When I am writing, I feel free.*
- *When I am writing, I feel like other kids.*
- *When I am writing, I feel like master cheetah comes through.*
- *When I am writing, I let myself go.*
- *When I am writing, I help people see what we see.*
- *When I am writing, there's a bunch of words floating in my head.*
- *When I am writing, I create a magical world.*
- *When I am writing, I don't have to talk. It's like instead I am talking to the blank paper and the paper doesn't respond. When I am writing I don't have to expect an answer.*

Meg supplied many creative "zine-ing" supplies for learners to use to personalize their zines, but two important stamps bearing the words *created by* and *written by* became a constant across the project. Learners stamped these words all over their zines, adding their name to each one. It was a simple act that declared ownership of their writing and creative expression.

"I feel good about myself. I am proud to be bilingual!" These learner words show how the beauty of bilingualism was woven into the Carrboro residency because learners were free to choose the language they wrote in. In the dual language program at Carrboro, half the learners' day of instruction is in English and half is in Spanish, but they rarely have the opportunity to write as they often speak, moving between both. After being encouraged to let their writing reflect their lived linguistic experience, learners created similes such as "I am strong like a gorilla or gentle como el viento" and poems such as "Juan, who wants my mama and the rest of my family to be feliz. Juan mi padre." Meg shared her experience of language in her family. When speaking about her loved ones, she often switched between Spanish and English. Meg asked, "Do any of you have that?" and learners chimed in with how language was used in their homes and families. Meg listened, thus recognizing the important role of language in learners' lives and explicitly honoring the value of Spanish and bilingualism.

"I feel good about myself. I am proud of my family." In preparation for writing a poem about "a person that matters," learners brought in photos of their family members and other loved ones. Meg talked to them about who was in each photo. Pictures of and poems about sisters, cousins, tías, moms, dads, padrinos, and friends filled the school library. The tone of the poems ranged from lighthearted, as in Kevin's poem about his sister Daysi telling him to "GET OUT" of her room, to Daniel's and Aylin's heartfelt tributes to their moms. Daniel wrote, "Estela mi mama es la mejor, pelo negro, manos normales, Y son ríe mucho" ("Estela my Mom is the best, black hair, normal hands, and she smiles a lot"). Aylin shared her mother's dreams with pride: "Lourdes my mami dreams about buying a big house for the family and dreams that we turn into people that will help my country and change the world." Many of the learners, including Aylin and Daniel, were able to read their "a person that matters" poems to the subject of their poem during the family celebration at the end of the week.

"I feel good about myself. I am proud to be Mexican!" The majority of the #MegMedinaWriters were of Mexican heritage, and all the learners were encouraged to share their heritage through their writing and the design of their zines. Something as simple as Meg's printing out flags from the countries of the Americas to add to the zines was an important moment. Almost every learner added flags to their zine. Learners were eager to share their heritage with Meg, too. Her Cuban roots meant she needed to be clued in on some important Mexican vocabulary. The group laughed hard as Angelyne explained the *chuchulucos* (snacks) line in one of her poems. Countering the false narrative that the Latinx community is monolithic is key, and what better way to affirm this than to celebrate the wonderful diversity in our Latinx learners!

"I feel good about myself. I am proud to be ME!" From start to finish, Meg Medina's residency was all about the #MegMedinaWriters themselves. Their first activity together before Meg arrived was making collages to introduce themselves to Meg, finding words and images that would share something important with her. All the writing that followed centered the learners: their memories, their families and loved ones, their identity. The zine was truly all about them.

The first exercise Matt did with his writers at Mount Vernon focused on using only two words to reveal an aspect of their identity. The two words that the learners used to describe their lives were incredibly powerful, as were their explanations: *Bloody Art* from Amy, who felt like she had to fight to draw. *Sunny Thunderstorm* from Hector, who told the group that his family helped him put a positive spin on everything. *Fun Life* from Fredyi, who told us he felt lucky to be Latino. And, of course, *Bolted Tombs,* which was the genesis of Maurice's moving poem. Julie loved this two-word writing exercise so much that she has incorporated it into other literacy activities. Learners can use the format to explore characters in fiction or to look deeper inside new characters that they are creating.

The second part of Touchstone 5 urges creation of a writing experience that "infuses the entire process with joy." These writers wrote hard, but they wrote joyfully. At all three schools, it was a joyful week! Joy was the foundation for a residency built around the idea—the truth—that every learner, every writer is unique and valued.

As part of the week with Charles at Northside Elementary, learners created "I am" poems that incorporated elements of themselves—things they loved, identified with, or connected to—and shared them out loud with others. They crafted poems for which they unabashedly pulled in parts of their identity and expressed pride in them, recording the pieces digitally to further spread the reach of their words. Mia stated, "I am black hurricanes / I am braided twisted hair / I am self-assured / I am a beautiful black QUEEN." She looked at herself and saw, looking back, a beautiful Black queen! Kathryn loved how Mia owned that truth with joy and lifted it up to share with the world.

Through their poetry the learners were able to speak to their true selves. Lashaun expressed himself by writing, "I am building train tracks to travel my world / I am an LA dreamer / I am sunny side up with a smile that shines / I am the author in a world of books." Natalie purposefully chose to begin her poem with "I am a beautiful shade of black" and then added, "I am the swag of Beyonce / I am an artist painting my world / I am a bright red tulip growing strong each day." It is powerful and beautiful to see learners showing joy and pride in their authentic selves.

TOUCHSTONE 6: Removes grading or high-pressure assignments. Focus is on welcoming and appreciating authentic voice and workshopping with learners.

—I'm free to create.

The wonderful reality about zines? There is no wrong way to create them! When Meg and Liz were planning Meg's residency, they considered writing a collaborative picture book, but Meg's zine idea really grabbed their imagination. Zines are adaptable. There would be no learner who did not finish in time or did not have enough work to share. Zines are personalized. Each learner can let their creativity loose in a zine, reflecting their own unique style! Any learner can participate, and learners with different writing skills all have entry points to the project.

Led by Meg, learners explored many aspects of figurative language and types of poetry during the week. They began with a color poem whereby Meg guided learners to explore imagery by combining two things that are the same color. "What two words can you put together that would make a really good picture?" she asked. She encouraged unusual word companions and pushed learners to make the harder choice of words: *"cherry fires, hot pepper pants, fall leaf feather, mango mole."* They moved on to similes with prompts such as "That old dog was sweet as a . . ." and "The monster's mouth was black as a . . ." These prompts led to original and creative similes, including "Her temper was sharp as a 1,000-degree knife" and "Her temper was sharp as a cactus and a savage porcupine."

Learners delved into childhood memories with Meg, bringing in toys they used to play with to write their "I remember that toy" poems. Meg asked them to answer questions in their poem. What does the toy look like? Who did they play with? Why is the toy important? Evelyn wrote, "The toy dog was important because it reminds me of my stepbrother and the toy dog always seemed like it was alive. I named him burrito and my sister named hers burrita. :)"

Learners were invited to choose someone important to them to write about in their "a person that matters" poem. Led by Meg, learners wrote about what their chosen person looks like, how they spend their time, what they always say to the learner, and what they dream of, crafting a beautiful pattern that repeated the person's name.

At our Writer's Cafe, Kalani was able to share this poem about his dad, who sat three feet away:

> My dad who I call Tony.
> He is playful and amazing.
> Tambien aveces me dice
> que vaya mos corriendo.
> El corre y yoenbici.
> He sometimes buys me things—
> not big, just up to 5 bucks.
> Also, Tony the one who
> wants papeles so I can go to
> Mexico with my family.
> Tony el que siempre dice—
> ay kalani,
> cuandoyohago algo que no
> está bien.
> Tony, who always loves me,
> who says goodbye after
> dropping me off at school.

Over the course of the residency, Meg focused on writing as *rewriting*. The writers experimented, edited, and created without judgment. She told the group, "We have first ideas and then better ideas," dedicating half of each session to pulling learners into workshopping pairs with her. In emphasizing the *process* of writing, Meg took the pressure off the final product. Whatever learners created was valuable and worth sharing and celebrating.

Charles also led learners through mini-lessons on specific poetry concepts combined with writing and revision time. Time was also dedicated to feedback and small, one-on-one conferences as learners crafted their poems. Charles even took time out to provide "boxing" sessions when learners needed a break. Learners spent time together talking through the process of poetry, sitting in the library wherever they felt comfortable. Providing space for joy and the freedom to create, centering learners and their identity, and lifting their voices made a lasting impact on our learners.

As Charles's residency came to a close, Northside's writers were celebrated for their work at a family reading. At the end of Leshaun's "I am" poem, he states, "I am a tall handsome Black boy. I am me." In a video of his reading, you see him glance toward his family and then you see and hear the validation he receives in return. Leshaun's family cheers and voices their pride in hearing him express himself. We should be celebrating together and cheering on our youth for sharing their voices with the world. This is powerful writing. Writing that they can hold up high, yet also close to their hearts. Working closely with an author and creating a piece that reflected their authentic selves made this experience so meaningful.

Matt workshopped in a way similar to that of Charles and Meg and shared his fun, relatable wisdom on writing throughout the week. "Real writing is revising," and "We must embrace the shittiness of our first drafts." Even when Julie had seventh- and eighth-grade learners in her mini-electives for the quarter before Matt came, she removed grading from the equation. The goals for the residency and its preparation were #OwnVoices reading, free creation, working on drafts, and celebrating writing that would live on. Learners were not working for a grade but writing for themselves.

Using the Equitable Model and Six Touchstones

Although the equitable writer-in-residence model was birthed during our weeklong residencies, this model can be used to guide any author or artist experience. We have used it for a spectrum of visits, including short, virtual ones. When bringing an author or artist to visit your school, be intentional. Consider that the actions you take that may seem like they are simply "how it is done" or "what people are used to" can reinforce the systems that deny opportunities to our learners from traditionally marginalized groups. Wearing the label of *writer* can be a powerful way for our learners to move through school and the world.

Shift your thinking and help others in your school shift their thinking about how a visiting author can impact your learners. Using these six touchstones, create experiences at your school that are inclusive and empowering. This framework and the idea of formulating an author visit centering equitable practices created real change in our schools. The impact has been broad and lasting. Create a similar impact by lifting the beautiful voices at your school! Your learners are ready.

Note: To read more about our experiences with the Steinfirst Artist-in-Residency Program, visit https://steinfirstartistinresidency.web.unc.edu/.

The Six Touchstones and Include

What better way to commit to "inclusiveness and respect for diversity in the learning community" (AASL 2018, 76) than by bringing BIPOC authors into our schools to create empowering writing experiences with our learners? Clearly, Liz, Kathryn, and I were beyond lucky to have amazing authors at our schools for a week, but this model is applicable not only for funded, intensive residencies. It works for *any* school visit, and we've applied it to a range of author and illustrator experiences, many with local authors.

Using an equitable writer-in-residence model is a clear way to realize the Create Competencies for school librarians.

- Building supportive writer groups aligned with the six touchstones is an ideal way to provide "opportunities for learners to interact with others who reflect a range of perspectives" (AASL 2018, School Librarian II.B.1.). Not only are learners exploring with a diverse group of learner-writers, they are having access to authors who are providing counter-stories to a single narrative. Learners who are participating in equitable, inclusive literacy activities are also illustrating diverse viewpoints (AASL 2018, School Librarian II.B.3.) by engaging in creative writing and exploring authors' #OwnVoices titles.
- Essential to equitable writing experiences and author visits is the inclusion of reflective resources. Our whole-school instructional threads allowed each learner to connect to the visiting authors before their visit and enabled us to integrate into the core curriculum texts that were representative of our learners' lived experiences. Having an author visit seamlessly supports the inclusion of diverse texts in classroom instruction. Once school stakeholders see their impact, the titles often find a permanent home in the curriculum. This is another way in which we can chip away at the traditional literary canon and challenge the normative position of whiteness in the curriculum. Our learners need activities that require them to both "evaluate a variety of perspectives" and "illustrate diverse viewpoints" (AASL 2018, School Librarian II.B.2., II.B.3.)—realizing this Competency from the AASL Standards supports our learners' right to inclusive resources throughout their schools.

Questions for the Reflective Practitioner

1. How can I use the AASL Standards and the Shared Foundation of Include to understand that bringing authors, artists, and speakers from marginalized communities to our schools improves the educational experience for *all* our learners?
2. How can I use the touchstones in the equitable writer-in-residence model to realize the Competencies under Include?
3. The Competencies under the Create Domain for school librarians foreground the development of opportunities in which learners are engaged with diverse perspectives. How will this goal come to life in my school library?

Moving Forward

WHAT CAN I DO TODAY?

Reflect on which communities of learners in your school have been previously excluded by not having an author or artist visit who identifies as being from the same community.

HOW CAN I BUILD ON IT TOMORROW?

Using the communities you've identified, look for authors and artists who would be representative of your learners for a school visit. Authors do not have to be *New York Times* best sellers to be impactful—look locally first!

ACTION STEPS

- Partner with a local bookstore, another school, or a PTA/PTO, or identify grant funding to build an inclusive visiting author experience for your learners.
- Use the empowering writing exercises that Meg Medina, Charles R. Smith Jr., and Matt de la Peña led with learners to build your own creative writing opportunities in the school library.
- Consider using the six touchstones of the equitable writer-in-residence model as a jumping-off point for addressing other growth opportunities in your school—from school assemblies to visiting scientists and experts to career day invitees.

7

Share with a Mental Wellness Curriculum

The *National School Library Standards* include helpful Evaluation Checklists that are directly tied to the six Shared Foundations and Key Commitments. Under Include, the school librarian is called on to develop and maintain "a teaching and learning environment that is inviting, safe, flexible, and conducive to learning" (AASL 2018, 175). We know that this straightforward guidance is both necessary and effort-filled to put into real action every day in our school libraries.

Creating school environments that are inviting and flexible is particularly meaningful when we look at the prevalence of mental health issues in our schools. One in five of our teen learners is living with a mental health condition, with the average delay between onset of symptoms and intervention being eight to ten years (NAMI 2016). How can we support the mental wellness of our learners through the school library?

We can use the school librarian Competencies under the Share Domain of Include to guide us in our efforts because we are directed to "facilitate experiences in which learners exhibit empathy and tolerance" (AASL 2018, School Librarian II.C.). By supporting the empathy and tolerance of our learners through a mental wellness lens, not only will we build inclusive learning environments, we can positively impact the social-emotional learning for school stakeholders. How do these ideas look when put into sustainable action?

Anita Cellucci, librarian at Westborough High School in Massachusetts, built a mental wellness curriculum at her school, prioritizing the school library as a stigma-free space. Her story serves as both inspiration and roadmap for the Include Shared Foundation and is filled with transferable ideas.

Mental Wellness Curriculum

Anita Cellucci

Creating a space that honors diverse ideas, fosters empathy, and provides a basis for equity has been the driving force from my first days as a school librarian. Developing a way to address mental health within the school library space was not an overnight decision or a quick fix. My entire reason for becoming a school librarian centered on the idea that a school library can be a refuge for those who are in need. Libraries as an antidote for toxic social issues is deeply ingrained in my philosophy about the function of a library in society, and I've always believed that school librarians can and should be catalysts for change within education. Transferring this belief to action was an important transition.

In my first year as a high school librarian, after working in elementary, middle school, and public libraries for fifteen years, I co-created a joint teen advisory board alongside the public library director. We focused on social issues, community service, and improvement of the town libraries for teens. Teens who participated had opportunities to reflect on their own place within a global community.

Collaborating with an English educator, we created a spoken word/slam poetry club. The poetry club provided a space for learners to write about their experiences and to prepare for and perform in an annual festival. The learners in the poetry club participated in active debates, informal discussions, and deep conversations about diverse perspectives. It was an active way to help teens develop empathy and tolerance for diversity. I've continued with both of these programs, and they are still vital aspects of the school library. During these first years in the high school, I wrote several grants to enable artists, poets, authors, and performers to visit the school and work directly with our learners. The majority of the grants were locally funded through an education foundation and cultural council. A passion for providing pathways for learner voice as well as creating an understanding within the community of the needs of teens was beginning to take hold and create impact.

Over the next several years, I continued to focus on learner voice. Collaborations with town entities was a priority because it brought a powerful validity to all our programs. Although I wasn't intentionally focusing on mental health during this period, I was providing inclusive practice that allowed me to become empathetic to issues that teens face. As an example, at this time I became a co-chair of a literacy project committee in the town. The committee had members from town departments such as Youth and Family Services and the public library, as well as counselors and educators. Our focus was to bring teen issues to light for adults in the community by having intergenerational conversations about these issues through YA literature. In our first attempt, we encountered pushback from adults but also created a way for teens to know that we saw them and understood. This process also reinforced my mission as a high school librarian. In addition, teens were taking ownership of the school library as their space, and the transformation was palpable.

Centering Mental Health

I eventually became keenly aware of mental health issues surrounding teens. I knew in my heart that these issues could be highlighted and, I hoped, helped through the school library. I also knew that doing so would take strategic planning and substantial education for the school community. My experience had shown me that educators, parents, and administrators took note of grants. A grant was a way to address a sensitive issue through a meaningful lens and, it was hoped, a budget. I decided to apply for the federal Library Services and Technology Act (LSTA) grant through the Massachusetts Board of Library Commissioners. The grant required that I research the issue and educate myself first. Providing a stigma-free space and access to knowledge and programming became my focus.

I began at the school level. My school is a participant in the MetroWest Adolescent Health Survey. According to the Education Development Center in Massachusetts, since 2006 the survey has been collecting self-reported data on high-priority health and risk behaviors, including substance use, bullying, mental health, violence, sexual behavior, and physical activity. The survey also captures data on emerging and evolving behaviors in the adolescent population, such as cyberbullying, sexting, prescription drug misuse (including opioids), and use of electronic cigarettes. The survey has shown and continues to show increasing trends in mental health issues of teens throughout the areas of Massachusetts that are surveyed. As I delved deeper into the trends of this data, I looked to the National Alliance on Mental Illness (NAMI), which reports that one in five teens lives with a mental health condition, with less than half receiving medical care. Research also tells us that 50 percent of mental health conditions emerge by age 14, and 75 percent by age 24 (NAMI 2016).

What I found astounding at this time was the lack of knowledge and understanding that the typical high school educator had about teen mental health. Most educators do not take classes or trainings that would help identify a struggling teen. In fact, the default often becomes a narrative that the learner is apathetic or unmotivated without any attention to the reason. Because mental health is a complex issue, I took courses to develop my own basic knowledge—NAMI Basics as well as a certification in Mental Health First Aid through the National Council for Behavioral Health. The courses were extremely helpful in writing and defending the grant.

The process of securing a federal grant is long and arduous. I was given a mentor to work with and a strict timeline. Writing this grant also opened deep conversations and solidified collaborative relationships with administration, with other educators, and with town departments such as Youth and Family Services and the public library. Interestingly, because this issue was new for libraries, some of my focus was on informing and educating the grant mentor and committee as well. This necessity only strengthened my conviction that this work was essential! In retrospect, I know that the committee was unsure about where this topic "fit" and soon moved me to the Innovative category.

Since my writing of the grant, a mental health category has been added to the LSTA Massachusetts grant process. More public libraries are now creating programming in this area and hiring counseling staff or those with dual degrees. The grant offered a pushing-off point and a way to bring validity to the issue within the school library space during a time when the connection between school libraries and mental health was not clear to those outside the field and also to some within libraries. The grant preparation process also helped me clarify and build a solid foundation in my own approach to inclusivity.

Grant Specifics: Learner Centered and Literacy Based

The target for the grant was a literature course offered to learners during their senior year of high school. The class, Psychology in Literature, offers learners an opportunity to read and critically analyze literature through a psychological lens. The culminating assignment of the course is a research project that uses Guided Inquiry Design with a therapeutic approach to acknowledge emotions that emerge while researching mental health and psychological topics.

During this unit, learners develop individual inquiry questions and reflect on their process and emotions throughout the research. In the grant year, learners shared their final reflective screencasts with ninth-grade learners who were studying mental health issues in their wellness course. In a face-to-face meeting, the younger learners were able to ask questions and have open and honest dialogue with the twelfth graders. In the beginning stages of the research, outside entities such as NAMI and the town department of Youth and Family Services presented to learners about resources as well as programs designed to dismantle stigma related to mental health. Throughout this project, it is typical that learners will self-report that they are themselves struggling with their mental health. The project has created a pathway for many learners to receive the support necessary from school staff as well as from outside-of-school resources.

Some aspects of the grant focused on integrating arts into the destigmatizing of mental health. Our collaborations with artists, poets, and authors focused on mental health topics during the grant timeline. As in previous years, I collaborated with the Massachusetts Literary Education and Performance Collective (MassLEAP) to have a Poets-in-Residence day. Three poets were in attendance, and their poetry focused on their lived experiences of mental health and addiction. Class groups attended throughout the day, and class members were invited to share their own poetry with a positive message for others. The culmination of this day was the creation of a mural with these poems. This mural continues to live in the school library, and both staff and learners continue to remark on the impact of the message.

Along with poetry, literature was a part of the grant implementation. A novel by a local author was chosen—*Alice Bliss* by Laura Harrington—and with grant funds, we planned programming tied into an author visit. Not only were learners involved in an assembly with the author, but classes could sign up to be part of a writing marathon. More than one hundred learners were writing in the school library with the author and sharing their thoughts and their personal reflections in small groups led by educators. Quotations from the book were used as prompts for writing.

Simultaneously, classroom educators were becoming trained in Mental Health First Aid by the National Council for Behavioral Health because Youth and Family Services and the public library were teaming up to bring this training through another grant. Because these town departments were aware of my grant, we worked together to bring the program to the high school. During the first training, I received certification along with ten other educators. This eight-hour training teaches a five-step action plan that is designed to help young people in crisis and noncrisis situations. Because the district saw the value in this training, there is now a coordinator who serves as the trainer for all educators in our district. Also during this time, the counselors brought additional mental health training to our school, and I was able to attend the ten-hour training for dialectical behavior therapy to help bring distress tolerance strategies, including mindfulness, to the classroom and school library.

Mental Health Curriculum in Our Library Today

Although the grant was implemented during the 2015–16 school year, it has continued to impact my school library and the school community. As a result, several collaborations, lessons, and programs have become part of the school library curriculum. There is a continuous fluidity to these programs in that each year more staff members become interested in participating and learners continue to share their voice in the programs' creation and implementation.

Because we knew that supporting teens' mental health consistently needs a multipronged approach, we worked with administration, which was fully supportive of continued implementation of and collaboration for programming in the school library. I have continued to collaborate with special education, the English language learner department, and school counseling, as well as educators of other disciplines to plan mental health initiatives. Although these collaborations look different, they are all focused on the wellness of learners and the promotion of the school library as a stigma-free and accepting space. The following are just some of the programs we've created:

- **Student Wellness Advisory Team.** Our primarily learner-led team is dedicated to promoting mental health awareness and dismantling stigma within our community. The learners are passionate about normalizing conversations about mental health and strive to implement initiatives that support the mental health of learners and instill a greater understanding of mental wellness. They've spearheaded activities such as these:
  - ***Mindful Making.*** This initiative allows learners to create in ways that are impactful to their state of mind, make an item to help with relaxation and mindfulness, or do both. The process is key—mindfulness strategies, as well as poetry and art, are integrated into the making process. Learners have made sensory kits and individual stress-less kits.
  - ***Meditation/Mindful Space.*** We created a meditation/mindful space within the school library to be used by small groups (such as bibliotherapy and dialectical behavior therapy) and by users seeking a quiet space for yoga, Mindful Making, and what we call a Mindful Minute. For the Mindful Minute, we have prepared mindfulness activities that are always available for anyone who would like to use the space (learners and educators). In addition, I lead scheduled mindfulness sessions after school and incorporate Mindful Minutes into classes that I teach in the space.
  - ***School Assemblies.*** We've supported assemblies about sound bath meditation and programs focused on suicide prevention, addiction, and general mental health.
- **Special Education Collaborations**
  - ***Small-Group Work.*** With small groups, we focused on habitudes, mindfulness, and reflective writing, built on the research by Angela Maiers (2012) found in *Classroom Habitudes,* the Collaborative for Academic, Social, and Emotional Learning (CASEL) competencies, and the work of people such as Daniel Goleman, Parker Palmer, and Rachael Kessler.
- **Literacy Collaborations**
  - ***Bibliotherapy.*** I work directly with mental health clinicians and wellness staff to create groups that allow learners who are dealing with anxiety, loss, depression, and other mental health issues to meet in a safe space. In these groups we focus on literature, dialectical behavior therapy strategies, mindfulness, and reflection.
  - ***Growth Mindset through Reading.*** I have co-taught literacy lessons and classes with the English department to reach learners using a therapeutic strategy of bibliotherapy as well as individual conferences to discuss the challenges that keep teens from connecting to reading.

- **Literature in the English Curriculum.** I have held professional discussions with the English department to help implement literature that not only is helpful for social-emotional learning but also reflects learners across a range of identities and experiences, including race, LGBTQ+, and mental health, and that is grounded in social justice.

In addition to searching out professional development related to mental health, I wanted to learn more specifically about trauma-informed practice. I took courses through the Center for Adolescent Studies: Trauma-Informed Practice, and the Advanced Trauma-Informed Care Toolkit Certificate for Youth Workers. The courses offered strategies and suggestions for working with youth impacted by trauma, and they helped me gain a foundational understanding of how trauma affects our brain and physical body.

None of the programs I've shared would have been possible without creating an inclusive environment with my learners, searching out professional development dedicated to mental health and social-emotional wellness, and continually demonstrating an understanding of and commitment to diversity in the learning community.

Mental Wellness Curriculum and Include

There is so much to learn from Anita's work in intentionally weaving mental wellness throughout her school library space and programming. Not only have her efforts impacted her learners but they have affected and educated other stakeholders for teen success—from colleagues in her school and district to families and social support staff in her community to grant-funding organizations! It is truly the Share Domain in practice.

Under Share, Include guides school librarians to give "learners opportunities to engage in informed conversation and active debate" (AASL 2018, School Librarian II.C.1.). Anita realized this Competency through several initiatives:

- Creating a poetry club in which debates and deep conversations about diverse perspectives were foregrounded
- Collaborating with the public library to create a joint teen advisory board through which teens had the opportunity to reflect on social issues affecting their community across a range of teen experiences and perspectives
- Designing writing marathons during which learners wrote with a local author—guided by book quotes as writing prompts—and then shared their thoughts in small groups

The other integral Competency under Share is that school librarians guide "learners to contribute to discussions in which multiple viewpoints on a topic are expressed" (AASL 2018, School Librarian II.C.2.). Anita's mental wellness curriculum demonstrates this Competency through the following projects:

- A Psychology in Literature unit in which learners use YA literature to discuss viewpoints, develop individual inquiry questions, and share reflections
- A Community Literacy Project that held intergenerational discussions about characters and perspectives in YA literature

A key contribution to the success of Anita's mental wellness curriculum is her reliance on searching out necessary trainings, resources, and professional development to support her own learning. Through the course of developing the curriculum, she completed numerous certifications and trainings. When we are working to successfully and meaningfully realize the Competencies under Include, seeking out necessary professional development is essential. The school librarian is always a learner, too!

Questions for the Reflective Practitioner

1. The Share Domain under the Include Shared Foundation requires that school librarians be "modeling and facilitating questioning techniques and group discussion strategies" to help "develop the types of skills [our learners] need to participate fully in a diverse community" (AASL 2018, 80). How do I do this in my own school library across grade levels?
2. The Include Shared Foundation foregrounds learning experiences in which learners exhibit empathy for diverse ideas. Where can I see these learning experiences in my own instruction?
3. How can I use the AASL Standards and exemplars like Anita's mental wellness curriculum to build a learning plan for myself that positively contributes to the social-emotional learning in my school library?

Moving Forward

WHAT CAN I DO TODAY?

Anita has a wealth of learner-centered activities in her school library that can positively contribute to mental wellness, including reflective writing, a reading garden, mindful making, yoga, spoken word poetry, and her Mindful Minute. Take a few moments to reflect on an initiative you would like to implement or grow in your own school library.

HOW CAN I BUILD ON IT TOMORROW?

Using the idea you identified in the preceding activity, determine what additional training, professional development, or resources would be necessary for you to implement or grow that initiative this year. For example, if you're interested in yoga, search out a certified instructor—starting with your school colleagues, families, and learners—who may be interested in either collaborating or volunteering in your school library. Or, if mindfulness is an area you'd like to grow, research mindfulness activities that you could incorporate into any school library activity, from booktalking and circulation to literature circles and guided research. Mindful Schools and the Association for Mindfulness in Education both have resource pages featured on their websites.

ACTION STEPS

- Access the free, self-paced online course titled Trauma Basics for Youth Workers available on the website of the Center for Adolescent Studies, search for upcoming courses in your area provided by Mental Health First Aid, or do both.
- Reach out to support staff at your school or in your district, including counselors, social workers, and school psychologists, to build collaborative programming through your school library.
- Incorporate more #OwnVoices books that feature characters with mental health conditions into your school library instruction and classroom collaborations.

8

Grow with Project READY

To build an inclusive school library takes the considerable internal work of growing our own equity knowledge—work that must be meaningful, consistent, courageous, and, at times, uncomfortable. It's not quick or easy, but it is an absolutely necessary foundational and ongoing piece. Implementation of the Include Shared Foundation does not—and cannot—happen without this internal groundwork!

The AASL Standards lay out the fundamental concept and Key Commitment of Include as "an understanding of and commitment to inclusiveness and respect for diversity in the learning community" (AASL 2018, 42). This understanding and commitment form the internal groundwork necessary to foster inclusivity in our school spaces. Additionally, the AASL Standards call on us to help "learners navigate varied perspectives and understand cultural relevancy" (AASL 2018, 42). How do we dive into this work?

Using the Grow Domain to guide us—because it centers pursuing personal growth—and our awareness of the internal work necessary to build inclusive school libraries and programs, we must commit to personally growing our own equity knowledge and capacity.

The first key Competency under Grow establishes that we must create "an atmosphere in which learners feel empowered and interactions are learner-initiated" (AASL 2018, School Librarian II.D.1.). Creating this sort of learner-centered atmosphere is possible only if, as school librarians, we are cultivating a space that not only is inclusive of *every* learner but also actively works to both honor and welcome our learners who are members of one or more marginalized communities.

When we reflect on the marginalization that is a reality in our schools, it's imperative that we understand the racial inequities that pervade and persist in education. Obviously, inequities exist for learners from other marginalized groups—including, but not limited to, learners with disabilities, learners who are members of LGBTQ+

communities, and English learners—and other chapters in this book cover programs and frameworks that are implementing Competencies that honor, welcome, and include learners from multiple communities. When we look at how race affects our BIYOC learners and how race intersects with membership in other marginalized communities to multiply inequities, it is clear that understanding—and disrupting—racial inequities is central to the Key Commitment of Include. Additionally, it is imperative that school librarians understand and disrupt the anti-Blackness that pervades so many U.S. systems—from criminal justice to healthcare to, yes, education.

To help school librarians implement Competencies from the AASL Standards, grow in their understanding of racial equity, and commit to this necessary, internal work, Project READY can be a powerful tool. It is a free, online, self-paced, anti-racist curriculum (available at https://ready.web.unc.edu) for school librarians to access at any stage in their racial equity journey.

Led by Drs. Sandra Hughes-Hassell, Casey H. Rawson, and Kimberly Hirsh, the Project READY team worked with current, practicing school librarians to build and refine the curriculum. It is accessible, engaging, and 100 percent necessary.

Growing Inclusive and Equitable School Library Services through Project READY

Kimberly Hirsh, Sandra Hughes-Hassell, and Casey H. Rawson

The Project READY curriculum is designed to support both school and public librarians committed to working toward racial equity and creating inclusive library programs and services for BIYOC.[1] In this chapter we will be looking at Project READY through the lens of school libraries and school librarianship. We recognize that developing an understanding of racial equity is a journey—one that people of color and Indigenous people in the United States have been on their whole lives, whereas many white people have never had to think about their race and how it impacts their lives. The curriculum is organized into three sequential sections. The first section (Foundations) focuses on basic concepts and issues that are fundamental to understanding race and racism and their impact on school library services. The second section (Transforming Practice) explores how these foundational concepts relate to and can be applied in school library environments. Finally, the third section (Continuing the Journey) explores how you can sustain racial equity work and grow personally and professionally in this area after completing this curriculum. No matter where you are on your own personal and professional racial equity journey, the curriculum offers opportunities to deepen and extend your understandings.

Race and racism are clearly complex topics with long histories and real consequences for BIPOC. Yet, when we first become aware of racial inequity, our first reaction often is to move straight from awareness of the injustices to potential solutions. This shortcut approach oversimplifies the causes and outcomes of racial inequity, often leads to "Band-Aid" fixes, and can even cause more harm than good. Even worse, when we use a trial-and-error approach in our work with BIYOC, those learners disproportionately bear the weight of our mistakes. Three related "shortcut" approaches to addressing racial injustice are also ultimately unhelpful or harmful:

- dealing with the immediate problem without considering its source
- ignoring the problem entirely and hoping it will go away on its own
- getting defensive or angry and refusing to think further about it

Racial Equity Work as a Cycle

To truly make progress toward racial equity, something more than a shortcut solution is required. We view the process of racial equity work not as a straight line but as an iterative cycle (figure 8.1). We have designed the Project READY curriculum around this cyclical model. As communities, social issues, organizations, and your

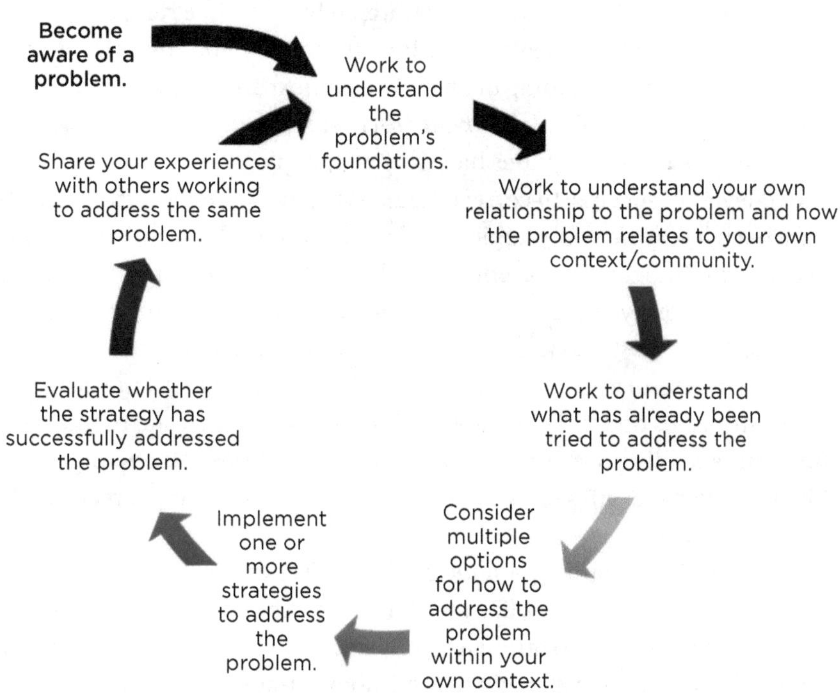

FIGURE 8.1 / **Cyclical model of racial equity work**

An iterative cycle of racial equity work was used to design the Project READY curriculum.

own personal knowledge evolve, you will need to repeat this cycle of learning, action, evaluation, and sharing.

In the context of racial equity work, the Project READY curriculum requires the following actions from school librarians:

1. *Work to understand the problem's foundations.* Institutional racism has a long, complex history in the United States. Understanding this history is critical to understanding our present circumstances. The first modules in the Project READY curriculum provide an overview of the history of race and racism, as well as current and past definitions of race and racism, how these issues manifest in systems and institutions today, and how they impact BIYOC.
2. *Work to understand your own relationship to the problem and how the problem relates to your own context and community.* Your own racial identity and life experiences will impact your racial equity work. It is critical that all people engaged in racial equity work understand their own positions in the systems and institutions that perpetuate racism, and how their own identities and cultures shape the ways they view others. White people in particular may never have spent much time exploring their own racial identities and cultures, and this curriculum has been designed to encourage that exploration. Similarly, racism manifests differently in different contexts. Inequities encountered by learners and staff in an urban elementary school library may be distinct from inequities encountered by teens in a rural high school library. Accordingly, strategies to address those inequities must be grounded in a thorough understanding of one's own context and community.
3. *Work to understand what has already been tried to address the problem.* For as long as racial inequities have existed, people have been trying, with varied levels of success, to correct them. Historically, many of these efforts have been led by racially marginalized people themselves, and communities of color and Indigenous communities already have a wealth of knowledge about racial equity work. Connecting with and learning from BIPOC communities is the best way to gain an understanding of specific strategies that may be successful within a local context. Other ways to gain knowledge about strategies that have already been found to be successful or unsuccessful include reading research from a range of disciplines, connecting with like-minded colleagues or other professionals, and speaking directly to the BIYOC you serve.
4. *Consider multiple options for how to address the problem within your own context.* Complex problems like racial inequity resist simple solutions. After taking the time to understand race and racism and your own role within systems of inequity, you can begin to think about strategies to address this issue within your own local context. Each strategy should be carefully evaluated

before implementation, with a focus on its potential impacts—positive and negative—on the communities you serve. People of color and Indigenous people in your school, library, and community should be involved in all steps of this process.

5. *Implement one or more strategies to address the problem.* Only after steps 1–4 have been explored will you be prepared to begin effectively implementing changes to your professional practice. Just as with earlier steps, the most successful implementations will involve working alongside people of color and Indigenous people in your learning community—working *with* instead of working *for*.
6. *Evaluate whether the strategy has successfully addressed the problem.* Of course, racial equity work must be undertaken for the long haul, and no single strategy will "fix" structural racism. With that said, all strategies we use to try to improve our practice should be assessed in terms of their impact on the BIYOC we serve.
7. *Share your experiences with others working to address the same problem.* There is a large and growing community of school librarians and other educators who have also undertaken the racial equity journey. Some will be ahead of you (in the sense that they have been working through iterations of this model for longer than you have), and some will be behind. All can benefit from an open exchange of knowledge about what is working, or not working, for other people. Becoming part of a community of people working toward racial equity can sustain and inspire your own journey, especially when setbacks occur. This community does not need to be limited by geography or discipline; digital learning environments have made it possible to share with and learn from a wider variety of people than ever before.

Can Individuals Really Make a Difference?

Racial equity is the work of a lifetime, and none of us are likely to see true racial equality in the United States within our lifetimes. However, immense progress has been made over the past several decades, and immense progress can be made in the near future. For you to benefit personally from your work with Project READY, and—more importantly—for the BIYOC you work with to benefit, you must believe that individual school librarians can make a positive difference in their school libraries and learning communities. Furthermore, you must believe that you, personally, have the power to create positive change.

Too often, we hear school librarians say things like these:

- This work is simply not politically possible for me because I work in a rural, conservative town.

- As a junior librarian, I don't have the authority to change my work environment.
- My library is a government institution, so we can't legally take a stand on these issues.
- My coworkers don't care about equity and inclusion, and I can't make them value this work.

These frustrations are common and human but ultimately unproductive. Instead of focusing on what you can't change, ask yourself, "What do I have power over?" "What change can I make?" "In what ways do I serve as a gatekeeper for information or resources at my organization, and how can I use those responsibilities to conduct racial equity work?" There may be understandable reasons why school libraries and school librarians haven't yet reached their potential in the realm of diversity and inclusion, but these reasons are simply not good enough, and never will be good enough, to justify the continued marginalization and oppression of youth of color and Indigenous people. As Paul Gorski has argued, "Students, families, and educators experiencing racism cannot afford to wait for us to saunter toward a more serious racial equity vision. They cannot afford to wait, in particular, for all white educators to ease into racial equity commitments at a pace of our choosing while they suffer the consequences of our casualness" (Gorski 2019, 58). We need to accept our ability and responsibility to engage in this work, and we must prioritize equity over the comfort of ourselves or our reluctant colleagues.

1. *Note:* Project READY: Reimagining Equity and Access for Diverse Youth was funded by a grant from the Institute of Museum and Library Services (Grant RE-40-16-0012-16).

Project READY and Include

Project READY clearly dovetails with the Key Commitment and school librarian Competencies under Include. For example, the cyclical model of racial equity work can be expanded and applied to build Grow Competencies addressing equity work across a spectrum of learner realities.

As you work through the Project READY curriculum, you'll be actualizing Competencies and Alignments from the AASL Standards Frameworks under Include. For example:

- The AASL Standards call on us to "explicitly lead learners to demonstrate empathy and equity in knowledge building within the global learning community by creating an atmosphere in which learners feel empowered and interactions are learner-initiated" (AASL 2018, School Librarian II.D.1.).

Working through modules 8, "Cultural Competence and Cultural Humility," and 9, "Racial and Ethnic Identity Development," of the Project READY curriculum provides learning aligned with these Competencies.

- Modules 19, "Student Voice and Agency," and 20, "Talking about Race with Youth," provide concrete examples to help school librarians initiate "opportunities that allow learners to demonstrate interest in other perspectives" (AASL 2018, School Librarian II.D.2.). Furthermore, these modules help us encourage learners to "acknowledge, appreciate, and celebrate differences and similarities through learner-led projects, displays, and initiatives" (AASL 2018, 80).
- To provide guidance in "showcasing learners' reflections on their place within the global learning community" (AASL 2018, School Librarian II.D.3.), Project READY modules 16a, "Building Relationships with Individuals," 16b, "Building Relationships with the Community," and 17, "Culturally Sustaining Pedagogy," are powerful access points.

In chapter 13 of the *National School Library Standards,* "Measuring School Librarian Growth," school librarians are specifically called on to do this work. "It is imperative that the school librarian be well-versed in a variety of perspectives and

Questions for the Reflective Practitioner

1. The school librarian Competencies under the Grow Domain stress showcasing our learners' place in a global learning community. How is this emphasis visible in my own school library practice?
2. How do I foresee learning through the Project READY curriculum as a way to implement AASL Standards Competencies related to equity and inclusion?
3. How will identifying my own entry into equity work—whether this work is new for me or already an essential part of my school library practice—help me develop a personal growth plan based on the school librarian Competencies?

strategies that foster inclusion" (AASL 2018, 148). The learning in Project READY provides these essential resources and strategies for building inclusive school libraries.

Moving Forward

WHAT CAN I DO TODAY?

Visit the Project READY website at https://ready.web.unc.edu and watch the landing page video introducing the curriculum.

HOW CAN I BUILD ON IT TOMORROW?

Download the Project READY journal and begin navigating the curriculum by learning about agreements in module 1a.

ACTION STEPS

- Identify school librarians in your district who are interested in creating a professional learning team (PLT), or identify an existing PLT with whom you can work through the Project READY curriculum and modules together.
- Identify other educators in your school who are interested in building their capacity for this work. Does your school already have an equity team? If so, are you on it? If your school does not yet have such a team, educators working through this curriculum together could be the seed that grows an equity team at your school.
- Reach out to key stakeholders in your school (administrators) or district (library supervisors) to introduce Project READY, sharing both your participation in this individually paced professional development and information about the curriculum via the website.

NOTE

1. BIYOC stands for Black, Indigenous, and Youth of Color. We use this abbreviation throughout the curriculum and this chapter to refer collectively to racialized (non-white) people. The umbrella term *people of color* has been criticized for erasing the unique experiences that Black and Indigenous people in the United States have had historically and that still impact their present realities—namely, the ongoing legacy of slavery that continues to impact Black Americans, and the legacy of Native colonization and genocide. Black Americans who have recently immigrated to the United States have a different relationship with our country's racial history, and the term *BIYOC* acknowledges the diversity of experience within the Black community.

PART III

School Library Alignments

The school library is a "third space." This characterization, embedded in the first Common Belief in the *National School Library Standards,* lays bare what can be so powerful—and beautiful—about school libraries. "The school library is a third space for learning, a space between the classroom and home, important for on-site, personalized, and self-directed learning" (AASL 2018, 11). By building this third space, school librarians can offer a place in which new learning can intersect with prior experiences from learners' homes, communities, and cultures.

This *transformative potential* of the school library as a third space is threaded throughout the school library Alignments in the Shared Foundation of Include.

- "Offering diverse learning experiences that allow for individual differences in learners" (AASL 2018, School Library II.A.2.). When we provide learning experiences that connect to our learners and recognize their assets and gifts, we are creating a meaningful third space.
- "Establishing and maintaining a collection of reading and information materials in formats that support the diverse developmental, cultural, social, and linguistic needs of the range of learners and their communities" (AASL 2018, School Library II.B.1.). Our collections should also serve as a third space—flooded with reading materials that our learners find engaging and reflective.
- "Implementing solutions that address physical, social, cultural, linguistic, and intellectual barriers to equitable access to resources and services" (AASL 2018, School Library II.C.1.). Third spaces—by their definition—do not have barriers. We cannot bridge the classroom and home if we are enacting or ignoring roadblocks in our learners' way.
- "Enabling equitable access to learning opportunities, academic and social

> support, and other resources necessary for learners' success" (AASL 2018, School Library II.D.2.). Third spaces are not exclusive. They are not built for a select few. A school library can exist as a third space for our learners only if it actively includes all of them.

As school librarians, we often have strong opinions about how our school spaces are named. For me, I am a Librarian, and my space is a Library.[1] You—or your district—may refer to you and your space by different names. Our administrators and classroom educators may refer to us by a multitude of names. *What our spaces are called is not nearly as important as what we are doing inside them.* Let's strive to build true third spaces—where our learners' communities and assets are celebrated and their learning goals and interests are nurtured.

How does the school library live as a third space in actual practice? The four chapters in this section answer that question while mirroring the four Domains under Include for school libraries. We'll **Think** with the #LibFive—a professional development program for libraries developed and led by eighth-grade learners and their school librarian.[2] By **Creating** a reopened school library that serves as a lighthouse for learners, a Colorado school librarian will show how inclusive literary experiences can build readers. A New Mexico district library supervisor will demonstrate how she **Shared** AASL resources with her librarians to better support LGBTQ+ learners and families. A North Carolina school librarian will offer strategies and experiences to help us **Grow** summer library programs through our schools.

NOTES

1. In building lifelong readers, we're also building lifelong library users. Where will our learners go in the future at college? The campus media center? Nope—the *Library*. And for the rest of our learners' lives, when they want to go to a community space for books, resources, internet access, and learning, where will they go? They will go to a public *Library*.

2. Full disclosure: that librarian is me.

9

Think with the #LibFive

As school librarians, we know that reflection is key to building effective school libraries. When we look at the school library Alignments for Include, the standards under the Think Domain explicitly incorporate this reflective piece: "Ensuring equity in the school library begins with an ongoing reflective analysis" (AASL 2018, 80).

This reflective analysis is required for every aspect of our school libraries, including our collections, instruction, programs, and physical spaces. In addition to engaging in self-reflection, it's necessary to seek feedback from our most crucial stakeholders, including other educators, counselors and student support staff, administrators, families, and, of course, learners. Our learners not only are our most significant end-users, they are the reason for our existence. Their feedback *for us* and assessments *of us* tangibly improve our school libraries to maximize their capacity to transform learners and learning.

Using the Alignments under Think that guide school librarians in "providing challenging and authentic opportunities that address the needs of the broad range of learners" (AASL 2018, School Library II.A.1.), we can design learning opportunities that gather this crucial school library feedback from our learners. School libraries—at their core—exist for our learners *and* through our learners. True inclusion in our spaces means inviting this reflective feedback from our most precious stakeholders—our learners. School librarians gain feedback in many ways, including informal conversations, suggestion boxes (either old-school or digital), usage data, and surveys.

Through sharing what came to be known as the #LibFive, I have the great pleasure and honor of introducing you to three of my former eighth-grade learners: Cesar Falcon, Jose Gomez, and Jaida Morris. Together, we embarked on a reflective journey to discover what inclusive school libraries—important third spaces for learning—both *are* and *do*.

#LibFive: Five Key Foundations for Building Inclusive Libraries

Cesar Falcon, Jose Gomez, Jaida Morris, and Julie Stivers

First, let's start with that hashtag! #LibFive is the abbreviation that three eighth-grade learners—*Cesar Falcon, Jose Gomez, Jaida Morris*—and I used to represent professional development we built for other school librarians unpacking Five Key Foundations for Building Inclusive Libraries. The #LibFive, though, is just the middle of the library story that birthed this educational professional development. This story begins in the way I believe every inclusive school library story begins—by *amplifying learner voice* with *consistency* and *joy*.

Consistency and Joy

Because we're talking about inclusion in our school libraries, *amplifying voice* is a necessary building block. Remember, we are *never giving* our learners a voice. Learners already have powerful voices. A school librarian's job is to provide a microphone and a space where learners are comfortable speaking their truths. School librarians must always ask themselves, "Whose voices are being amplified?" and "Conversely, whose voices are being silenced?" Inclusion is about welcoming, but it is also about disrupting—disrupting inequities and disrupting the silencing of our learners.

Learners are not going to trust us with their true selves if we are not centering and honoring learner voice each day, with *consistency*. What does this look like in a school library? It's using classroom strategies that invite learner input, selecting classroom texts that reflect learners, building real time into the curriculum for creative writing, welcoming learner expression—yes, even during "structured" time—and building author visits within an equity framework—and those are just examples that happen during class time.

Consistently amplifying learner voice happens just as much—or more—in the extra moments. From collecting books with superheroes that look like our learners to welcoming and cherishing learners' personal writing to allowing space for creativity, honoring learner voice has to happen every day—in seemingly small ways. Otherwise, a specific large-scale project like the #LibFive could never have incubated in my school library. As school librarians, we can build inclusive school libraries successfully and authentically only if we're truly centering our learners—with consistency. Jaida and Jose and Cesar would never have developed the #LibFive project with me if they didn't trust and know that I valued and centered their voices before we ever even started.

This is why I say that the #LibFive is just the middle of our school library story. The beginning is consistently happening with all my learners in those everyday moments with that other crucial foundation: *joy*. If our learners don't feel joyful in our school spaces, we're not doing it right.

Building inclusive school libraries takes intentionality and effort on our part, but it's not drudgery. It should be work infused with joy—*on both sides*. Inclusion must be brought to life with both consistency and joy—otherwise, it's just a word, and our learners know the difference.

Building the #LibFive

The learners at my alternative, academic-recovery school come to us from their base schools and are able to rewrite their own school stories. Some of that rewriting naturally happens in the school library. Many of our learners have experiences at multiple schools, and they become frequent library users for the first time in our school library. That is both powerful and humbling! I wanted to help other school librarians build inclusive school libraries in which learners from traditionally marginalized communities are centered and cherished. I knew this message would be more meaningful—and authentic—coming from some of my wonderful learners themselves. Creating this learner-led professional development became the central focus of an enrichment/remediation period I had with three amazing eighth graders.

To prepare for building this school library professional development, Jaida, Cesar, and Jose eagerly learned about research that directly related to our topic. We began with Dr. Kafi Kumasi's research (2012), which found that many learners of color felt like outsiders in their school libraries and that it often seemed like a place that was "owned" by the school librarian.

To build a foundation for thinking about school libraries and youth, I shared findings from the powerful Hanley and Noblit study (2009), which found that for youth of color, positive racial identity leads to academic success. From there, we moved to unpacking the state of representation in books today by exploring the Diversity in Children's Books 2015 infographic (Huyck, Dahlen, and Griffin, 2016). This exploration led to discussions of #OwnVoices, counterstories, and the necessity of building reflective collections.

Inspiration for the #LibFive project also came from an initiative of the Blue Ribbon Mentor-Advocate Program—a learner support program in the Chapel Hill-Carrboro (North Carolina) City Schools—called the Student Six. The Student Six is a learner-led professional development program centering on six culturally sustaining strategies for educators to use to better connect with their BIPOC learners. We dove into the six strategies and watched videos of student trainers Erika Franco-Quiroz and Jotham White talking about their experiences. Jaida, Jose, and

Cesar then embarked on their own action-based research. They conducted school library walks. They thought about the school libraries at their base schools and their experiences there. We brainstormed about what makes a school library feel truly welcoming. We spoke to other learners about their past school library experiences.

The Key Foundations

We initially came up with eleven ideas for what school libraries and school librarians can do to be inclusive. We spent months on this project, eventually winnowing our list to the five biggest ways that school libraries can build inclusive programs and spaces:

1. See me! Listen to me.
2. Show me on the shelves and walls. Read those books yourself.
3. Graphic novels and manga are not extra.
4. Show the joy in our stories.
5. Make the library a sorting-free zone.

These ideas might seem obvious or too simple, but I would implore those thinking along those lines to think again. These guidelines are powerful *because of* their simplicity and, when done well, can result in empowering school libraries and programs.

1. SEE ME! LISTEN TO ME. — *Jose Gomez*

Greet us. Be excited to see us. *At my last school, no one ever smiled at me when I came in the library.* Learn our names. Say them correctly. Find out what we're interested in. We have things to say, and in the classroom there may not be time. Please let us tell you things!

This quote from Pedro Noguera (2003) shows this foundation, too: "For voice to be meaningful, there must be those willing to listen."

2. SHOW ME ON THE SHELVES AND WALLS. READ THOSE BOOKS YOURSELF. — *Jaida Morris*

I need to feel wanted, welcomed, and seen. That is *not* possible if I don't see myself in school library displays and on the shelves. I want to read books that have characters that share my experiences and interests.

I don't want you to only have diverse books. I want to *talk* with you about them. It means so much to me that Ms. Stivers has read the same books, and then we get to talk about the characters and plotlines. Together.

I can see myself *all over* the books in my Mount Vernon school library. I love these covers [figure 9.1]—isn't it clear how I can see myself in them? In just a minute, I picked up all these books which were on display in the library that looked like me. They are so beautiful! Before Mount Vernon and Ms. Stivers, I didn't know that all of these books were out there. Remember, diverse books are good for all readers!

FIGURE 9.1 / **Jaida's book covers**
These are some of the covers that made Jaida feel seen in the library

3. GRAPHIC NOVELS AND MANGA ARE NOT EXTRA. ***Cesar Falcon***

Please understand how much kids love these books. They are *not* less important than other books. Reading equals reading, and we want shelves and shelves of these books in our school libraries.

They are *more* than gateway books, they are *books*. Period. Please get them in the classroom, too, so they are used during lessons like they are here at Mount Vernon. We looked at research with Ms. Stivers that showed us that graphic novels contain more complex vocabulary than text-only books—up to 20 percent more!

4. SHOW THE JOY IN OUR STORIES. ***Jaida Morris***

"Black People Look Good!" We did this exercise in the beginning of the year and I was writing down things about my Mount Vernon school library that I liked. That was the first thing I wrote down: *Black People Look Good*. I wrote it because I could look around and see covers that didn't only show Black people dealing with slavery or civil rights. I could see beautiful covers with Black people living happy or interesting lives in the present day or in a future world.

Collect books for your school libraries that show BIPOC youth just having adventures. Do *not* only include books that are focused on struggle. When you show the joy, happiness, and normal lives of Black or Brown teens in books, you are showing the joy and happiness of *me*.

These are book covers [figure 9.2] from the Mount Vernon school library I've read this year that demonstrate this idea.

FIGURE 9.2 / **Jaida's joyful book covers**
In the Mount Vernon school library, Jaida read these books that showed the "joy in our stories."

5. MAKE THE LIBRARY A SORTING-FREE ZONE. *Cesar Falcon*

We can get sorted in school all day by grades, how smart our teachers think we are, even by how we dress and look. Don't sort me in the school library! I never feel "sorted" here [at the Mount Vernon school library]. It feels completely different and that's why I'm here in the library. All. The. Time.

Please think about sorting at your book fairs, too. [See chapter 16, "An Inclusive Book Fair Model," for more on sorting related to book fairs.] This is what some of my classmates had to say about sorting:

- *I always felt like the librarian at my old school gave me and my friends this look when we walked in. Like this evil kind of stare. Like she had already decided something about us.*
- *This one year, my teacher at an old school stopped at the book fair for us to buy books on the way back from lunch. If you had money with you, you got to shop at the fair. If you didn't you sat on the floor in the entrance to the school library. Our classmates came back with bags of books and we just sat there on the floor, waiting.*

- *I never had money to buy anything at the book fairs at my other schools so I couldn't get anything. It didn't feel right to be in the school library and not be able to get books.*

Putting It All Together

Jose Gomez

These five reasons help explain why we love our school library so much. It's why we started coming to the school library, it's why we love Ms. Stivers, and it's why we read more. We want every school library to also do these five things really well for *all* learners, but especially for learners like us who never felt welcome at our school libraries before this one.

The #LibFive as Professional Development

We unveiled our #LibFive concept—*Five Key Foundations for Building Inclusive Libraries*—at our district conference, WCPSS (Wake County Public School System) Convergence, in spring 2018. Feedback from our district librarians was overwhelmingly positive. Presenting with Jaida, Jose, and Cesar—who did the majority of the speaking—was my proudest moment as an educator. Project READY filmed our #LibFive presentation several weeks later in our Mount Vernon school library and has embedded the learning into its anti-racist curriculum. (See chapter 8, "Grow with Project READY.")

The #LibFive professional development was shared at ALA's 2018 National Conference during the Young Adult Library Services Association (YALSA) Presidential Program Panel on Youth Activism and during a concurrent session at 2018 SLJ Teen! Live. The #LibFive can be universally applied to any school library—or any library that serves youth. The #LibFive infographic shown in figure 9.3 can be copied and shared.

The #LibFive's deceptively simple messages are necessary for every school library. There are no half measures or qualifying conditions. Intentionally committing to carrying out these five foundations—with consistency and joy—will help all school librarians build inclusive school libraries.

FIGURE 9.3 / **#LibFive: Key foundations for building school libraries**

Mount Vernon school library learners developed these five key foundations for building inclusive libraries.

#LibFive and Include

The ideals of the #LibFive partner beautifully with Competencies and Alignments across the Shared Foundation of Include. When we look specifically at the Alignments for School Libraries under the Think Domain, we find these guidelines:

- School librarians can support balanced perspectives and "authentic opportunities" (AASL 2018, School Library II.A.1.) by leveraging Jaida's wisdom and building collections that reflect learners through authors, stories, and characters with shared experiences and with BIPOC characters that are not focused solely on struggle or trauma.
- "Offering diverse learning experiences" (AASL 2018, School Library II.A.2.) can be realized by embedding graphic novels in the curriculum, which Cesar implores school librarians to do.
- We are called on to provide "a comprehensive variety of resources" (AASL 2018, School Library II.A.3.). Three of the #LibFive foundations—Show me on the shelves and walls; Graphic novels and manga are not extra; and Show the joy in our stories—dive into inclusive ways to provide a comprehensive variety of resources. School librarians can use the language of the AASL Standards and the foundations in the #LibFive to strengthen collections.

The third Common Belief in our *National School Library Standards* is that "learners should be prepared for college, career, and life" (AASL 2018, 11). Designing creative opportunities that include public speaking, writing, and connected learning is a powerful way to prepare our learners. Similar opportunities inviting learner voice—on a range of topics including your school, your community, social justice issues, our nation, or our world—can be created and scaffolded for any age level. By partnering these creative opportunities with the Alignments under the Think Domain, we are building school libraries that allow our learners to thrive. For example, during the creation of the #LibFive, Jaida, Jose, and Cesar investigated, analyzed, and reflected on resources and their own experiences.

Questions for the Reflective Practitioner

1. As I look at the key foundations in the #LibFive, which foundation is currently the strongest in my school library? Which represents the biggest growth opportunity?
2. What "challenging and authentic opportunities" (AASL 2018, School Library II.A.1.) have I initiated in my school library?
3. How can building a collection with a "comprehensive variety of resources" help my school library support balanced perspectives (AASL 2018, School Library II.A.3.)?

Moving Forward

WHAT CAN I DO TODAY?

Print the #LibFive infographic. Consider placing it on your desk or near your work space so you can have a visual reminder of the learning and experiences provided by Cesar, Jose, and Jaida.

HOW CAN I BUILD ON IT TOMORROW?

Select one (or more) of the five foundations to focus on as a growth opportunity in your school library. Consider your school's leadership or school improvement goals or personal growth objectives in making your choice.

1. See me! Listen to me.
2. Show me on the shelves and walls. Read those books yourself.
3. Graphic novels and manga are not extra.
4. Show the joy in our stories.
5. Make the library a sorting-free zone.

ACTION STEPS

- Reflect on your current methods for gaining learner feedback. Either strengthen an existing method—such as editing a survey you've already used—or brainstorm a new way to invite and include learner voice.

- After you've chosen a #LibFive foundation as a growth opportunity, enlist learner feedback to make it happen! For example, if you choose foundation 3, you could build a learner team that suggests titles and series to buy for your collection. You could also enlist learners' help in building manga and graphic novel displays or begin an anime club to cross-promote with your new manga collection.
- Identify an issue or opportunity in your school or library that you can explore with your learners. The possibilities for their input and design are infinite—from lesson planning ideas and club offerings to suggested policy revisions and changes in physical layout. Our learners have so much to offer!

10

Create and Be the Lighthouse

Our very first Common Belief as a profession articulates our purpose—and expresses a fundamental right of our learners. "The school library is a unique and essential part of a learning community" (AASL 2018, 11). What happens when our learners are denied this educational right?

Large, urban districts—from Philadelphia to Chicago to Los Angeles—have been eliminating school librarian positions at alarming rates. Nationwide, public school districts have lost 20 percent of their school librarians since 2000, even as learner populations have grown. For example, from 2008 to 2018 in Denver Public Schools, learner enrollment *increased* by 25 percent, but the number of school librarians *decreased* by 60 percent (Sparks and Harwin 2018).

This educational malpractice is putting our learners at risk. A multitude of statewide studies have found that schools with high-quality school library programs have higher reading test scores and, for high schools, higher graduation rates. These studies were controlled for key factors including learner-teacher ratios, demographics, and funding levels and found that "the benefits associated with good school library programs are strongest for the most vulnerable"—including BIPOC learners, learners from families who are socioeconomically disadvantaged, and learners with disabilities (Lance and Kachel 2018). Educational malpractice, indeed!

The AASL Standards and the Shared Foundation of Include set forth a key Alignment for School Libraries under the Create Domain that can guide school librarians as they establish necessary groundwork in opening or reopening a school library. "The school library represents all members and their place in a global learning community by organizing facilities to enhance the use of and ensure equitable access to information resources and services for all learners" (AASL 2018, School Library II.B.2.).

We often hear stories and statistics about the toxic trend of school library closings and librarian layoffs. But what happens when a school or community recognizes the transformative potential of this third space and fights back? When a school library is reinstated? Restaffed? Rebirthed?

Denver school librarian Julia Torres reopened a shuttered school library on a shared-school campus. Hers is a story of Include in meaningful action, offering guidance for both new and experienced school librarians.

Be the Lighthouse

Julia E. Torres

I may go, but I will leave behind all my thousand & one lives—
a bookmad girl never dies. —Amanda Lovelace

I have been called many things—among them "well-spoken" (what does that even mean?), "mysterious" (only to those who don't take the time to uncover my secrets), "savage" (my learners call me this—and I love it), "unfettered" (definitely), "fiercely independent" (my mother calls me this), and "wild" (my hair certainly is). . . .

I suppose I accept these labels, and yet, my nearest and dearest know why I am Toni Morrison's Beloved. I am Zora Neale Hurston's Janie. I am Maya Angelou's "caged bird." I am Nella Larsen's Clare. I am Audre Lorde, Angela Davis, June Jordan, Nikki Giovanni . . . and a thousand more.

Every learner deserves the chance to find themselves reflected in the pages of their favorite book, to get so lost in a story that time disappears, and the only pursuit that matters is reaching the bottom of the page so that it can be turned, so that a story can unfold, so that the invisible thread between reader and author, past and present, imagination and reality strengthens and tightens to become an unbreakable cord.

Unfortunately, in some cases, books have become objects from which youth feel alienated because they do not see themselves reflected on the pages, they do not identify with the authors who wrote them, or see a connection between the time periods in which the books were born and the times we are living in now—sometimes even the language in which the books were written. This feeling can change, of course, when school librarians and other educators collect books within an equity framework and seek to disrupt the traditional literary canon.

Even so, for several years now, in many urban school districts, school libraries and school librarians have begun to disappear. Disappearance is of course a euphemism. The deliberate underfunding of school libraries has caught on—especially in communities with high populations of immigrants, or families and learners labeled "low income," or both. Stealing books and access to them from youth has been a deliberate choice. How do I know? This is exactly what happened at my own school—Montbello in Denver. We spent several years without a school librarian, and the physical space was taken over by other school programs. Eventually, amid public outcry, the board voted. Tax money was "re-allocated." A new school library remodel, inventory, and school librarian position were funded.

Because I am known as the book-mad lady on campus, I was asked to design library programming for all five schools on our Montbello campus in late April of 2018. By May, I was asked to apply for the position as campus librarian. Within five days at the end of May and the beginning of June, I resigned from my position as language arts teacher, got hired as the campus librarian, moved everything out of my classroom, delivered the commencement address at our school's graduation, and saw 90 percent of the school library's outdated inventory removed from the building to make way for what was to come: creating a transformative school library.

I was able to come full circle. I have the chance to live my dream—to help kids fall in love with books and with reading again. It was my intention to keep teaching, reading, growing, and learning beside the learners in my community and perhaps (if I am really fortunate) to set a model in place that catches fire in more cities around the country and world that are experiencing this same disturbing trend.

> ". . . a bookmad girl
> never dies."
> Her love for ideas
> words
> language
> just multiplies
> (and so)
> let the journey
> Begin.

Fast forward to the beginning of my inaugural year as Montbello librarian for five schools—two middle schools and three high schools—on one campus. A small catch: the school library isn't open yet. I don't actually have a physical space! Because there are five schools in one building, and space is at a premium, the fight for physical square footage happens every year. As they say, the devil is in the details. For me, the most important detail is making sure that youth are not forgotten in all the shuffling, reshuffling, and adult chaos that bubbles up at the beginning of the year.

So, I got to it and created the school library website so that learners could begin to check out e-books right away—either on one-to-one school devices or on personal phones and devices. I am still very much learning to be a school librarian for grades 6–12 because I haven't been in a middle school since 2005. Being a teacher-librarian who needs to be a lighthouse for everyone—rather than just a select few—to find safe harbor is challenging . . . but I had Angie Thomas, Jason Reynolds, Nic Stone, and Elizabeth Acevedo to help me.

I did more than thirty classroom visits in the first two weeks. For each one, the objective was clear—get learners who haven't had a school library for as long as seven years to at least consider giving reading a chance. I am in the school library to help learners find their way to developing rich, varied, and full reading lives that they can use as guiding lights through their time in the school system and beyond.

During each visit, I took classes through the website and asked them to tell me honestly whether they enjoyed reading. Predictably, the older the children are, and the longer they've gone without a school library, the smaller the number of hands raised stating that they do enjoy reading. Most classrooms had just 20 to 30 percent of learners answering in the affirmative.

After taking learners through our new Montbello Library website and showing them how to check out e-books, I talked to them about Project LIT, a literacy initiative started by high school learners and their English teacher in Nashville, Tennessee, and the exciting events we had coming up for the year. I also read aloud from *The Hate U Give* by Angie Thomas, *Long Way Down* by Jason Reynolds, *Hope Nation* (a collection edited by Rose Brock in which YA authors share personal moments of hope and inspiration), or *The Poet X* by Elizabeth Acevedo. I let learners choose which one they wanted to hear. I've read from each of these books so many times, but it never gets old, because the response is the same every time. Learners love to be read to, and I love reading to them. They especially love it when the books speak their language—tell the stories of their lives—which sometimes, in some ways, is my life too. After the read-aloud, I ask for thumbs up, to the side, or down as an answer to the question, "Based on what I've read so far—would you keep reading?" Each time, more than 90 percent of learners gave an emphatic thumbs-up.

When I saw the way learners responded to the read-alouds, nudged one another, and said, "Miss, do you have any more copies of that book in the library?" I knew the school library, though not physically open yet, was well on its way to achieving its goal.

When I pitched Project LIT Montbello, I did a short booktalk for each of the nine Project LIT books, and I raised enough money to purchase fifty copies of each title.

In order for the school library to be successful, I have to work hard to gain these learners' trust. They need to know that reading is fun, not just something adults try to get them to do to earn a score on a test—they're too smart for games like that. I need to remove labels like *nonreader, not proficient,* or *low level* from our vocabulary. My most important job is to help learners reclaim their reading lives and know that somewhere among the stacks, both physical and virtual, there is a book waiting just for them. I want them to know that reading poetry, manga, graphic novels, song lyrics, Instagram photo captions, all of it counts and that they are emphatically not

#MontbelloReads High School Selections for Our 2018–2019 Campus Book Club

August/September: *The Hate U Give* by Angie Thomas
October: *Tradition* by Brendan Kiely
November: *Odd One Out* by Nic Stone
December: *Pride* by Ibi Zoboi
January: *Allegedly* by Tiffany D. Jackson
February: *On the Come Up* by Angie Thomas
March: *Speak: The Graphic Novel* by Laurie Halse Anderson
April: *When I Was the Greatest* by Jason Reynolds
May/June: *The Poet X* by Elizabeth Acevedo

nonreaders just because they don't like to read the things that schools and adults tell them they need to.

When I scheduled Jason Reynolds to Skype into our school library* and speak with our learners, I knew I had to educate my colleagues about the incredible value of this literacy event. I went to other educators individually and spoke about how this experience would specifically support their curriculum. I also searched our library system to find every learner who had checked out a book by Jason—and then I wrote individual passes to get them out of class!

Too many folks assume that because we pour love, resources, and money into literacy in early childhood, once children have a firm foundation, they no longer need support in developing or maintaining reading lives. Let me assure you that is not true. I am one of just five secondary education librarians in my school district, and there are many districts that have none at all. I am new to this. I do not know details of what it will take to change conditions that result in the removal of secondary school libraries from America's schools, especially urban school districts (the first to have school libraries removed). But I know that the accompanying work is to remove the shame and stigma that too many learners feel about their reading habits, that reading that reflects their tastes, lives, languages is not good enough—an unfair burden for them to carry, placed upon them by adults.

School libraries, and school librarians, are the lighthouse by which so many learners find their way through the storm. It benefits all of us when we create, value, preserve, and protect those literacy lighthouses.

At our first #MontbelloReads Campus Book Club meeting, we talked about what we were willing to bring to the group and what we hoped to get out of participating this year. One girl said simply, "More words." For me, that was everything.

---

*This excerpt is adapted from text originally printed in "Hold Fast to Dreams" (June 23, 2018) and "Be the Lighthouse" (September 17, 2018) on *juliaetorres.blog*.

Being the Lighthouse and Include

Julia is creating a powerful school library and programming at Montbello, and it is easy to see the school library Alignments for Include illuminated in her work. "The school library represents all members and their place in a global learning community by:

- "Establishing and maintaining a collection of reading and information materials in formats that support the diverse developmental, cultural, social, and linguistic needs of the range of learners and their communities" (AASL 2018, School Library II.B.1.).
    - By prioritizing reflective literature—in both print and digital formats—and accessing and promoting literary opportunities such as author visits and holding regular book clubs on campus that give learners from five schools the chance to come together around great books, the Montbello school library is meaningfully supporting its learners.
- "Organizing facilities to enhance the use of and ensure equitable access to information resources and services for all learners" (AASL 2018, School Library II.B.2.).
    - When Julia was unable to use her physical library, she brought the school library to her learners, visiting every class and providing access to literature via read-alouds, booktalks, a newly created website, and checkouts from the new e-book collection.
- "Featuring learning opportunities that include diverse viewpoints" (AASL 2018, School Library II.B.3.).
    - Julia organized yearlong book clubs that created learning opportunities through reading, discussion, and activities that championed the diverse perspectives not only of authors and characters but also of her learners.

I was incredibly lucky to meet Julia as a learner myself when she was a visiting teacher-in-residence for our WCPSS teen Summer Writing Institute. As a facilitator, I was thrilled to learn alongside our teen writers about creative writing with Julia. As an educator, I was even more excited to learn more about culturally sustaining pedagogy, inclusive teaching methods, and restorative classroom strategies simply by seeing Julia in action with our teen writers.

Questions for the Reflective Practitioner

1. What barriers have I overcome in my school library and school to ensure "equitable access to information resources and services for all learners" (AASL 2018, School Library II.B.2.)? What growth opportunities related to this Alignment still exist in my school library?

2. When my school library is a lighthouse for my learners, how can this help me realize the school library Alignments under the Include Shared Foundation?

3. How can building a collection that supports "diverse developmental, cultural, social, and linguistic needs" (AASL 2018, School Library II.B.1.) help my school library represent learners and their place in a global learning community?

Moving Forward

WHAT CAN I DO TODAY?

Literacy initiatives like book clubs featuring texts from authors representing multiple and intersecting communities can be used to build excitement for reading in your school. Visit diversebooks.org—or any of the resources listed in the Action Steps for chapter 5, "Think with Read Woke"—to find potential book club selections and ideas.

HOW CAN I BUILD ON IT TOMORROW?

Julia is the cofounder of Disrupt Texts—"a crowdsourced, grass roots effort *by* teachers *for* teachers to challenge the traditional canon in order to create a more inclusive, representative, and equitable language arts curriculum that our students deserve" (disrupttexts.org). Explore the website—including the mission statement and information on disrupting specific classroom texts—for information on inclusive literacy strategies.

ACTION STEPS

- Advocacy is a key piece in rebuilding, maintaining, and safeguarding our school libraries. Explore the *AASL Advocacy Toolkit* for resources and support.
- Read-alouds and author visits are a foundational part of Julia's school library practice for both middle school and high school learners. Whether or not these are already key parts of your booktalks, identify a new high-interest title—or group of titles—written by BIPOC authors for read-alouds in upcoming booktalks. Julia has shared that giving her learners the opportunity to engage with authors directly has been transformative for her program. Using the equitable model highlighted in chapter 6, "Create with an Equitable Writer-in-Residence Model," invite authors to visit your school library virtually or in person to read their work and speak with your learners.
- An engaging school library website was essential as Julia was building a new program. Consider giving your website—or selected pages—a refresh after asking for learner feedback on its usability and engagement. Use the Competencies and Alignments under Include for support in improving its structure and message.

NOTE

1. Read more about Julia's work and Jason's visit in *Denver Teacher Librarian Brings Students Back to Library* (2019) by K. Yorio (https://www.slj.com/?detailStory=denver-teacher-librarian-brings-students-back-to-library).

11

Share through LGBTQ+-Inclusive School Libraries

The fifth Common Belief that the AASL Standards define as central to our profession is that "intellectual freedom is every learner's right." (AASL 2018, 13). When we are not providing a rich collection and curriculum that includes multiple and intersecting identities, we are denying our learners this fundamental right. An area of collection development and school library programming that often falls short in this regard is the meaningful and intentional inclusion of the LGBTQ+ community—from authors to stories to history.

It's a foundational—and comforting—concept that school libraries can be safe spaces for learners. I'd suggest that we also aspire to building *brave* spaces, where learners have the freedom—and feel safe and comfortable enough—to be their full selves.

Just as we cannot discuss Include without addressing who has been *excluded,* we cannot create safe spaces without also addressing our learners who *feel* unsafe and *are* unsafe as a result of our school climate, policies, resources, and curriculum. The Gay, Lesbian and Straight Education Network (GLSEN) National School Climate Survey tracks school experiences of lesbian, gay, bisexual, transgender, and questioning (LGBTQ+) youth in schools, including challenges faced and supportive school resources. GLSEN's most recent data show that progress on safety in schools for LGBTQ+ youth, though slightly improved from the 2017 data, has not shown as much positive change as had been trending since the early 2000s. GLSEN found that schools nationwide continue to be hostile environments for many LGBTQ+ students, who experience discrimination and victimization and are subjected to anti-LGBTQ+ language. Many LGBTQ+ students avoid school activities as a result or even miss school entirely (Kosciw et al., 2020).

As school librarians, we can—and must—work to disrupt the victimization and hostile school realities for our LGBTQ+ learners. The first Alignment under Share calls on our school libraries to implement "solutions that address physical, social, cultural, linguistic, and intellectual barriers to equitable access to resources and services" (AASL 2018, School Library II.C.1.). AASL has published a toolkit—*Defending Intellectual Freedom: LGBTQ+ Materials in School Libraries*—framed in solutions that address this school library Alignment for building LGBTQ+-inclusive collections, instruction, and spaces. Implementing this key Alignment not only creates a safer school library—and school—for our LGBTQ+ learners, families, and colleagues, it positively impacts learning for all school stakeholders. An important thread running through all of the Competencies and Alignments under Include is that diverse learner identities are assets that transform and advance learning for all of us, not challenges to overcome!

Rachel Altobelli, director of library services and instructional materials for Albuquerque Public Schools, was the AASL member guide to the 2018 ALA Emerging Leaders team that developed the LGBTQ+ Resource Guide, Applied Framework, and Infographic, and she used the guide to lead professional development in her district. She shares her experiences with that professional development, as well as tools for us to build LGBTQ+-inclusive school libraries.

LGBTQ+-Inclusive School Libraries

Rachel Altobelli

Include, as a Shared Foundation and as a concept, forms the bedrock of so much of what we do in school libraries. Learners with an inclusive mindset will more easily gain competence in the other five Shared Foundations—Inquire, Collaborate, Curate, Explore, and Engage. Before learners begin to explore the richness of the Include Shared Foundation, they need to know they are a cherished part of their school, fully inside and in charge of their educational experience. If learners feel that they are on the outside, ignored entirely, or perhaps grudgingly tolerated, how can we ask them to "demonstrate an understanding of and commitment to inclusiveness and respect for diversity in the learning community" (AASL 2018, 76).

All Learners Need to See Themselves

Lesbian, gay, bisexual, transgender, and queer/questioning (LGBTQ+) learners are at risk of feeling unrepresented, unwanted, and alone. Especially in elementary schools, some educators may imagine that no LGBTQ+ learners are present, and, therefore, no need exists to court controversy and potential challenges by providing LGBTQ+ materials. It's equally easy to look around a school that prides itself on being inclusive, see the happy faces gathered together in Genders and Sexualities Alliance groups (GSAs), Queer-Straight Alliance groups (QSAs), or other groups, and assume that the hard work has been done, even though not all learners are out and some may live in far from supportive home environments.

LGBTQ+ learners are everywhere, at all ages and levels, and they are still at increased risk for a host of issues, including bullying, assault, and suicide. According to the Centers for Disease Control and Prevention (CDC), although most LGBTQ+ learners lead happy lives, and supportive schools are an important factor for their success, "some LGBTQ+ youth are more likely than their heterosexual peers to experience difficulties in their lives and school environments, such as violence" (CDC 2017).

I think and write and deliver professional development about this topic because it's personal for me, and it's safe for me to do so because I'm insulated by the privilege that comes from being a white, cisgender person who has a secure job in a school district where I can be out. I remember the many years I spent feeling like there was something wrong with me, because I didn't know it was possible to be a happy, successful lesbian. Even though I looked like many of the characters in books, I never really felt safe or at home in any of my schools or school libraries. When I looked inside the books on the shelves, I wasn't really there.

I want better for LGBTQ+ learners today, but they are still underrepresented in children's and YA literature, and they are still too often reduced to a single facet of their identities. Outside school libraries, textbooks and other instructional materials are likely to omit entirely the existence of anyone, past or present, who isn't straight and cisgender. This is the environment that LGBTQ+ learners exist in. How often have you seen LGBTQ+ representation in a traditional textbook, or even in a novel that's assigned reading? If you have seen LGBTQ+ representation in a traditional textbook or assigned novel, was the LGBTQ+ character also white, or also male?

If you did come up with some examples, that's wonderful! Now compare the number of books you thought of to the number of books you can think of in which a cisgender, straight, and white teenage girl must rescue her dystopian society from itself while choosing between two attractive yet very different boys.

LGBTQ+ learners, along with learners with many other identities, will often look around at the books, materials, stories, and textbooks that surround them and find themselves either left out or presented as problems to be solved or avoided. For LGBTQ+ learners of color and learners with intersectional identity from marginalized communities, these issues are amplified. Additionally, LGBTQ+ learners, in most cases, do not have their LGBTQ+ identities in common with their families of origin, which means they are at risk of feeling like the "other" both at home and at school. Our learners don't have the privilege that comes from being the adults in our institutions, so they need us to be brave advocates for them. As we are advocating, it can be helpful to surround ourselves with any librarian's traditional tools—resources and information that we can share with all learners, including other educators.

Initial steps could be buying #OwnVoices books with LGBTQ+ representation, or attending Safe Zone training and then displaying a Safe Zone sign. These actions send important signals to learners. For school librarians who already have books and signs, there is still so much more that can be done. For example, many books with LGBTQ+ characters (especially older titles) feature those characters struggling with the coming out process, and these books are often the only ones owned by school libraries. Although these stories are important, it's equally important (if not more so) to have books with LGBTQ+ characters doing other things. Lauren Barack, writing in *School Library Journal,* stated that teens and tweens "want to see more genres featuring LGBTQ learners as characters, even if gender orientation isn't the main plot point" (Barack 2014). After all, coming out is—we hope—not the main or only event in an LGBTQ+ person's life.

Beyond acquiring a wonderful rainbow of diverse LGBTQ+ materials, how we present information and resources also matters. In our professional development, I shared my personal feelings about LGBTQ+ genre labels: I'm not a fan. If I had walked into my middle school or high school library and seen all the LGBTQ+-themed books shelved together, perhaps with a helpful rainbow sign, I would have walked right out of that school library and never returned.

I'm just one person, though, and learners today live in a very different world. They may even ask their school librarians to group the LGBTQ+ books together, or label them, because they are out and proud and happy and safe and secure and bursting with pride. This confidence is what we want for all our learners, and it brings me a great deal of joy to see it—it hasn't been *that* long since I was in school, and I was so far from being out, we weren't even in the same zip code.

Even as we celebrate this glorious confidence, we have an obligation to remember that LGBTQ+ youth can be in very different places from each other. In our professional development session, we shared how we've talked to many school librarians who get wonderful input from their learners in GSAs or other LGBTQ+ groups. Those learners certainly have a better idea of what it's like to be young and LGBTQ+ right now than I do, but they may or may not have a good idea of what it's like to be young and LGBTQ+ and fully or partially closeted. The LGBTQ+ learners who are coming out or will come out are often in a very, very different place from learners who are not ready to come out yet, sometimes for safety reasons, and the learners who *are* out don't necessarily know what the learners who aren't out need.

Even if some learners like the idea of LGBTQ+ or rainbow stickers, I still advise sticking to the general principle that groups of people are not genres. To do otherwise reduces LGBTQ+ people to one facet of their identity, instead of focusing on what they are choosing to do with their lives (even if those lives are fictional). I do like digital LGBTQ+ resource guides because of two crucial points. One is privacy, but the other is the inherent flexibility of online organization—in a digital environment, a book can fit into more than one category, without having to buy multiple copies or cover the spine entirely in stickers.

Professional Development Centering LGBTQ+ Learners

In my district, we use the AASL resource guide, *Defending Intellectual Freedom: LGBTQ+ Materials in the School Library,* as a place to begin gathering those resources and information. It's a rich resource, equally well suited for school librarians to explore individually or for use in a group setting.

The guide was the primary resource my district used in several beginning-of-the-year in-service sessions I co-facilitated with Sara Cook, the school librarian at Jefferson Middle School and a committed advocate for all her learners. We combined information from the guide with information she has gathered from her learners. Their real-life questions let us all take a moment and ponder things like subject headings—what does it say to learners when they must search for the term *homosexuality* in their school library catalogs? (I realize that we use technical vocabulary in many cases, but at this point in history, someone using the word *homosexual* is often a fairly strong sign for an LGBTQ+ person that they are not in a safe or welcoming situation. Try Googling *homosexual* and then either *gay* or *lesbian* or *queer* and compare the results.)

The goal of the professional development sessions was to provide a safe and nonjudgmental space for school librarians to learn and discuss. Not everyone has the same level of knowledge when it comes to correct vocabulary, and many school librarians are new to buying LGBTQ+ materials. Our learners need us to show them they matter!

In our professional development, Sara and I tried to allow time and space for conversations and sharing, because everyone's school and situation are different, and there are seldom perfect answers that apply universally. Although there were both small-group discussions and full-group questions, we didn't require any kind of share-out from the small groups. Sometimes, when adults are the learners, we feel safer talking to just a few fellow learners, with no pressure to formally share what we discuss.

The result was rich and rewarding—and challenging—conversations and questions. One question in particular is difficult to write about, because it's awkward, and, in the moment, it was hard. After small-group discussions, a school librarian from my district raised her hand and asked for advice about a learner. Her concern for the learner, whose parents were not particularly accepting, was clear and palpable. Why, she wondered aloud, couldn't the learner simply be "normal," because it would be so much easier?

I have heard variations of this question many times, often asked by well-meaning individuals, but it never loses its sting. When we wonder why learners don't fit easily into predetermined boxes, we ask them to give up pieces of themselves. A learner who isn't "normal"—whatever that means—is a learner who is other, who is outside, and who can never be centered in their own educational experience.

In a professional development context, where school librarians are the learners, I believe it's important to accept questions like this one as honest attempts to grow. Sara and I addressed the word choice of "normal" but also assumed that the question came from a place of caring. When we are learning to "[contribute] to discussions in which multiple viewpoints on a topic are expressed" (AASL 2018, Learner II.C.2.), there are bound to be some growing pains and unintended missteps.

When our youth are the learners, though, we do need to watch for viewpoints expressing that certain categories of people are inherently wrong, bad, or other, and that have the potential to stifle or harm the young people to whose education and future we are devoted. Because LGBTQ+ learners may not be fully out, or even consciously aware of their identities, school librarians should assume they are present in every school, grade, and class.

Knowing that LGBTQ+ learners are present in all schools, whether or not their existence is known to their educators, school librarians have an excellent opportunity to model "articulating an awareness of the contributions of a range of learners" (AASL 2018, Learner II.A.1.). Part of being aware of the contributions of a range of learners is becoming aware of how groups and communities define themselves and what words are preferred.

Technology can help us answer our own questions. If you or your educator partners are unsure about pronoun use with transgender or nonbinary learners, useful resources abound on the web. A quick online search of *trans etiquette* produces a list of websites answering pronoun and name questions. Two places to start are GLSEN's "Supporting Trans and GNC Students" and GLAAD's "Tips for Allies of Transgender People." Of course, this profusion of information, especially when surrounding potentially sensitive topics, must be rigorously evaluated. Who else—if not the school librarian—will teach learners (and fellow educators) how to make such evaluations? Always, the ultimate resources on correct pronouns are your learners themselves.

Learners with any kind of LGBTQ+ identity will notice an attention to language, and they will notice a lack of attention to language, and they will use this information when deciding whether the school library (or the school itself) is a place that includes them.

The advantages of learners feeling embraced and centered in their own educational experience are many, and powerful, and brings me to something that happened recently, a few months after our LGBTQ+-focused professional development. As I stood with a school librarian in her recently flooded school library, she told me how she'd recently purchased more books for her K–8 school featuring LGBTQ+ characters.

Adding materials to her collection was wonderful, but what she did next was both simple and beautiful. Once the books arrived, she worked with her middle school–level GSA learners, and they picked a book for her to read to the kindergarten learners. It may seem like a small thing, but it will resonate through the lives of her learners, supporting them in ways she may never know.

For these middle school GSA learners, when they "[reflect] on their own place within the global learning community" (AASL 2018, Learner II.D.3.), their input and value as engaged learners will be clearly present. Middle school learners will often have already experienced being the other, but these learners have now experienced being the experts. For the kindergarten learners, perhaps they will move through elementary school seeing and learning about a wide variety of lives and perspectives and, therefore, will never learn to divide their fellow humans into "normal" and "other" categories.

From the beginning of their K–12 experience, these kindergarten learners will have begun "demonstrating interest in other perspectives during learning activities" (AASL 2018, Learner II.D.2.). For the kindergarten learners who are LGBTQ+, their perspectives will be included, making it easier for them to be interested in other perspectives. For the learners who aren't LGBTQ+, they will live in the world and will be better placed to be inclusive global citizens if knowledge of the rich diversity of humanity is a part of their learning experience from the very beginning.

Of all the Shared Foundations, I find Include to be the most central, because I believe learning springs most effectively from a place of security, agency, and inclusion. When learners see that they and their classmates are recognized by their schools, they are more likely to feel safe enough to explore the wide variety of viewpoints and perspectives that school librarians and libraries offer. If school libraries are inclusive spaces and school librarians work to promote representation, LGBTQ+ learners have a foothold of safety within their schools.

LGBTQ+-Inclusive School Libraries and Include

Our learners are always paying attention to what we do—and what we fail to do. Omission and silence speak loudly! Rachel pointed out that "learners with any kind of LGBTQ+ identity will notice an attention to language, and they will notice a lack of attention to language, and they will use this information when deciding whether the school library (or the school itself) is a place that includes them." This truth is powerful for all our learners across a range of identities. Welcoming Schools has a wonderful resource on LGBTQ+-inclusive language—*Defining LGBTQ Words for Children*.

For our school libraries to realize the Alignments under the Share Domain, we must

- Commit to "implementing solutions that address physical, social, cultural, linguistic, and intellectual barriers to equitable access to resources and services" (AASL 2018, School Library II.C.1.). Rachel's professional development addressed the soft censorship that can happen when school librarians themselves are the barrier to learners having equitable access to resources by not collecting a rich array of fiction and nonfiction titles that center or are created by members of the LGBTQ+ community, or both.
- Facilitate "opportunities to experience diverse ideas by promoting the use of high-quality and high-interest literature in formats that reflect the diverse developmental, cultural, social, and linguistic needs of all learners and their communities" (AASL 2018, School Library II.C.2.). Reflecting the LGBTQ+ identities of our learners and families—whether they are visible or known—is a key piece of this Alignment. Resources on collecting LGBTQ+-inclusive materials are centered under the Curate section in AASL's resource guide, *Defending Intellectual Freedom: LGBTQ+ Materials in School Libraries.*
- Work on "constructing a learning environment that fosters the sharing of a wide range of viewpoints and ideas" (AASL 2018, School Library II.C.3.). Rachel advanced this Alignment by leading professional development in her district using the AASL LGBTQ+ guide as a key resource. The guide is flooded with essential questions and activities, making it an almost turnkey professional development resource for professional learning teams or district librarian groups. The guide is also written for the school librarian as an independent learner. As with all equity and bias work, so much of our development is internal, and the essential questions in the guide can be used as writing prompts for this internal work.

I met Rachel when she served as the member guide for our ALA Emerging Leaders team as we were developing AASL's guide, *Defending Intellectual Freedom: LGBTQ+ Materials in School Libraries*. Rachel was key to developing a guide that firmly rests on the standards and is organized explicitly through the six Shared Foundations. The guide is a meta-example of the *National School Library Standards* not only because it's structured on the Shared Foundations but because its messages and resources also illustrate Include. It can also be used as an example of the ways in which the AASL Standards can be comprehensively applied to any school library opportunity.

When we work through the AASL Standards to construct our own school libraries as brave school environments in which our learners can feel safe, it's crucial to address harassment *and* include lessons and resources in the school curriculum that are LGBTQ+ inclusive. Learning for Justice is an essential resource on both of these fronts and has a wealth of equity-based online professional development that is free and easily accessible for school librarians. On the Learning for Justice website, you can access *Speak Up at School* and learn strategies for how you and your learners can respond to biased remarks. You can also find *Best Practices for Serving LGBTQ Students,* which has resources for building intersectional lessons that incorporate LGBTQ+ history and perspectives.

Because we are intentional about creating LGBTQ+-inclusive school libraries through the AASL Standards Alignments, it's crucial that we use an intersectional approach and do not view LGBTQ+ history or communities through a narrow lens. Our LGBTQ+ learners are whole people with many identities that span races, nations, languages, and disabilities. Their whole selves need to be seen, validated, and supported.

A final note on the powerful learning and experiences that Rachel shared with us. The question that a school librarian asked during the professional development session about why a learner just couldn't be "normal" reflects the implicit bias that our LGBTQ+ learners and colleagues face daily. Responding to this question is an opportunity to unpack how we can be advocates and accomplices in professional learning spaces. In a room full of school librarians, the work of responding to a harmful statement questioning the normalcy of our learners should not have rested solely on the presenters' shoulders. There could have been—should have been—a chorus of school librarian voices calling our colleague out and reminding them that straight does not equal normal. Saying nothing communicates at best complicity; at worst, agreement. We cannot carry out the Shared Foundation of Include if we are not advocates for our learners, wherever we are. Yes, we are called on to respect diverse perspectives, but that does not include perspectives that are rooted in ignorance and bias—perspectives that harm or other a learner or group of learners. That's harassment, not a perspective, and it doesn't live in the Domains, Competencies, and Alignments under Include.

Moving Forward

WHAT CAN I DO TODAY?

If you haven't already, download or print the AASL's resource guide, *Defending Intellectual Freedom: LGBTQ+ Materials in School Libraries,* and view the infographic and applied framework. The resource guide is easy to find with a quick online search for *AASL and LGBTQ Guide.* It can be directly accessed at https://standards.aasl.org/project/lgbtq.

HOW CAN I BUILD ON IT TOMORROW?

The LGBTQ+ resource guide is organized according to the six Shared Foundations in the *National School Library Standards*—you can read it linearly or jump among the interconnected foundations. Pick one and dive in!

Questions for the Reflective Practitioner

1. The school library Alignments under the Share Domain include the guidance that challenges to materials should be addressed through "established, detailed, and approved processes that uphold the American Library Association's Library Bill of Rights" (AASL 2018, 81). How are such processes represented in my own collection management plan? (The LGBTQ+ resource guide contains resources to help with this!)

2. Under Share, the standards call on libraries to honor "all school community members through displays" (AASL 2018, 81). Is this true for my displays? Are books centering characters from a wide range of identities authentically and seamlessly included in every display and genre in my library?

3. How do I foresee learning through the AASL LGBTQ+ resource guide as a way to implement standard Alignments related to equity and inclusion?

ACTION STEPS

- Conduct a shelf audit in your school library (see appendix B, "Shelf Audits"). How many books feature main characters who self-identify as queer or as members of the LGBTQ+ community?
- If you haven't already, identify a Safe Zone or Safe Schools training to attend.
- In your own collection, look at the cataloging of nonfiction books that deal with sexuality and gender. Do the assigned subject headings reflect a view that classifies cisgender and heterosexuality as "normal" and, therefore, designates the wide range of orientations and gender identities that fall out of that narrow range as a "social problem"—as old Dewey numbers did? Re-catalog and label where necessary, and ensure that you are collecting new nonfiction resources for learners.

12

Grow with Northside Neighbors

U**nless our school library is situated in a year-round school, we** typically say goodbye to our learners in the beginning of summer. For the most part, our collections may sit on our shelves waiting for the end of summer to be in learners' hands again. This is the traditional calendar model for school libraries—but is it enough?

Wait. Just wait, you may be thinking. Summer breaks are necessary and healthy for educators. For school librarians. After all, if we're doing it right throughout the year and devoting time and energy to our programs and learners, we need a break. Absolutely. During that last week of school in June—after a full year of supporting and nurturing our learners and their literacy—even my eyelashes are tired. And yet, could we do both? Could we build a way to connect with learners during the summer and still benefit from a necessary break?

The Grow Domain includes "the school librarian's responsibilities to enable equitable access to learning opportunities and resources necessary for learners' success" (AASL 2018, 150). We know that there are disparities in summer opportunities available to our learners. As school librarians, could we help level those disparities? Disrupt those inequities?

Elementary librarian Kathryn Cole says yes. After identifying key community collaborators, she has built a powerful summer learning program that has transformed and grown her school library into a beautiful community hub—a valued and valuable third space.

Northside Neighbors: School Libraries as Community Spaces

Kathryn Cole

What if our school libraries opened up wider to provide access and oppor-tunity whenever possible? What if, instead of shutting down for the summer months, we made an intentional choice to remain open? What if school libraries served as community spaces throughout the year for our learners and their families? What if . . . ?

Those "what ifs" became the reality that guided our work in establishing a summer library program at Northside Elementary School in Chapel Hill, North Carolina. Our aim was to provide learners in our school neighborhood walk zone with school library services grounded in access, equity, and engagement during the summer. What started as an idea to provide more summer access to our school library collection quickly became a community hub of engagement, exploration, laughter, and relationships.

Community Background

Nestled in the historic African American community within our small university town, Northside Elementary School has a rich and vibrant history. Although the current building was constructed in 2013, our school has a deep legacy as a Rosenwald School that served the Northside Neighborhood's Black community during segregation. Many alumni still live in the area and share memories of their days spent learning at the original Northside. The educators who worked in the school also lived among the learners and their families, and there existed a mutual trust and familiarity between home and school. When *Brown v. Board of Education* forced school systems to begin the process of desegregation, Northside learners and educators were integrated into local white schools, and Northside Elementary was closed. The building continued to serve as a site for education in other ways, including housing a local prekindergarten program.

Over the last few decades, the Northside neighborhood has witnessed many changes as a result of gentrification and local community demographic shifts that included the influx of refugee families along with an increase in college learner housing. Because of this shift, the Northside Neighborhood Initiative was developed. This initiative is a community partnership that pursues a shared vision for the historic Northside Neighborhood: a family-friendly, multigenerational community that balances the needs of long-term residents, new owners, renters, and learners.

Our school is an important symbol in this community and serves as a vital partner in sharing the community's history and vision for equity and inclusion. One floor of our new building includes a dedicated history walk with enlarged, wall-mounted photographs along with a timeline that shares the history of our school. We foreground this history that often went ignored or unnoticed. Helping our learners understand and learn from the people who came before them is an integral part of their education at Northside today. Equity and inclusion drive our work from a historical perspective and for current classroom practices. Centering equity in our current practice means we examine barriers that inhibit opportunities and actively work to dismantle those barriers in policy and practice.

Our school is also home to a district-wide Newcomers program for newly arrived immigrants in grades 3–5 who have little or no English proficiency and either little or interrupted formal education in their native countries. Our school library actively connects to this program and collaborates with the instructors to create meaningful learning experiences that integrate literacy and inquiry with hands-on learning opportunities.

Our school library plays an integral role in our equity efforts, and our Northside Neighbors Summer Library Program was part of our overall commitment to ensuring that our marginalized populations have access to summer learning opportunities. Summer reading sign-up data from the public library revealed that many families in our school neighborhood walk zone were not able to access the programming being offered during the summer months. Lack of direct public transportation from our school neighborhood to the public library created a barrier for many of our families. Communication was also key. For many of our neighborhood families, English is not their primary language, and public library publications were not shared in multiple languages. With so many local neighborhood learners not accessing the public library's summer program, learners in our school community missed out on opportunities to explore, create, and get books in their hands during the summer.

We wanted to provide learners in our community with more opportunities for engagement during the summer, while also providing book access. We had the community space, we had the books, we had the people—we just needed a plan for action.

Keeping the School Library Open When School Is Out!

Keeping the school library open and accessible during the summer was the primary goal of the Northside Neighbors program. When school libraries close up and schools slow down, our aim was to do the opposite. We wanted the active space our school library had become during the school year to remain that way during the summer for our community. In 2015 we began to brainstorm ways in which our school library could remain open and provide programming and services to neighborhood youth. By opening our school library during the summer, we could run a program similar to that of the public library but do so in a space that learners and their families were already familiar with and could easily access. Through purposeful planning, intentional community partnerships, and active outreach, we developed a program that continues to run strong years later.

Working closely with our public library system, we are able to use our school library as an extension of the public library's summer reading program, thereby ensuring that learners who may not be able to visit the main branch during the summer have an experience similar to that of their peers. This partnership includes visits from the local youth outreach librarian, who runs a biweekly program. We also partner with our school district's Food for Summer program to ensure that learners have access to lunch daily while in the building. And our local Public School Foundation, along with the support of community sponsors, provides funding for staffing, visits from local performers and artists, and supplies needed for various activities.

As the school librarian, I oversee and plan the summer program and then work with other educators in our building to coordinate the week-by-week activities. Before the school year ends, plans are made, calendars created, and special programs booked. We also seek learner feedback to guide what our summer program will entail. Because this is a program designed specifically for neighborhood youth, we want it to reflect their interests.

The final step is program promotion and outreach. We actively share information with families during family literacy nights each spring, make neighborhood visits, send home translated flyers, and discuss the program with learners before school lets out to ensure that they know the official start day.

Equity, Access, and Engagement

For seven weeks during the summer, we open our doors four hours a day, three to four days a week, and our school library quickly becomes a community center. At ten o'clock on the dot, our neighborhood youth walk up together to partake in everything from read-alouds to gaming to creative art and science activities that incorporate the use of our school library makerspace. Our Northside Neighbors summer library program provides a space in which learners can check out books, relax, socialize with friends, and access a multitude of resources to explore during the summer break from school.

Although the initial idea was to open the school library with flexible hours that featured a few program options throughout the week, we quickly noticed a need to alter our plan that first summer. When learners arrived, they wanted to stay and engage in activities over the course of the four hours. So, we did. We saw a need and we filled it. We made the space less like a traditional library and more like a community center. Learners are able to walk up and stay for the duration, access books, and engage in programs and activities planned alongside free-choice options. And the real beauty of this program is how it engages not just current learners but former learners and siblings, creating broad family connections to our school library. This outcome also means we have to think strategically about programming and activities that can incorporate a wide age range because we have had children as young as 4 and as old as 15 coming together. We think about ways our older youth can serve as group leaders and use their expertise and skill to model for our younger learners.

We provide experiences that allow for making, creating, exploring, and having fun! Although we plan out many activities, we also ask our youth what kinds of things they want to engage in. We take their feedback and build our program around their input, ensuring that their voice is at the heart of what we engage in each summer. Although our school library serves as the main hub of activity, we utilize many spaces across our school, including the garden, the playground, the cafeteria, and the learning lab. We also incorporate walking field trips and utilize our public transit system. We've gone swimming, visited our local university's planetarium, and walked to nearby parks, greenways, and creeks. We take advantage of using our entire neighborhood as a learning space, with our school library serving as the heart and center.

We incorporate STEAM-based activities throughout the summer. We've made slime, created fidget spinner art, and applied design thinking principles when building water slides using common household items. We've built with LEGOs, created green screen projects, folded and raced paper airplanes, and constructed our own water shooters using PVC pipe, duct tape, and foam noodles. We have focused on global studies as we traveled around the world while also exploring our own identities and connections to self. We learned about wishing traditions around the world before creating our own wish portraits, participated in oral storytelling and drumming traditions from Sierra Leone, West Africa, and read about the history and cultural traditions of yoga before trying it ourselves.

One year we made it our mission to focus on building a better world through a series of projects. Our learners learned how to make pet toys for our local animal shelter, built and painted birdhouses for our school campus, designed stepping-stones and painted signs to beautify our garden landscape, and built our own Little Free Library for the larger Northside community.

Every summer, we connect our activities to literacy and fill our summer days with read-alouds of every kind. Each program begins with a related story. Before building water shooters, learners read *Whoosh! Lonnie Johnson's Super-Soaking Stream of Inventions* by Chris Barton. In preparing to create our own Little Free Library, we looked at digital images of ways in which libraries provide books to kids all over the world and read *Inside the Books: Readers and Libraries around the World* by Toni Buzzeo along with *Waiting for the Biblioburro* by Monica Brown. Before a local theater troupe came to perform their production of Anansi tales, we read various versions of this traditional African trickster tale and even performed our own skit (complete with upcycled costumes). And one summer we read lots of stories that featured dogs while we visited with Libby, a therapy dog, who made weekly visits to our library.

We've also connected stories to our garden projects. We read about farmer Will Allen through the book *Farmer Will Allen and the Growing Table* by Jacqueline Briggs Martin. We discovered the important work he has done with his local community to create gardens in urban landscapes where food deserts once existed. We then connected that story to our own school garden as we not only planted but also harvested a bounty of fresh vegetables that the learners took home each visit. Our garden became a hub of activity and served as a community connection that allowed not just our learners but their families to get involved. Through many laughs, a lot of sweat, and plenty of dirt under our nails, we planted, weeded, watered, and enjoyed tomatoes, cucumbers, peppers, melons, and more all summer long.

Just as the public library offers special guest programs, we coordinate with local artists and performers to do the same. We have welcomed puppeteers, hip hop dancers, local farmers (along with their goats), and University of North Carolina college athletes into our school library to oversee special programs. Strategically layered throughout the summer, these programs allow our learners interactive and engaging opportunities to explore the arts, nature, health and wellness, and more. Learners have explored the world of birds and then watched a macaw fly across the school library with Birdman Dave and have gotten to hold snakes and pet giant tortoises when they learned what it means to be a herpetologist from The Traveling Tortoise visit. These experiences enhance summer learning and provide engagement in ways not typically explored during the year. We connect each visit with literacy before or after by exploring stories and books related to the topic our visitors bring before us. And when possible, we also use these visits as a springboard to inspire our creative side as we design and make something based on the focus of the visit.

Each summer wraps up with an experience to celebrate all the learning, reading, and growing we've done. From a trip to the local bowling alley to an overnight camping trip, we end our time together with *joy!* We build experiences that create lasting memories. And when we look back at pictures captured throughout the summer, we reminisce, laugh, and smile as we revisit each individual memory. Finally, we wish each other well until we get to do it again.

Starting Your Own Program

We strategically planned a program and sought out a community sponsor through our Public School Foundation to fund this program throughout the summer. This funding ensures that we can pay for staffing, special guest performances, educational programs, and supplies necessary to create a host of engaging activities. However, it's possible to do the same with little to no funding using only local talent and resources. If multiple days a week isn't an option, consider opening your school library one day a week throughout the summer for families to access resources and programming. Even if nothing but the collection is made available, it creates an opening that wasn't there before to engage families in your school library.

Consider flexible options for hours that you could operate a program. If your school is located in an area in which children can walk to your building, you may consider opening for a few hours during the day. If your school is more isolated or transportation is necessary to get to your school, then you may want to offer open hours during the evening when parents may be more available to bring children. You can also alternate hours to ensure that you provide the same opportunities to families who may not work traditional workday hours.

Another approach may be to visit local neighborhoods and take your program to the learners! A summer school library program doesn't have to exist in the physical constraints of a school building. Put some books and a few supplies in a tub and visit a neighborhood where your learners live. Meeting our families where they are to provide programming can be very powerful and build community connections between home and school. Learners could make weekly requests for books of interest that could be checked out and delivered each visit. Alternatively, the school librarian could take a handful of books to share and leave for learners to enjoy until a return visit. Either approach allows books from the school library to be utilized and enjoyed during the summer while also providing programming opportunities in neighborhoods. And depending on your school community and locale, a local neighborhood program may be better attended than if it were hosted at the school.

Staffing a Summer Program

When establishing a summer school library program, it can be overwhelming to think about how to acquire funding to pay for staffing. An alternative model could involve volunteers. Create a schedule with other staff members from your school in which people sign up for one rotation (or more if they desire) during the summer. Rather than spending money on local performers or guest programs, invite staff members to share or showcase a special talent with learners. This can be an opportunity for staff to lead an activity with learners that educators never seem to find time for during the school year. Consider asking your music, art, physical education, drama, or other teaching specialists in your building to lead a program that introduces a new skill or engages learners in a special project. What talents and skills could families in your school community have and be willing to share with learners? Is there a chef, an artist, a landscape architect, someone who knows how to sew? Invite them to be a part of your program.

You could arrange storytimes with local community helpers by inviting government officials, firefighters, school board members, and others to engage in a weekly program that would simultaneously build relationships across the community. Local high school learners may be available to organize programs and activities while also acquiring service hours. Something as simple as an organized kickball game combined with a read-aloud and conversation can be fun and engaging for area youth.

Low-Cost Program Supplies

If you would like to begin a summer program, you can start small with little more than read-alouds and access to the collection. A quick and easy activity to pair with a read-aloud would be bookmarks that children can make and take when the program ends. Many activities involve little to no cost. Buy some inexpensive sidewalk chalk and create a poetry walk on the sidewalks at your school, have a bubble parade, use recycled plastic bags and some duct tape to create handmade soccer balls, lead a nature hike, build a puzzle. If you have access to physical education equipment, borrow a few items such as jump ropes, hula hoops, and basketballs to use during the summer.

For many STEAM-based activities, everyday household objects or low-cost items from the dollar store are all that is needed. Straws, popsicle sticks, coffee filters, rubber bands, cotton swabs, pipe cleaners, buckets, and more can go a long way when thinking creatively. You can also request items from your faculty or community before summer begins. Recyclables such as paper towel rolls, milk jugs, bottle caps, and mixed-part plastics can be repurposed when creating and building using design thinking. Another person's trash can be a makerspace treasure and incredibly useful for a summer program. It never ceases to amaze me what learners can do with a few random objects and a big imagination.

Reflections on Community

Each year, as the summer comes to a close and our programming ends, I am encouraged to think about and reflect on how we can continue to cultivate these relationships beyond the summer. How can we include more families from our neighborhood, build lasting partnerships, and learn from and with one another? I find myself reflecting on how our school library can offer services and programs important to our community and serve as a gathering space to meet the needs of our families. More than anything, I recognize how our school library has become more than just a library. It has become an inclusive community hub—a place for kids in our community to feel welcome, to engage, and to know that there is always a place where they can seek refuge even when they have moved on from our school. This program we have started is such a gift to all participants, including other educators and me. It has cultivated community relationships, provided hours of engagement, and created opportunities for kids to learn from and with one another. Our school libraries have to be more than just books. We have to create inclusive spaces that extend the definition of a school library. School libraries can be the heart of what community-based, inclusive education can and should be for our youth. Sometimes, it just takes asking, "What if . . . ?"

Northside Neighbors and Include

The framework of Northside Neighbors partners beautifully with the Competencies and Alignments across the Include Domains. When we look specifically under Grow for school libraries, we find the following:

- The very first Alignment under Grow is that the school library must ensure "that all learning needs are met through access to information and ideas located in a diverse collection of sufficient size for the learner population" (AASL 2018, School Library II.D.1.). Kathryn has built a diverse, reflective collection that prioritizes #OwnVoices titles and foregrounds the use of read-alouds to blend with every activity. Her awareness of her learner population and families in her community is evident through every aspect of her intentionally built summer program.
- The second Alignment calls on the school library to enable "equitable access to learning opportunities, academic and social support, and other resources necessary for learners' success" (AASL 2018, School Library II.D.2.). Northside Neighbors lives this Competency through its wealth of inclusive activities across a wide variety of subjects, interests, and locales.
- Finally, the school library is charged with "clearly and frequently articulating the school library's impact when communicating with administration, faculty, staff, learners, parents, and the community" (AASL 2018, School Library II.D.3.). To gain funding and support, Kathryn articulated the value of summer learning for Northside's learners. She was able to recruit staff members to join Northside Neighbors and is diligent in finding local artists and experts—who reflect her learners—to enhance the program each summer. One of the most powerful aspects of Northside Neighbors is its welcoming framework for family members. Communication is a key piece of this Alignment, and Kathryn works to make sure that families in her community—across multiple languages—are aware of her summer library offerings. Kathryn's school library has become a true community space—it is the Grow Domain in beautiful action.

Questions for the Reflective Practitioner

1. How am I meeting school library Alignments that show my school library is building empathy and equity?
2. How would opening my school library at least once during the summer—or virtually—help meet school library Alignments related to "equitable access to learning opportunities, academic and social support, and other resources necessary for learners' success" (AASL 2018, School Library II.D.2.)?
3. How do I plan on "clearly and frequently articulating the school library's impact" (AASL 2018, School Library II.D.3.) during this school year?

I am lucky enough to call Kathryn a co-conspirator because we work in neighboring districts to build our school libraries into equitable and transformative school spaces. I have always admired her Northside Neighbors program but had honestly never seriously considered it as an option for my school because of scheduling and transportation concerns. My goal for this guide is that the chapters serve as both inspiration and roadmap for readers. It's working for me! I'm going to use Kathryn's ideas and strategies to start planning and designing a summer learning program for my school library, including exploring virtual options. Who's with me?

Moving Forward

WHAT CAN I DO TODAY?

Reflect on your school, learners, and summer opportunities. Like Kathryn, ask yourself, "What if . . . ?"

HOW CAN I BUILD ON IT TOMORROW?

Refer to Kathryn's advice on starting your own program, staffing a summer program, and finding low-cost program supplies. Identify one idea you'd like to start implementing for next summer.

ACTION STEPS

- Speak with your administration about the possibility of building a summer school library program for your learners.
- Identify collaborators at the building level. Is there a colleague who would be interested in organizing this program with you? Identify possible programming leads.
- Start researching possible funding through grant opportunities, local businesses, and your PTA/PTO/PTSA, and keep a running list of potential volunteers!

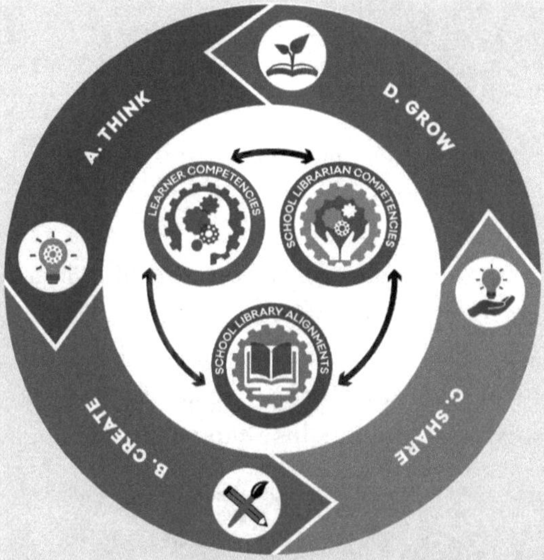

PART IV

Across Include

As school librarians, we are not progressing through the Domains, Competencies, and Alignments under Include in isolation. The three frameworks—Learner, School Librarian, and School Library—are most powerful when we are approaching them interdependently. The AASL Standards are explicit about this interdependence: "No standards set or Shared Foundation can be effectively executed independent of the other two sets" (AASL 2018, 17). The AASL Standards are not silos, accessed one at a time, separate for each program or activity. Instead, they are linked—across Domains and frameworks and through our roles of leader, instructional partner, teacher, information specialist, and program administrator.

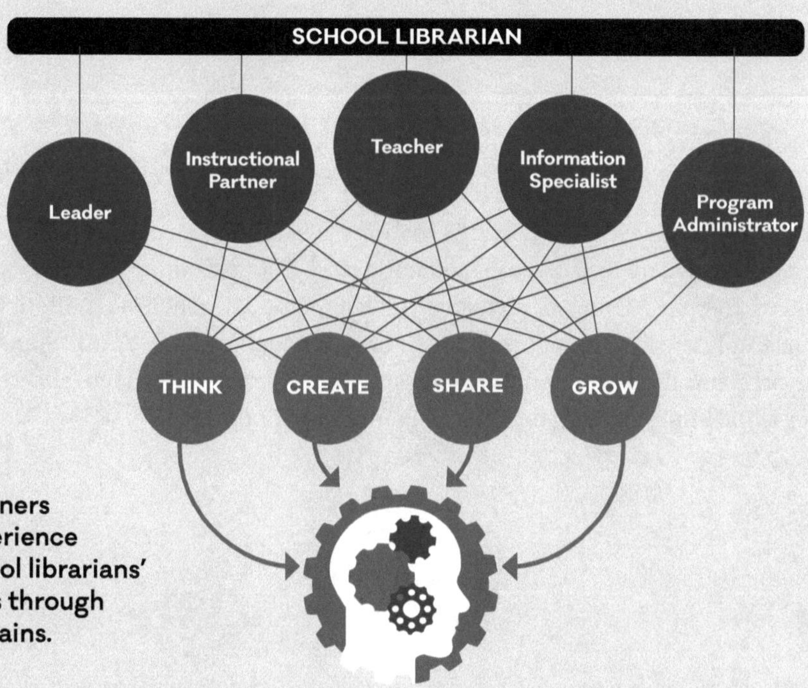

Learners experience school librarians' roles through domains.

We've just explored twelve school library initiatives that each accessed a multitude of Competencies and Alignments from across numerous "boxes" in the Include Shared Foundation. One Domain in one framework—one box—was the focus of each chapter in the first three parts of the book. This last section is going to switch that focus. We won't be diving deep into one box. Instead, each of the chapters in this section will touch on multiple standards from across Include, demonstrating how robust the Competencies and Alignments are and how inclusive school libraries, programs, ideas, and research live out, across, and through this Shared Foundation.

SHARED FOUNDATION II.

Include

KEY COMMITMENT

Demonstrate an understanding of and commitment to inclusiveness and respect for diversity in the learning community.

Domain	LEARNER DOMAINS AND COMPETENCIES	SCHOOL LIBRARIAN DOMAINS AND COMPETENCIES	SCHOOL LIBRARY DOMAINS AND ALIGNMENTS **The school library facilitates the Key Commitment to and Competencies of INCLUDE**	Domain
A. Think	**Learners contribute a balanced perspective when participating in a learning community by:** 1. Articulating an awareness of the contributions of a range of learners. 2. Adopting a discerning stance toward points of view and opinions expressed in information resources and learning products. 3. Describing their understanding of cultural relevancy and placement within the global learning community.	**School librarians direct learners to contribute a balanced perspective when participating in a learning community by:** 1. Engaging learners to articulate an awareness of the contributions of a range of learners. 2. Guiding learners as they adopt a discerning stance toward points of view and opinions expressed in information resources and learning products. 3. Differentiating instruction to support learners' understanding of cultural relevancy and placement within the global learning community.	**The school library supports balanced perspectives through resources and learning opportunities by:** 1. Providing challenging and authentic opportunities that address the needs of the broad range of learners. 2. Offering diverse learning experiences that allow for individual differences in learners. 3. Providing a comprehensive variety of resources.	**A. Think**
B. Create	**Learners adjust their awareness of the global learning community by:** 1. Interacting with learners who reflect a range of perspectives. 2. Evaluating a variety of perspectives during learning activities. 3. Representing diverse perspectives during learning activities.	**School librarians establish opportunities for learners to adjust their awareness of the global learning community by:** 1. Providing opportunities for learners to interact with others who reflect a range of perspectives. 2. Devising learning activities that require learners to evaluate a variety of perspectives. 3. Designing opportunities that help learners to illustrate diverse viewpoints.	**The school library represents all members and their place in a global learning community by:** 1. Establishing and maintaining a collection of reading and information materials in formats that support the diverse developmental, cultural, social, and linguistic needs of the range of learners and their communities. 2. Organizing facilities to enhance the use of and ensure equitable access to information resources and services for all learners. 3. Featuring learning opportunities that include diverse viewpoints.	**B. Create**
C. Share	**Learners exhibit empathy with and tolerance for diverse ideas by:** 1. Engaging in informed conversation and active debate. 2. Contributing to discussions in which multiple viewpoints on a topic are expressed.	**School librarians facilitate experiences in which learners exhibit empathy and tolerance for diverse ideas by:** 1. Giving learners opportunities to engage in informed conversation and active debate. 2. Guiding learners to contribute to discussions in which multiple viewpoints on a topic are expressed.	**The school library facilitates opportunities to experience diverse ideas by:** 1. Implementing solutions that address physical, social, cultural, linguistic, and intellectual barriers to equitable access to resources and services. 2. Promoting the use of high-quality and high-interest literature in formats that reflect the diverse developmental, cultural, social, and linguistic needs of all learners and their communities. 3. Constructing a learning environment that fosters the sharing of a wide range of viewpoints and ideas.	**C. Share**
D. Grow	**Learners demonstrate empathy and equity in knowledge building within the global learning community by:** 1. Seeking interactions with a range of learners. 2. Demonstrating interest in other perspectives during learning activities. 3. Reflecting on their own place within the global learning community.	**School librarians explicitly lead learners to demonstrate empathy and equity in knowledge building within the global learning community by:** 1. Creating an atmosphere in which learners feel empowered and interactions are learner-initiated. 2. Initiating opportunities that allow learners to demonstrate interest in other perspectives. 3. Showcasing learners' reflections on their place within the global learning community.	**The school library builds empathy and equity within the global learning community by:** 1. Ensuring that all learning needs are met through access to information and ideas located in a diverse collection of sufficient size for the learner population and supported by reliable hardware and software. 2. Enabling equitable access to learning opportunities, academic and social support, and other resources necessary for learners' success. 3. Clearly and frequently articulating the school library's impact when communicating with administration, faculty, staff, learners, parents, and the community.	**D. Grow**

To showcase the power of Include in action, four school libraries and their programs or models are shared in this section: "Disabilities and School Libraries," "Comics, Manga, and Inclusion," "Selecting and Using Children's Books about Indigenous Peoples," and an inclusive book fair model called #TrueBookFAIR. These examples will demonstrate the interdependence of the AASL Standards Frameworks and their components across learners, school librarians, and school libraries while implementing the Shared Foundation of Include.

13

Include and Disabilities

In the *National School Library Standards,* a vital Best Practice for the Include Shared Foundation centers on the creation of an accessible space. "Use furniture that is adjustable and moveable to meet the needs of all individuals, as well as small and large groups. Arrange materials and equipment so they can be easily accessed by all learners" (AASL 2018, 82). Accessibility of our space and collection—and our instruction—is key for us as school librarians. To meet these Competencies and Alignments with fidelity requires us to build our accessibility capacity and understanding for our stakeholders with disabilities—including learners, colleagues, and families.

North Carolina middle school librarian Ness Shortley shares research, insights, and her own experiences with inclusively serving learners with disabilities. This chapter can inform our thinking about inclusion across the frameworks and Domains.

Disabilities and School Libraries

Ness Shortley

School libraries should be warm and welcoming places for all learners— including disabled learners. Given that disabled people comprise one-fifth of the population of the United States and that nearly 90 percent of disabled children attend public schools (Brault 2011), it is practically guaranteed that your school library has patrons with a variety of disabilities both visible and less visible. But how often do we think about disabled learners (including colleagues and families) when we're designing our spaces—or, as is more likely, when we're working with the space we've inherited? How often do we think of disabled people when we're developing our collections or thinking about instruction? When we're collaborating with classroom educators? How do we think about disabled learners? In short, how do we include disabled learners and other community members in our school libraries? To explain how I include disability in my own library practice, I'd like to share some important background research about disability in education and how I have transferred that knowledge and experience to my own school library space and instruction.

Disability Models

The way we think and talk about disability undergirds everything else: how we treat disabled people, how we view accommodations, the kinds of stories we tell and seek out for our collections, and more. Many frameworks explore how we view disabled people, but we'll explore four of them briefly because they affect every part of our practice:

- The charity model of disability puts forth a perspective that disabled people exist so that nondisabled people can show how good they are (Retief and Letšosa 2018). Disabled people should be pitied, and their life is terrible and painful. It's from this idea that we get phrases like "she suffers from anxiety" or "he is confined to a wheelchair." This model is also visible in a lot of media created by nondisabled people about disabled people. In books and movies like *Me Before You* by Jojo Moyes and *Wonder* by R. J. Palacio, Will and Auggie, respectively, exist to show readers and moviegoers alike how good or bad the nondisabled people in their lives are, while simultaneously conveying that disabled lives are less valuable than nondisabled ones.
- The medical model of disability focuses on the disabled person's body or mind and the ways it is different from a nondisabled person's body or mind. Basically, those who subscribe to the medical model view disability as a problem or deficit that exists within a person. Disability activists and many scholars find this model limiting at best and harmful at worst; under the medical model of disability, the disabled person must want to get well and must work to the exclusion of all else to do so. The goal is to be, functionally, nondisabled. The goal is a cure. Disability also becomes something for the individual to overcome rather than something that can be navigated with accommodations (Mairs 2008; Quayson 2007).
- The social model focuses on disability as a social construct; it marks the difference between impairment and disability and focuses on how the environment excludes certain types of bodies (Retief and Letšosa 2018). Some of the ways the environment might disable people include a lack of ramps to get into buildings, inadequate or missing captions for movies, policies that police how people must be or act, and unnecessary job restrictions. In short, the

social model focuses on fixing institutions and attitudes instead of people.

- The identity model, which is closely related to the social model, also holds that disability is socially constructed but takes this concept a step further, arguing that disability is a positive identity, much like queerness or Blackness, and includes the ideas that intersectionality (Crenshaw 1989) compounds the marginalizations of our learners and that each identity affects the other (Retief and Letšosa 2018). From this model comes the idea of disability pride. The push for #OwnVoices literature—that is, books written by people who hold the cultural identities they're writing about—is a relevant example.

These frameworks can help us identify our latent biases about disability and disabled people, as well as help us frame the ways we think about accommodations and inclusion. By interrogating our deeply held and often unconscious beliefs about disability, we can better serve our learning community: learners, parents, families, and colleagues in our schools. Using the identity model of disability will help school librarians create loving and safe spaces for disabled learners in schools.

Language of Disability

There has been a lot of discussion about the language that should be used when referring to disabled people: Should it be disabled people? People with disabilities? The disabled? People with special needs? Other euphemisms, such as handicapable, differently abled, or physically challenged? Generally speaking, euphemisms in our school spaces should be avoided. Disabled people don't have special needs; they have needs, full stop, the same way nondisabled people do. Many disabled people view such terms as paternalistic.

Some, often nondisabled, people have argued for what is known as people first language (e.g., a learner with autism) instead of identity first language (e.g., an autistic learner). With the people first construction, the learner comes before the disability or impairment, and supporters of this construction say it centers a person's humanity before their disability. Educators who prefer people first language suggest that it eliminates stereotypes and generalizations because it focuses on the learner rather than the disability. Still, many disabled people prefer identity first language over people first language, arguing that disability is inextricable from who they are. Indeed, many of the loudest proponents of people first language are nondisabled people, who can be uncomfortable with disabled identity.

For disabled learners and families who prefer identity first language, their disabilities are intrinsic and are crucial to their experience, similar to the ways race and ethnicity, gender identity, and sexual orientation affect how people experience the world and how people are treated. Regardless, the preference of the disabled learner (or learner with a disability, as the case may be) should be respected and followed.

It's also important to take care that language doesn't reinforce stereotypes about disabled learners. The following are some guidelines to consider when talking about disabled learners, family members, and colleagues:

- Remember that disabled people are people, with many of the same hopes, dreams, foibles, and ambitions as nondisabled people.
- Generally speaking, don't turn disability into a noun: avoid such terms as *the blind* and *the disabled.*
- Avoid words that imply victimhood or tragedy, such as *suffers from, afflicted with,* and *overcome by.*
- Recognize that mobility aids—such as wheelchairs, canes, walkers, scooters, and crutches—represent freedom for disabled people. Avoid constructions (such as *confined to*) and comments that imply that using these and other aids is giving up or otherwise negative.
- Avoid using disabled people as inspiration or imply that nondisabled lives are more valuable than disabled lives.
- Recognize that disability isn't something to be overcome and that disabled people are not inspirational simply for living their lives.
- Recognize the extent to which ableism affects disabled people's lives with barriers. For example, a wheelchair user is impaired by stairs or by too-steep ramps.

Which broad terms to use when describing disabled and nondisabled people is not the only issue when dealing with language and disability. People use language associated with disability in their everyday speech—for example, by describing surprising or outrageous events as "crazy" or using "retarded" or "lame" as a casual put-down, much the same way that people use "gay" as a generic insult. As school librarians building inclusive spaces, we have to push back on the use of these terms, with learners and colleagues.

Disability Representation in Books

Scholars, activists, educators, and others have long talked about the importance of representing authors from all walks of life, all colors, all creeds, all genders, all sexualities, all body shapes and sizes, and all levels of ability. Bishop (1990) coined the idea of windows, mirrors, and sliding glass doors. Learners of all ages need to see themselves in literature, and this analogy helps illustrate why. Mirrors allow children and teens to see their own experiences reflected back at them, while windows allow them to see into other worlds and cultures—and sliding glass doors allow them to use their imaginations to walk on through. Still, certain learners have many more mirrors than others; white, cisgender, heterosexual, nondisabled boys have the most mirrors, and the further away a learner gets from that identity, the fewer their mirrors become.

Data from the Cooperative Children's Book Center (CCBC) show how abysmal the representation is for Black, Indigenous, Asian, and Latinx people; center staff have begun tracking other areas of marginalization—namely, disability, gender, religion, and sexual orientation—and found that these identities are poorly represented, too. When learners are limited in who they see in the media they consume, they are limited to single stories (Adichie 2009) about their world, which can limit their imagination and cause them to view those not like them as other and less than. Learners also need to see those who are different from them in literature, to help them build empathy for those who do not look or act like them and to build cultural competency. Disabled learners, too, need relevant and authentic representation in picture books and in middle grade and young adult literature, and nondisabled children, teens, and adults need to see depictions of disabled people being the heroes of their own stories.

School libraries have an incredible opportunity to be inclusive in a way that classroom educators may not: through the representation of disabled people in our collections. But how do school librarians judge the quality of the representation in books and other media? What should school librarians be looking for when we're thinking about adding books to our collections and weeding resources with stereotypical and outdated depictions of disabled people?

Literary and disability studies scholars have noted that disabled characters in media tend to fall into one of several categories. These tropes, for the most part, are stereotypical or one-dimensional representations of disabled people that do not allow them to be fully fleshed-out and well-rounded characters; indeed, disabled characters in media often serve to move the plot forward or to show character development in other, nondisabled characters. Some of the more common tropes include disability as a shorthand for evil (e.g., Captain Hook), disabled characters whose bitterness about their disability consumes them, disabled characters as eternal children or holy innocents, cosmetic disability (e.g., Luke Skywalker's mechanical hand) where the disability has little impact on the story, inspirational disability (e.g., Auggie in *Wonder*), and helpless disability.

Positive portrayals of disabled people include high expectations for what the disabled character can accomplish, showing the disabled character's agency, showing their positive impact on society, and showing them in relationships with disabled and nondisabled characters in which both benefit (Curwood 2013). Myers and Bersani (2008) noted that books with ableist messages can distort "perceptions of people with disabilities and [help] maintain biases and myths about disabilities." Their guidelines for evaluating books for children and teens can help readers more critically engage with media:

- Does the book ignore disabled people?
- Do the illustrations promote a stereotypical depiction of disabled people? For example, do the disabled people always look or seem happy? Is the disabled character shown in a leadership role, or are they there to convey some sort of message?
- Is the story line ableist? Is the disabled person there to add tension to the plot or problems for the main characters? How are the disabled characters portrayed—as flat and one-dimensional or as fully realized people? Are they stereotypes?
- Does the author use ableist language? For example, is the disabled character "confined" to a wheelchair? Does the author use ableist metaphors, such as *lame, crazy,* or *blind*?
- Do the disabled characters have agency? Does the disabled character get to be the hero, or do they have to be rescued by the hero?
- Does the book support positive self-image for disabled children and teens?
- Is the author disabled? Are they disabled in the same way as their character? Is the work #OwnVoices? If not, have they done research and hired a sensitivity reader?

Furthermore, school librarians should ask themselves whether common perceptions of disability and tropes are supported or disrupted in the text, what purpose the disabled character serves, and who benefits and who loses as a result of the representation of disabled characters (Dunn 2015). Keeping these things in mind can help us as school librarians develop collections that authentically and accurately capture the experiences of disabled people.

Making Our School Libraries Inclusive

How accessible and inclusive is the physical space of our school libraries? As the school librarian, we may not have much say in the design of our spaces, the kind of furniture that is in place, and more, but there are steps you can take to make your school library and your programming more inclusive. Legally, because of Section 504 of the Rehabilitation Act of 1973 and the Americans with Disabilities Act of 1990, we cannot exclude disabled people from participating in and benefiting from our school libraries, and, of course, we wouldn't want to.

In the physical space of my middle school library, I've

- ensured that a wheelchair user or disabled learner using mobility aids such as a cane, crutches, a powerchair, or a walker can navigate the physical library and can access the same spaces that nondisabled learners can;

- removed anything that could stick out from shelves or anywhere else, such as power cables, rugs, and low-profile stools that might impede a blind or visually impaired person;
- ensured that my circulation desk, book return area, and multiple library computers are accessible to wheelchair users;
- worked to create environments that meet the needs of different learners, creating a semi-private, quiet space for learners who get distracted or overstimulated in loud environments and also a space where being quiet is not required; and
- identified accessible computer accessories: the school library has a computer with a trackball for those who cannot easily manipulate a laptop trackpad or mouse; speech-to-text software is available for visually impaired, blind, and learning-disabled users; and wrist rests are available for learners with mobility impairments, such as carpal tunnel or juvenile rheumatoid arthritis.

I work to make our collection inclusive by prioritizing authentic and accurate representations of disabled people. We have a variety of formats (e.g., large-print books, e-books, audiobooks) available for checkout. Our digital resources, including databases and catalogs, can be accessed using adaptive technology, including screen readers. Our collection development policy includes language stating that digital resources will be made accessible. I work with our special education teachers to stay abreast of individualized education programs (IEPs) and 504 plans, which keep me aware of the accommodations disabled learners are entitled to.

School librarians have an opportunity to make the school library a safe space for neurodiverse learners, especially autistic learners, learners with attention deficit hyperactivity disorder (ADHD) or obsessive-compulsive disorder (OCD), those with sensory issues, those with auditory processing disorders, and those with mental illnesses, such as anxiety. Requiring disabled and neurodivergent learners to engage in the same ways as their nondisabled and neurotypical peers can cause disabled and neurodivergent learners a lot of harm. Requiring learners to make eye contact, to keep still, to not hold something in their hands—for example, for fidgeting or stimming (self-stimulating behaviors)—can lead to maladaptive behaviors, emotional dysregulation, and negative self-regard. Schools often require conformity of learners; this expectation is especially difficult for disabled learners. But the school library can be a space that allows disabled and neurodiverse learners to be their whole selves. Additionally, we can help other educators in our schools build inclusive practices for their neurodiverse learners by modeling best practices in the school library.

Finally, how do learners discover or obtain these accessible resources? For some, having to ask for them may be an insurmountable barrier. If learners and other stakeholders have to ask for the resource, it's not as inclusive as it could be. I'm extremely transparent about the resources available for our learners, and I promote these with all classes.

Even if we have the most accessible school library imaginable, it won't all be perfect for every disabled individual; what's accessible for one disabled learner may be distracting, harmful, or otherwise inaccessible for another. I've learned that there are no one-size-fits-all solutions. However, by seeking out inclusive collections, building welcoming spaces, and including disabled learners, educators, and parents in making the school library an accessible place, we go a long way toward making our school libraries an inclusive space for all.

Disabilities, School Libraries, and Include

Learners with disabilities are vital—and present—members of our school library community. To ensure equitable access, we must be intentional in our language, our frameworks, and the construction of our physical spaces. Additionally, we must create spaces where neurodiverse learners can be comfortable and learn in a barrier-free environment.

I've relied on Ness's experience with building a disability-inclusive school library to inform and improve my own practice. The guidance and strategies that Ness shared clearly connect to Competencies and Alignments across Include.

- "Learners adjust their awareness of the global learning community" (AASL 2018, Learner II.B.). By building a collection that includes #OwnVoices stories in which diverse characters are change agents in their own lives, Ness is helping all her learners become aware that disability is a natural and valued aspect of our global community.
- "Creating an atmosphere in which learners feel empowered" (AASL 2018, School Librarian II.D.1.). By adopting strategies that welcome neurodiverse learners—abandoning an outdated need for eye contact, understanding the importance of fidgeting or stimming—Ness is building a space where all learners can feel comfortable and empowered.
- "Organizing facilities to enhance the use of and ensure equitable access to information resources and services for all learners" (AASL 2018, School Library II.B.2.). Ness has restructured her library to make it physically accessible for all her learners.
- "Implementing solutions that address physical, social, cultural, linguistic, and intellectual barriers to equitable access to resources and services" (AASL 2018, School Library II.C.1.). Ness's commitment to understanding and implementing the accommodations needed by learners with IEPs or 504 plans shows this Alignment in action.

Questions for the Reflective Practitioner

1. How can I organize—or reorganize—my school library facilities to "ensure equitable access to information resources and services for all learners" (AASL 2018, School Library II.B.2.) to align with the AASL Standards?

2. What solutions can I put in place to remove barriers for disabled learners that may be present in my school library?

3. After reading what Ness shared about disability models and literature tropes, how will this information shape my assessment of books featuring disabled characters?

Moving Forward

WHAT CAN I DO TODAY?

Do a walk-through of your space, assessing elements that could be barriers for your learners and other stakeholders.

- Check for wheelchair and mobility aid access. Are shelves and stacks browsable? Is the circulation desk accessible? Is there at least one computer, desk, or table that is accessible?
- Check for shelves and power cables that could impede a visually impaired learner or adult.
- Are stairs and elevators clearly marked? Is there signage in braille?
- Are there telecommunication devices or staff trained in sign language?
- Are there private, quiet spaces for learners who get distracted or overstimulated in loud environments?

HOW CAN I BUILD ON IT TOMORROW?

Identify resources to purchase for your collection that are disability positive. Visit Disability in Kidlit (disabilityinkidlit.com) for posts and reviews, including an Honor Roll—a vetted list of books that the site recommends. A Novel Mind (anovelmind.com) includes a searchable database of titles centering mental health and neurodiversity.

ACTION STEP

- Invite other stakeholders—including learners—to do an accessibility walk-through of your space. Use the observations from your walk-through to address and modify flagged elements. Share your informal space audits with your administration to spark conversations about ways to continue to make school library resources and services more accessible. This dialogue could result in securing financial support to make even more structural changes—including furniture and technology.

14

Graphic Novels and Inclusive Practice

A vibrant graphic novel collection—including "traditional" graphic novels, comics, and manga—is vital to an inclusive school library. Two Include Best Practices champion this collection effort: "Provide up-to-date print and digital collections" and "focus on resources in multiple formats" (AASL 2018, 82). When we think about *up-to-date* titles in *multiple formats,* there is no clearer model than a graphic novel. Simply put, our collections are not up-to-date or inclusive if we are not devoting energy and resources to building a strong graphic presence.

To demonstrate the why and how of building a robust graphic collection, New York high school librarian Juan Rivera is going to share his experiences through an inquiry lens. The Domains do not exist in isolation from each other but, rather, form a dynamic loop of inquiry that we can leverage to improve our school libraries. Juan Rivera took a vital element of his school library—comics, manga, and graphic novels—and applied the four Domains and the school library Alignments under Include to demonstrate why a strong collection of resources employing serial art to tell stories is so essential.

Comics, Manga, and Inclusion

Juan Rivera

When I was eight years old, I moved to Lexington, Kentucky, from rural Puerto Rico. Though my mother was from Kentucky and English was her native language, I spoke only Spanish as I entered third grade. At the time there weren't many Spanish speakers in Lexington, and at first I was placed with a speech pathologist to "correct" my Spanish and help me learn English. I remember phonics cards and reading groups named after birds. I had great, supportive educators.

However, a lot of my learning happened after school when I went to the corner store. In addition to getting candy, I picked up comics and devoured them—*Richie Rich, Casper the Friendly Ghost, Donald Duck and Scrooge, Archie,* and, later on, *Mad Magazine.* I loved the color and the stories. Combined with great educators, my love for comics helped me move up to the Flying Eagles reading group in a year. My school also had a welcoming and attractively stocked school library with a great school librarian who organized a Reading Is Fundamental program and Scholastic book clubs. I became a reader.

Flash forward and now *I* am the school librarian, and books featuring storytelling through sequential art have exploded in school libraries. Manga, comics, and graphic novels have become essential to school library collections. The AASL Standards can help school librarians as learners, teachers, and program administrators to deepen any element of practice. For example, in May 2018 my colleague Jill Ehlers and I presented *The Power of Manga, Comics, and Graphic Novels through the Lens of the AASL Standards Framework for Learners* at the New York Library Association Section of School Librarians (NYLA/SSL) Conference.[1] In that presentation, we focused on how to use the six Shared Foundations—Inquire, Include, Collaborate, Curate, Explore, and Engage—as a way to deepen our understanding of how to use manga and comics to strengthen our school libraries and enhance learning.

Comics are a great way to incorporate the Shared Foundation of Include. Each of the four Domains of Think, Create, Share, and Grow can help us explain and explore how comics help school librarians create inclusive school libraries and programs.

Think

Why can I use comics to meet the needs of a wide range of learners and support "balanced perspectives through resources and learning opportunities" (AASL 2018, School Library II.A.)?

Why and how do comics help realize the school library Alignments for Include under the Think Domain? I've found that it is important to not only have a rich comics collection but also understand how to articulate the ways in which comics meet learner needs. These conversations can be had with administration, other educators and reading specialists, and families. Luckily, before I became a school librarian, I had done some extensive research into manga and comics and came armed with ideas about how comics, manga, and graphic novels meet the needs of a broad range of learners. Here are some key points:

- Manga and comics have the potential to help English learners (ELs)—those learning English as a new language—learn in a naturally scaffolded way (Kunai and Ryan 2007).
- Comics meet the needs of a wide range of learners. The graphic section of our school library brings together learners receiving special education services, AP students, and learners receiving EL support. They are connected by their love of the comic format, and it is a wonderful example of how a school library can bridge learners from across the school. As a library student, I spoke to #leadoutloud Syracuse school librarian Sue Kowalski. Though the regulars for her school library's manga collection included a variety of readers, a high proportion of readers on the autism spectrum were passionate about the format.
- Comics, manga, and graphic novels can lead learners to contemplate, write about, and explore the world. For example, one of my former learners wrote the following about the Naruto series:
    - I've been reading this series for over eight years now. Basically what I love about Naruto is that the series teaches you about the pain and struggle of a kid longing to be accepted by his peers. But through many hardships he learns how to overcome his own demons while still trying to be recognized by his village. It's funny because Naruto reminds me of myself as a teenager. (E. J. Joyner, pers. comm. to Juan Rivera on July 5, 2014)
- Manga and other forms of storytelling through sequential art can provide learners with a "home run" experience with reading. This successful and motivated reading can lead to even more academic success in other areas (Henken and Krashen 2015).

In short, there are many reasons to include comics in your collection! It's important to revisit and articulate all the reasons and research that support their inclusion.

Create

How can I establish, maintain, and organize a comics collection that supports the "diverse developmental, cultural, social, and linguistic needs of the range of learners and their communities" (AASL 2018, School Library II.B.1.)?

We have already established the why for including graphic novels, manga, and comics in the school library. Now we can delve into the "how" of making an inclusive collection that responds to the needs of more learners. As a new and solo school librarian, I have relied on a few basic moves:

- Make the comics collection central and secure to ensure access and visibility and to safeguard a valuable resource.
- My school library is shaped like a backwards *L* with the circulation desk at the crook of the *L,* allowing a view of all exits. Early on, I decided to put most comics on carts right next to my desk. This position takes advantage of traffic flow exposure while allowing me to have conversations and increase my visibility. Graphics are more than 80 percent of my circulation! Since I became a school librarian at this school and made comics central to the collection and space, circulation has quadrupled.
- Include the community as you grow your collection. Conversation is key. One reason my collection is so popular is that I listened to people like our library tech, who is a virtual walking encyclopedia about manga and comics. Learners will also tell you what they want if you create an atmosphere in which they are comfortable telling you.
- Seek diversity of viewpoints in your collection. I rely on several resources to get comics and graphics that go beyond what our community may know about. Specifically, I have relied on the New York Public Library's Best Books for Teens, *School Library Journal,* and YALSA's Great Graphic Novels for Teens. For school librarians serving younger learners, the Association for Library Service to Children (ALSC) creates a Graphic Novels Reading List each year, helpfully categorizing by K–2, 3–5, and 6–8.

Share

How do I share my comics collection in ways that help learners overcome barriers and that "[facilitate] opportunities to experience diverse ideas" (AASL 2018, School Library II.C.)?

To fully leverage your robust, diverse comics collections, it's crucial to promote them with both your learners and your educator colleagues. I've found it works best to employ a multilevel approach to reach as many learners as possible.

- Let your learning community know that you have manga, comics, and graphic novels in addition to all your other resources. For example, when I learned that all grades at the high school have a grade-level orientation, I asked for a few minutes to introduce myself and the school library and highlighted the graphic novel collection.
- Reach out to your special education and EL educators and invite them to bring their learners to the school library. Emphasize how comics can improve fluency and vocabulary through their naturally scaffolded and highly motivating content.
- Generate organic conversations with your learners to get ideas for new titles, series, authors, and illustrators.
- Keep your collection central, visible, and accessible.

Grow

How do I reflect on whether the school library is using comics to "[build] empathy and equity" (AASL 2018, School Library II.D.)?

After building and promoting our comic collections, it's necessary to reflect on how well they are reaching all our learners, particularly those from marginalized groups. Also, what steps can you take to grow your collection even further?

- Get out of your comfort zone. Attend a comic con or a presentation that challenges your thinking. Comic conventions now include more library, educational, and diversity programming, and library and education conventions now include more comics and manga. The New York Public Library and New York Comic Con collaborate on an annual event. Presentations on this day devoted to librarians, educators, and the general public have included the following:

- "#Representation Matters in Your School Library"
- "Graphic Novels, Mental Health, and the Challenges That Inspire Authors"
- "Teaching Race, Culture, and Comics"
- "Pop Culture Pride: Cultivating Queerbrarianship at Your Library"
- I was able to attend "LGBTQ+ in Children's Graphic Novels" during which Mariko Tomaki, Brooklyn A. Allen, Ethan M. Aldridge, Natalie Riess, and Gina Gagliano addressed the power of comics to address gender fluidity and many more issues related to the LGBTQ+ community. One of the speakers also sang the praises of school librarians who were able to do "psyops" and make LGBTQ+ youth feel safer and okay by including more LGBTQ+ materials in school libraries, especially in rural areas.

- Stay calm and be prepared to defend your collection. If you are creating a diverse and challenging collection, you should be prepared to defend it. Do not censor in anticipation of challenges. Review and share your collection development policy with your administrator and learning community. Get acquainted with the materials of the Comic Book Legal Defense Fund and ALA's Office for Intellectual Freedom.

Comics, Manga, Graphic Novels, and Include

In addition to the specific school library Alignments that Juan used to demonstrate an inclusive comics lens, his graphic collection and programming highlight multiple Competencies and Alignments under Include:

- "Creating an atmosphere in which learners feel empowered" (AASL 2018, School Librarian II.D.1.). By collecting titles in graphic formats and being able to articulate how this approach meets the needs of multiple learner groups, Juan is building a space where his learners grow into empowered readers.
- "Promoting the use of high-quality and high-interest literature in formats that reflect the diverse . . . needs of all learners" (AASL 2018, School Library II.C.2.). By building a strong graphic format collection, Juan is utilizing multiple formats in his school library to both reflect and reach learners with a variety of needs and interests.

I was lucky enough to meet Juan when we were part of the 2018 ALA Emerging Leaders team that had the privilege of developing the *Defending Intellectual Freedom: LGBTQ+ Materials in School Libraries* toolkit for AASL. Each member of our six-person team chose a Shared Foundation to focus on for developing materials, and Juan spearheaded the work under Inquire. His commitment to an inquiry focus can be seen in the way he took a key library element—comics—and used the Domains and school library Alignments under Include to set up a cycle of inquiry and explore the importance of comics in school libraries from multiple angles.

Moving Forward

WHAT CAN I DO TODAY?

Explore your graphic novel and manga collection and choose a book to read.

HOW CAN I BUILD ON IT TOMORROW?

Identify at least ten more titles to buy for your collection. The following resources can help:

- YALSA's Great Graphic Novels for Teens
- *School Library Journal,* especially the "Stellar Panels" column and the blog *Good Comics for Kids*
- "Best Graphic Novels by Native Writers," American Indians in Children's Literature

Questions for the Reflective Practitioner

1. In what ways does my school library promote comics and graphic novels as a way to align with the Domains under Include?
2. How would I advocate that comics and graphic novels "[facilitate] opportunities to experience diverse ideas" (AASL 2018, School Library II.C.)?
3. How could I follow Juan's inquiry model in identifying an element of my own school library practice to explore across the four Domains—for learners, school librarians, or school libraries?

- "Graphic Novels," Social Justice Books (Teaching for Change)
- Comic Book Legal Defense Fund
- ALSC's Graphic Novels Reading Lists for grades K–2, 3–5, and 6–8

ACTION STEPS

Identify activities to celebrate the comic format at your school library—for example:

- Start a comic book, manga, or anime club (or any combination of all three).
- Partner with a local comic-book store to celebrate Free Comic Book Day.
- Invite a comic artist to visit your school library.
- Partner with your art educator to develop a comics art club.
- Have a comics-only or manga-only event that is co-developed with your learners.

NOTE

1. Visit bit.ly/aaslcomic for more on our NYLA/SSL presentation.

15

Critical Indigenous Literacies

The ***National School Library Standards*** **recognize that school** librarians inhabit multiple roles—often at the same time. An essential role we should always manifest is that of learner. "School librarian Competencies intentionally parallel those of the learner, and emphasize the integrated nature of a comprehensive learning environment" (AASL 2018, 44). As we guide learners in critically reviewing texts, we must also build our own capacity in this skill. When we engage with Native or Indigenous texts, we often must unlearn what we've previously been taught.

To learn—and unlearn and relearn—in this field, it's essential that school librarians are accessing teaching from Native scholars, authors, and educators. Dr. Debbie Reese, tribally enrolled at Nambé Pueblo, was an assistant professor in American Indian Studies at the University of Illinois at Urbana-Champaign (UIUC). Prior to that, she taught in UIUC's College of Education and its School of Information Sciences (now an iSchool). Her work on Critical Indigenous Literacies holds foundational learning for school librarians as they implement Competencies and Alignments across Include.

Selecting and Using Children's Books about Indigenous Peoples*

Debbie Reese

In 1863 President Lincoln issued a proclamation stating that the last Thursday of November would be a national day of thanksgiving. In 1990 President George H. W. Bush issued the first presidential proclamation that designated November as National Native American Heritage Month. With these two proclamations occurring in the same month, many educators use November as the time to read aloud or assign children's books that feature Native peoples. In this chapter, I ask school librarians to rethink literature used to teach learners about Indigenous peoples. In situating the experience of Native peoples across time, I begin with a clarification of terms.

I am tribally enrolled at Nambé Pueblo, which means I am counted on the Nambé census. Most Native people prefer to name their specific tribal nation because being specific helps non-Native people learn that we are far more diverse than what the terms *American Indian* or *Native American* evoke. Historically, *Indian* was commonly used, but over time, more people began using *Native* instead. Most recently, *Indigenous* has emerged as an alternative, as seen in the movement to replace Columbus Day with Indigenous Peoples Day. I use the terms *Native* and *Indigenous* interchangeably, unless referring to a specific tribal nation.

More than five hundred federally recognized tribal nations exist in the United States today, with distinct systems of governance, languages, locations, material cultures, religions, and, of course, stories! Some people are taken aback by the word *nation* as applied to Native nations because of the tendency to group Native peoples with other minority groups in the United States. However, that framework fails to encompass our single most important attribute: Native nationhood. Without this recognition, our status as sovereign nations whose people were—and are—Indigenous to this continent is erased. We were not the first Americans because Native nations predate the United States of America by hundreds of years. In fact, European and then U.S. leaders entered into diplomatic negotiations with leaders of Native nations who inhabited the lands from the beginning. The outcomes of those negotiations were treaties, much like the ones the United States forges with foreign nations today. Nonetheless, depictions of Native peoples as primitive or uncivilized are one

---

*Adapted from an article originally published in *Language Arts* from the National Council of Teachers of English. Reese, D. 2018. "Critical Indigenous Literacies: Selecting and Using Children's Books about Indigenous Peoples." *Language Arts* 95(6), 389–393. Copyright 2018 by the National Council of Teachers of English. Used with permission.

of the reasons our nationhood is difficult to accept or understand. In fact, Native peoples had/have distinct cultures passed down from many generations with complex practices and traditions—hardly primitive. Therefore, the larger culture needs to unlearn and rethink how the identities of Indigenous peoples are represented and taught.

Expanding Critical Literacy: Inclusion of Indigenous Peoples

The theoretical term I highlight in this chapter is *Critical Indigenous Literacies* (Reese 2013). Critical literacy encourages learners to read between the lines and ask questions when engaging with literature: Whose story is this? Who benefits from this story? Whose voices are not being heard? Although these questions may seem difficult, Vasquez (2014) wrote that even in early childhood, learners are capable of asking these critical questions when approaching texts. Adding *Indigenous* to critical literacy asks readers to think of those questions when they read stories that have Indigenous characters in them.

Critical Indigenous Literacy forefronts the historically marginalized treatment of Native stories—and, by extension, Native people. In addition, a critical literacies perspective gives voice to how stories are presented and told about people and their history. For example, our creation stories are just as sacred to us as Genesis is to Christians; we do not view them as folktales. In many school library catalogs, however, *The Story of the Milky Way: A Cherokee Tale* by Joseph Bruchac and Gayle Ross (1995) is likely to appear under "Cherokee Indians—Folklore." *Beaver Steals Fire: A Salish Coyote Story* by the staff of the Confederated Salish and Kootenai Tribes (2005) is most likely categorized as "Salish Indians—Folklore." In fact, both are religious stories explaining some aspect of how the world was created.

In contrast, Peter Spier's (1992) *Noah's Ark* is not labeled "folklore" but "Bible stories—O.T." In fact, all three are creation stories, but the Christian story is treated differently. This difference in the ways in which Native and Christian creation stories are treated privileges Christianity, perpetuating institutionalized racism that keeps in place the ideologies of a society that is predominantly Christian. One group of creation stories is categorized and treated as fiction whereas the other group of creation stories is accepted as truth. Despite efforts by Native people to get their stories accurately categorized, there has been little or no movement, which raises critical questions: Whose voice is not heard in the way that stories are categorized? Whose ideologies are implicitly valued by categorical labels?

Another problem is the "myths, legends, and folktales" books that are marketed as Native. They are ubiquitous and mostly written by people who are not, themselves, Native. These authors may not have the knowledge needed to accurately depict aspects of Native traditions, some of which are part of our religious dances. In *Dragonfly's Tale,* for example, Kristina Rodanas (1995) shows Pueblo people having a food fight—a misrepresentation of a "throw." During the harvest dance, food items (such as ears of corn) are tossed to others as a way to share foods. Rodanas depicted this important community value and spiritual activity as the sort of mischief American kids sometimes engage in. Misrepresentations like these lead to similar critical questions: Who is telling these stories? How are these stories being represented? Who does this story belong to?

School librarians and other educators can make choices that do justice to Native stories by choosing books written by Native writers. Both *The Story of the Milky Way* (Bruchac and Ross, 1995) and *Beaver Steals Fire* (Confederated Salish and Kootenai Tribes, 2005) are #OwnVoices stories—a hashtag created by Corinne Duyvis to describe a book that is written by someone who is of the particular culture being depicted. The idea is that the quality of a story is improved when the person creating that story is an insider who knows what to share and how to share it with outsiders. As a child, I was taught what can—and cannot—be shared with outsiders. A history of exploitation has made Native writers mindful of what they disclose.

To capture this concept, I have been adding a "curtain" to Bishop's (1990) "mirrors, windows, and sliding glass doors" metaphor when I talk or write about Native stories. This is a way to acknowledge and honor the stories behind the curtain—those that are purposefully kept within Native communities. Native communities resisted historical oppression and continue to preserve our culture by cultivating our ways in private spaces—behind the curtain. Although Native people share some of our ways publicly in the present day, there is a great deal that we continue to protect from outsiders. Furthermore, it conveys the importance of how #OwnVoices knows what belongs within the community and what knowledge can be shared outside our communities.

We Can Do Better: Rethinking Native Stories in School Libraries

Let's turn now to Native American Heritage Month and its intersection with Thanksgiving. Many school librarians read aloud children's books about the "First Thanksgiving." Some classes or grade levels take part in reenactments, with kids dressing up like Pilgrims and Indians or, perhaps, Wampanoags. Most of these books and activities default to stereotypes whereby Native people are shown in feathered headdresses and fringed clothing—items worn by Plains Indians rather than anything the Wampanoag people would have worn. When educators use Thanksgiving as the vehicle for their instruction about Native peoples, they are inadvertently locating Native lives in the past.

There are better ways to bring Native stories and books about Native peoples to learners. I focus on Cynthia Leitich Smith's (2000) picture book *Jingle Dancer* to illustrate how school library collections depicting Native people could be improved. The key ideas are to choose books that are tribally specific (that name a specific tribal nation and accurately present that nation), written by Native writers, set in the present day, and relevant year-round, keeping Native peoples visible throughout the school year.

CHOOSE BOOKS THAT ARE TRIBALLY SPECIFIC.

Select books about Native peoples who are or were residents of your specific state. I recommend using websites like the National Congress of American Indians and the Smithsonian's National Museum of the American Indian for information on tribal nations. Smith's picture book is about Jenna, a little girl who is doing the jingle dance for the very first time at an upcoming powwow. In the author's note, Smith shares that Jenna is a citizen of the Muscogee Nation, pertinent to children in Georgia, where the Muscogee people originated, or in Oklahoma, where they are today. Therefore, focusing on the local context empowers tribal nationhood within the states of origin rather than focusing on politically constructed holidays like Thanksgiving.

USE PRESENT-TENSE VERBS TO TALK ABOUT NATIVE NATIONS.

A school librarian in Georgia might say, "Today, the Muscogee Creek Nation is in Oklahoma. Before Europeans arrived on what became known as the North American continent, the Muscogee Creeks were in Georgia." To go even further, use the provocative but accurate word *invaded* instead of *arrived.* While reading *Jingle Dancer,* which is set in the present day, show the Muscogee Nation website as a complementary source. Jenna's house is in an everyday neighborhood, and she is wearing clothes similar to those worn by kids in the classroom. She is a person of the present day.

CHOOSE BOOKS BY NATIVE WRITERS.

As noted earlier, Smith is Muscogee Creek. Introducing her as the author is another opportunity to use a present-tense verb. Because Smith and her character are Muscogee Creek, *Jingle Dancer* is an #OwnVoices story. As such, Smith is writing from her personal knowledge of Muscogee families and communities as they come together to help a child prepare for and participate in a ceremonial dance for the first time. Jenna needs specific clothing, learns the steps and music, and understands the meaning of the dance from her tribal community. At one point in the story, Jenna is feeling overwhelmed by all that she has to do. In a matter-of-fact way, Jenna's great-aunt tells her about the story of Bat, which is a Creek creation story. As a result, we learn that Creek families share creation stories with each other to instill strength and as a way to carry on when feeling low or overwhelmed.

USE BOOKS BY NATIVE WRITERS YEAR-ROUND.

Jingle Dancer can be used any time of the year. It is only one of many books available. A school librarian doing a unit on lyrics in pop music with a middle school educator might consider using Eric Gansworth's (2013) *If I Ever Get Out of Here*. It is tribally specific, set in the present day, and an #OwnVoices story. Every chapter title in the book is the name of a song by the Beatles or Paul McCartney. (If you're a fan of either one, you'll love the discography Gansworth has on his website!) Gansworth's book is about the relationship that develops between Lewis, a Native boy living on the Tuscarora Reservation, and George, a white boy living on a nearby Air Force base.

Each year the market is flooded with problematic books that publishers market to school librarians and other educators, but there are also gems worth reading. I read as many as I can and create "best of" lists at my website, American Indians in Children's Literature (https://americanindiansinchildrensliterature.blogspot.com). Visit! See what you'll find for your school library collection.

For Further Reading

Hirschfelder, A., P. F. Molin, and Y. Wakim. 1999. *American Indian Stereotypes in the World of Children*. Lanham, MD: Scarecrow Press. ISBN 978-0-8108-3613-6

- This very useful text has eight chapters with several short essays in each one. It also contains an extensive bibliography of books and articles that educators can study to gain a depth of knowledge about the ways Native peoples have been depicted over time.

Jones, G. W., and S. Moomaw. 2002. *Lessons from Turtle Island: Native Curriculum in Early Childhood Classrooms*. Saint Paul, MN: Redleaf Press. ISBN 978-1-929610-25-9

- Written especially for educators—by two educators—this book takes a close look at issues regarding how Native content is taught. It features lesson plans built on children's literature that can provide learners with accurate and authentic knowledge.

Recommended Children's and Young Adult Books

Here is a list of recommended books in a range of genres, all written by Native authors with tribally specific content.

Bowwow Powwow, Brenda Child, illustrated by Jonathan Thunder (Minnesota Historical Society, 2018)

A Day with Yayah, Nicola I. Campbell, illustrated by Julie Flett (Crocodile, 2018)

Fry Bread: A Native American Family Story, Kevin Noble Maillard, illustrated by Juana Martinez-Neal (Roaring Book Press, 2019)

Hearts Unbroken, Cynthia Leitich Smith (Candlewick, 2018)

Hungry Johnny, Cheryl Kay Minnema, illustrated by Wesley Ballinger (Historical Society Press, 2014)

If I Ever Get Out of Here, Eric Gansworth (Arthur A. Levine Books, 2013)

In the Footsteps of Crazy Horse, Joseph Marshall III, illustrated by James Mark Yellowhawk (Abrams Books, 2015)

Indian No More, Charlene Willing McManis with Traci Sorell (Tu Books, 2019)

An Indigenous Peoples' History of the United States for Young People, Roxanne Dunbar-Ortiz, adapted by Jean Mendoza and Debbie Reese (Beacon Books, 2019)

Kamik Joins the Pack, Darryl Baker, illustrated by Qin Leng (Inhabit Media, 2016)

The Marrow Thieves, Cherie Dimaline (Cormorant Publishers, 2017)

Mission to Space, John Herrington (White Dog Press, 2016)

The People Shall Continue, Simon J. Ortiz, illustrated by Sharol Graves (Lee & Low Books, 2017)

Rock and Roll Highway: The Robbie Robertson Story, Sebastian Robertson, illustrated by Adam Gustavson (Henry Holt, 2014)

The Water Walker, Joanne Robertson (Second Story Press, 2017)

We Are Grateful: Otsaliheliga, Traci Sorell, illustrated by Frané Lessac (Charlesbridge, 2018)

We Are Water Protectors, Carole Lindstrom, illustrated by Michaela Goade (Roaring Rock Press, 2020)

When We Were Alone, David A. Robertson, illustrated by Julie Flett (HighWater Press, 2016)

You Hold Me Up, Monique Gray Smith, illustrated by Danielle Daniel (Orca Book Publishers, 2017)

Young Water Protectors: A Story about Standing Rock, Aslan Tudor and Kelly Tudor (Eaglespeaker Publishing, 2018)

Critical Indigenous Literacies and Include

Dr. Reese's scholarship is essential for every inclusive school library because her work always foregrounds the reading learner. How are learners affected by the text? What are they seeing? What are they not seeing? How are depictions of Native people affecting their identity development? Her lens for reviewing children's literature is an exemplar not only for Native or Indigenous texts but also for strategies on critically reviewing youth literature in general.

Using a Critical Indigenous Literacies framework connects to key elements of the AASL Standards Framework for Include.

- Under Learner for Think: "Adopting a discerning stance toward points of view and opinions expressed in information resources and learning products" (AASL 2018, Learner II.A.2.). Because critical literacy centers the asking of significant questions when reading text, it supports learners—including school librarians as learners—in "adopting a discerning stance."
- Under School Library for Share: "Promoting the use of high-quality and high-interest literature in formats that reflect the diverse developmental, cultural, social, and linguistic needs of all learners and their communities" (AASL 2018, School Library II.C.2.). Titles that are tribal-specific and written by Native authors represent a more realistic picture of Native youth and

Questions for the Reflective Practitioner

1. In what ways does my school library help learners adopt a discerning stance toward points of view in texts?
2. How can my school library support more realistic depictions of Native nations and communities, not just in my school library but throughout the school?
3. How will the addition of recommended #Own-Voices Native texts help my school library meet Alignments related to facilitating opportunities for learners to experience diverse ideas?

push against the harmful "people of the past" narrative. These recommended books are examples of high-quality literature that can reflect diverse cultural, social, and linguistic needs of learners and families.

Moving Forward

WHAT CAN I DO TODAY?

Visit the American Indians in Children's Literature website and access the Best Books page. Identify books to purchase for your school library!

HOW CAN I BUILD ON IT TOMORROW?

Check the cataloging in your collection. Are creation stories treated equitably? If not, make a plan to recatalog, relabel, and reshelve so that all creation stories—no matter the religion or nation of origin—are placed in the same category.

ACTION STEP

- Embed #OwnVoices Native literature in your school library curriculum—all year long. Work with classroom educators to help in the selection of class texts, using Dr. Reese's framework.
  - » Choose books that are tribally specific.
  - » Use present-tense verbs to talk about Native nations.
  - » Choose books by Native writers.
  - » Use books by Native writers year-round.

16

An Inclusive Book Fair Model

Equitable access is a core principle of our profession. In the school library Alignment under Include in the Share Domain, we are specifically called on to implement "solutions that address . . . barriers to equitable access to resources and services" (AASL 2018, School Library II.C.1.). Seems straightforward, yes? However, there are events at school libraries across the country for which access is not equitable—for which learners literally have to buy themselves access. I'm speaking, of course, about traditional school book fairs. Surprised? I know that they are well loved by many school librarians and other educators, but consider the traditional book fair model. Is it inclusive to turn our school libraries into mini-stores each fall and spring, becoming for-profit satellites for publishers? My answer to this question would be no. For my own school library, the #TrueBookFAIR was born out of that no.

#TrueBookFAIR

Julie Stivers

The typical school Book "Fair" does not align with its name. Learners are unintentionally sorted into two groups—those who *can* afford to purchase items at the event and those who *cannot*. This outcome is particularly egregious because a school library should be a "sorting-free" zone. We should not be sorting based on grades, test scores, or reading levels. Or, of course, the ability to purchase books. It goes against all a school library stands for but is common practice.

And yet. And yet. Book Fairs can generate excitement for reading. They offer a pathway to more books in the home. There is high educator interest. During my first year as a school librarian, I wondered how I could create a program that generated reading excitement, increased the number of self-chosen books in the home, and championed reading for pleasure—all while preventing inequitable sorting by excluding learners. I decided to build a different kind of fair.

Planning a Different Kind of Book Fair

When building new programs in our school libraries, there are often two foundational steps that we need to take—finding the money and securing administrative support. Of course, at times, this is one colossal step because our administrator typically controls our school library budget. I'd encourage you to look beyond traditional budget channels when planning new programs. In the case of my new book fair idea, I spoke to our Family Engagement Committee chair, who happened to be our school social worker. We had additional funds left in our Title 1 budget that year for family events. When I pitched my May book fair idea to her, I stressed that more books in the home could offset summer learning loss and that with a family event, we could champion literacy across ages. The Family Engagement chair was sold, and with that endorsement and a promised $300, I pitched the idea to my principal. My sell was straightforward. Let's build excitement for reading, the school library, and our school by giving away new books to learners at a nighttime event. Embedded in that sell was also the trust that my principal had in me to organize and promote the event. Again, this was my first year, but I had already proven to him that I could create excitement for literacy because he had seen the changes I'd made with my space and collection.

I now had the money. I had a night circled on the calendar. My plan was to create my own fair—where no money would be allowed in the door. Instead, every learner in the school would come and "shop" for books, with everyone leaving with at least two new, self-selected books. To make this goal financially feasible, I chose a publisher's warehouse sale as my primary source for materials.

To elicit buy-in from the start, I queried learners for book suggestions—by title, interest group, and genre. The conversations during those planning and feedback sessions were illuminating. Many learners told me that they had always loved and hated book fairs in previous schools—loved seeing all those new books but hated that they were never able to buy anything. One learner, Zach, summed it up perfectly—and unknowingly named the event—by saying, "Seriously. They were Book UNFairs. You are having an actual BookFAIR." The #TrueBookFAIR was born.

Inaugural #TrueBookFAIR

And a BookFAIR it was. I did not simply buy whatever books I could get. I purchased books that were reflective of my learners, their experiences, and their interests, prioritizing #OwnVoices literature. To celebrate family reading, I made additional purchases of picture books, board books, and early chapter books to allow learners to gift reading material to their younger family members. Importance of family and inter-age collaboration and support are key components of the cultural ethos of the majority of learner groups at our middle school. Having reading material for a variety of ages—in addition to teen—allowed this event to honor and recognize this cultural strength of our learners.

The program was a powerful literary experience for our school. I was able to purchase more than four hundred books that were reflective of my learners in terms of race, ethnicity, interests, and author. I structured the event to "look" like a typical fair, with signage, displays, and genre groupings. Learners were engaged . . . and disbelieving. "I can pick whatever book I want?" "I don't even need to look at the price?" "What about this one?" Yes. Yes. *Yes*. My learners were not only excited about their own new books but making plans about reading certain books to—and with—specific family members.

When I reflected on and evaluated this program, I first noticed the measurable data. Every book gone. Every learner with more reading material to keep that—and this is key—had been self-selected from a fair collection that was intentionally, reflectively, and lovingly curated. An additional number of school conversations centered on reading that happened in the days leading up to, during, and after the #TrueBookFAIR. The number of stories recounted after the fair detailed reading between family members. In my school library, I encourage learners to check out books for family members and was thrilled that this framework organically carried over to our #TrueBookFAIR program.

The unmeasurable data can be trickier to unpack. The #TrueBookFAIR directly led to more books in learners' hands, which can be a key component of lifelong reading and improving literacy. Additionally, learners were able to own books by authors that I had been promoting both in the school library and in language arts classes. When connections can be made between learners' outside interests and our curriculum, we know that learning is more meaningful.

To honor learner voice, I used quick surveys to assess the event and gather feedback on how to improve the event. The feedback was unanimously positive, and the suggestions were thoughtful and direct. Learners suggested that I increase the number of days, increase the number of #TrueBookFAIRs, and include learners in a buying field trip to the warehouse!

Reflection is a key piece of our school library programming and is a necessary tool in improving each year for our learners. Those reflective data, however, also need to be shared with stakeholders. In addition to sharing highlights with administration, I shared at staff meetings and with the broader community via social media.

#TrueBookFAIRs Today

#TrueBookFAIRs have become an essential piece of our inclusive school library. We hold two a year, and our spring fair includes a family night during which every family member selects a new book to keep. It can be difficult for families to attend nighttime events, so the #TrueBookFAIR always extends through school days during which every class visits the fair to "shop" for two new books to keep. There are five key components of our #TrueBookFAIRs.

- Its premise is always the same: learners select new books to keep from a bespoke fair collection that I have intentionally and lovingly curated to reflect our learners and their interests. There is no cost for our learners.
- Self-selection + ownership + reflective books = literacy magic. Our administration financially supports the base fair collection. I visit the Scholastic warehouse sale for the bulk of my fair "shopping" and hustle for donated new books and ARCs (advanced reader copies) all year to supplement.
- The fair collection is key! #OwnVoices literature is foregrounded. Learners' interests are leveraged to carefully curate, and all books are *new*.
- #TrueBookFAIRs also support whole-family literacy by curating collections for younger family members.
- Our spring, end-of-May #TrueBookFAIR is a strategy to guard against potential summer reading loss. Learners' socioeconomic status or summer situation should not be a barrier to accessing books.

With physical schools closed in favor of virtual instruction in the spring of 2020 due to the COVID-19 pandemic, I did not abandon my hopes for a spring #TrueBookFAIR. I brainstormed multiple options—from getting grant funding for learners to choose e-books to access on their school-issued devices to organizing a digital "shop" with curbside pickup. Adding to the uncertainty about schedules and safety, I knew that funding would be an issue because our school budgets were frozen. DonorsChoose came to my rescue.

I have used DonorsChoose in the past to procure funding for classroom sets of #OwnVoices titles to be used as class texts and to supplement my own school library budget for collection improvements. I never share my DonorsChoose grant requests with family or friends and do not promote them on social media. All my projects have been funded by strangers through the DonorsChoose site. I have found that people want to help us get reflective, engaging books into our learners' hands.

DonorsChoose reached out to me in spring 2020 as part of its Keep Kids Learning Program, and I applied—and was accepted—for one of these grants, which arrived in the form of a big box store gift card. This is obviously not normally a place I would shop for school library books, but I scoured the store's site and built a Virtual #TrueBookFAIR collection filled with titles across formats and genres I knew my learners would be interested in (as always, foregrounding reflective, #OwnVoices titles!). I designed a digital shop and visited Google Meet classes to promote the fair, booktalked selected titles from my digital shop, and explained how learners could select a title to keep. Using learner orders, I then purchased the books with the DonorsChoose-provided gift card.

I had originally planned to distribute the titles with learners' end-of-school closing procedures via curbside pickup, but because of timing and school constraints, I committed instead to safely delivering the titles to my learners' homes during the summer. I realize that this approach is an impossibility for most school librarians—a curbside pickup model could be ideal for operating a fair in a virtual landscape.

Reframing School Book Fairs

Books at home matter. Self-selection matters. Reflective books matter. Removing barriers to participating in book fairs matters! Why can't all our learners have access to self-selected, new books to keep? Why can't a school library be part of that?

Yes, I am part of a small school community. Our most recent #TrueBookFAIR had more than nine hundred books, though, costing only $500. It's a hustle that I invest my time, energy, and heart into all year. Other school librarians could start with one grade level.

Also, yes, I understand that for some, profits from fairs fill their shelves. That's another problem—we shouldn't be relying on financial support from families and communities to build our collections. All school libraries need administrative and school financial support to build inclusive collections, driving academic achievement across subject areas. Book fair profits should not be a foundational collection development strategy.

The significance of the #TrueBookFAIR lies in its intentional design: reflective, #OwnVoices books + inclusive framework – school sorting = a meaningful, literacy-rich, culturally sustaining school library event.

#TrueBookFAIR and Include

Each #TrueBookFAIR I organize at our school strengthens my belief in its framework. In chapter 9, "Think with the #LibFive," we heard from my learners who co-created learner-led professional development. In talking to their classmates about traditional book fairs at previous schools, they heard problematic stories about treatment at fairs; for example,

- *This one year, my teacher stopped at the book fair for us to buy books on the way back from lunch. If you had money with you, you got to shop at the fair. If you didn't you sat on the floor in the entrance to the library. Our classmates came back with bags of books and we just sat there on the floor, waiting.*

No learner should ever experience this in a school library—even if there is a book fair going on. Especially when there is a book fair going on! Those elementary school learners sat on the floor—grouped in a line because they had no money with them to purchase a book—while their classmates shopped. It's inexcusable.

The #TrueBookFAIR represents Competencies and Alignments under the Include Shared Foundation:

- "Creating an atmosphere in which learners feel empowered" (AASL 2018, School Librarian II.D.1.). My school library is always open, and my learners are always able to access resources—including during book fairs. Exclusion from any school library activity does not create an atmosphere of empowerment.
- "Implementing solutions that address . . . barriers to equitable access to resources and services" (AASL 2018, School Library II.C.1.). By building a pathway to increased book ownership, the #TrueBookFAIR addresses an economic barrier.
- "Enabling equitable access to learning opportunities" (AASL 2018, School Library II.D.2.). Again, equitable access means equitable access, no matter what program the school library is offering! There is no time-out from offering access.

Questions for the Reflective Practitioner

1. In what ways does my school library enable "equitable access to learning opportunities" (AASL 2018, School Library II.D.2.)?
2. Are there any ways in which learners are sorted during book fairs in my school library? What are some ways that I can reduce or eliminate sorting of learners at the book fairs hosted in my school library?
3. How do I create "an atmosphere in which learners feel empowered and interactions are learner-initiated" (AASL 2018, School Librarian II.D.1.)?

Moving Forward

WHAT CAN I DO TODAY?

Reflect on any book fairs you hold (or that are held) at your school. How inclusive are they? Is anyone excluded from participating because they do not have funds to purchase books?

HOW CAN I BUILD ON IT TOMORROW?

Identify strategies from the #TrueBookFAIR that you could implement in your school library. Remember, you could start with just one grade level!

ACTION STEPS

- Identify funding for your own inclusive book fair. Don't be daunted! The trick in getting people to say yes to you and your school library is to be unrelenting in showcasing both the joy and engagement in your program. Speak with administration about the importance of an inclusive framework for literacy-rich events. If necessary, search out funding from your community or via grant applications. Your PTO/PTA/PTSA and local businesses are also potential avenues for support.
- If you are an elementary school librarian, enlist the talents and energy of middle and high school learners from neighboring schools to help organize your own inclusive fair.

Conclusion: Intersecting the Shared Foundations through Include

The Shared Foundations that anchor the *National School Library Standards* are linked through and across a tapestry of Domains, Competencies, and Alignments. The Shared Foundations were not created to be implemented in isolation. Instead, they are designed to mirror our own school librarian positions—interconnected and dynamic, with a myriad of opportunities and functions that support, enrich, and sustain one another.

Inquire

Key Commitment: *Build new knowledge by inquiring, thinking critically, identifying problems, and developing strategies for solving problems.*

Inquiry is at the heart of improving our individual school library practice. Because so many of the Competencies and Alignments under Include require self-reflection and dedicated learning—and unlearning—Inquire is a key ally of Include. As we learn a more accurate history of both the United States and the world, it allows us to think critically about social issues today—applying our learning to decolonizing our teaching methods and framework.

The first Best Practice under Inquire explicitly calls for supporting "learner voice and choice" (AASL 2018, 74), a key tenet of inclusive teaching practices. The Inquire Best Practice that calls for engaging in professional learning by accessing articles, books, posts, and presentations is tailor-made for Include. Expanding our own personal learning teams (PLTs)—both virtual and site-based—is necessary for inclusion. We need to be actively seeking out scholarship from BIPOC educators, in addition to educators from other marginalized communities.

CHAPTERS ILLUMINATING INQUIRE + INCLUDE

- Chapter 4, "Grow with Loudness in the School Library"
- Chapter 8, "Grow with Project READY"
- Chapter 13, "Include and Disabilities"
- Chapter 14, "Graphic Novels and Inclusive Practice"
- Appendix A, "Annotated Bibliography of Foundational Scholars and Resources"

Collaborate

Key Commitment: *Work effectively with others to broaden perspectives and work toward common goals.*

Work effectively with others. That simple-sounding sentence contains so much to unpack! Working effectively with others implies community and respect. It implies empathy and an understanding that your collaborators are going to look, think, and learn differently from you. It implies that you've had practice working in groups and circles and that you understand that common goals are effective and reachable. Without Include, that phrase—work effectively with others—will be hollow.

School librarianship is overwhelmingly white. For our profession to reflect reality and our learners, we must work to diversify our ranks. As we work toward this longer term goal, we must be collaborating today with BIPOC community members to provide our learners with a richer and more realistic picture of our world.

CHAPTERS ILLUMINATING COLLABORATE + INCLUDE

- Chapter 1, "Think with the Learning for Justice Social Justice Standards"
- Chapter 3, "Share with Restorative Practices and Circ^2"
- Chapter 6, "Create with an Equitable Writer-in-Residence Model"
- Chapter 11, "Share through LGBTQ+-Inclusive School Libraries"

Curate

Key Commitment: *Make meaning for oneself and others by collecting, organizing, and sharing resources of personal relevance.*

In the introduction to this guide, I sought to debunk the myth that Include can be driven primarily through Curate. That myth is categorically not true—having an inclusive collection is not enough to build an inclusive school library, and it is not enough to meet the Competencies and Alignments of Include. One hundred percent true. The following statement is also 100 percent true: *Include partners beautifully with and through Curate.*

Because Curate centers making meaning by collecting, organizing, and sharing resources, it follows that the value in making meaning is made more significant and powerful when those resources are personally reflective of our selves, our experiences, and our interests. To marry Curate and Include is to build, use, promote, and share a collection that reflects the wide diversity of identities in your school—across races, languages, religions, disabilities, gender identities, body sizes and shapes, sexual orientations, life experiences, and countries of origin.

The Best Practices for Curate—from establishing advisory boards to building collection policies to ensuring digital access—are impossible without the lens of Include. Inclusive practices are not bits of equity to be scattered on our programs. Inclusive practices are the foundation on which Curate builds those beautiful school library collections that attract and sustain our learners.

CHAPTERS ILLUMINATING CURATE + INCLUDE

- Chapter 5, "Think with Read Woke"
- Chapter 15, "Critical Indigenous Literacies"
- Chapter 16, "An Inclusive Book Fair Model"
- Appendix B, "Shelf Audits"
- Appendix C, "Diversity in Publishing Infographic"

Explore

Key Commitment: *Discover and innovate in a growth mindset developed through experience and reflection.*

Include and Explore celebrate together with joyous discovery. Best Practices for Explore—from ensuring that "learners have time to share ideas and wonderings" to having books and resources that "spark and support exploration of personal interests" (AASL 2018, 110)—are made more meaningful through Include. With inclusive Competencies and Alignments partnering with Explore, your school library will ensure that all learners experience the joy of a curious, free space that reflects their interests.

Supporting learners as they innovate through a growth mindset is an example of how we can nurture with high expectations, a key tenet of culturally sustaining pedagogy and Include. Building a culture of reading is explicitly mentioned through Explore. With a collection and literacy instruction foregrounded in Include, a whole-school reading community is attainable.

CHAPTERS ILLUMINATING EXPLORE + INCLUDE

- Chapter 2, "Create by Slamming in the School Library"
- Chapter 7, "Share with a Mental Wellness Curriculum"
- Chapter 10, "Create and Be the Lighthouse"
- Chapter 12, "Grow with Northside Neighbors"

Engage

Key Commitment: *Demonstrate safe, legal, and ethical creating and sharing of knowledge products independently while engaging in a community of practice and in an interconnected world.*

The creation and sharing of knowledge products are cornerstones of Engage and are enhanced through Include. By using culturally sustaining instructional methods, school librarians can empower learners to have agency in their own safe dissemination of information and creative artifacts. Engaging in a global society is modeled through Include. In order to engage responsibly in an interconnected world, learners must exhibit empathy, have an understanding of cultural relevancy, and recognize their own context within the global community. Include and Engage partner effectively for learners in this way.

In evaluating information and thinking critically about sources, Include Competencies center the evaluation of multiple perspectives as indispensable. Because Engage requires providing a space for learners where they can share information, the community-building foundation of Include is imperative.

CHAPTER ILLUMINATING ENGAGE + INCLUDE

- Chapter 9, "Think with the #LibFive"

Annotated Bibliography of Foundational Scholars and Resources

This appendix includes resources and information on foundational scholar-ship that provide insight into the Shared Foundation of Include in both research and practice. This list is not intended to be exhaustive but to give an overview of additional resources for school librarians. New scholarship will continue to be written. Today. Tomorrow. Some of it, maybe, by you. Build a wide professional learning network—inclusive of the scholars and educators mentioned here—to stay abreast of resources that will help your school library live the Competencies and Alignments under Include.

Interpretations of ALA's Library Bill of Rights explicitly make this call:

> Libraries are essential to democracy and self-government, to personal development and social progress, and to every individual's inalienable right to life, liberty, and the pursuit of happiness. To that end, libraries and library workers should embrace equity, diversity, and inclusion in everything that they do. (ALA 2017)

Everything that they do! Let's dive deeper into resources to support us.

AASL Position Statement on Diversity in the Organization

A key AASL Position Statement concerns the importance of diversity in the organization (AASL 2011) because diversity of identity in its many dimensions and intersectionalities enriches schools and our learners.

> In [the school] setting, diversity provides rich opportunities for school librarians to collaborate with educators and administrators to create meaningful learning experiences that foster cultural competence, sensitivity, appreciation, and respect for differences in the school library and classrooms. Persuasive benefits of fostering an inclusive environment are learner success and empowerment. (AASL 2018, 215)

The school librarian profession is not yet diverse enough in race, nationality, ethnicity, language, culture, and religion. As we work to change this reality, it's important that we address this need for the benefit of our learners *now* in our school libraries by bringing in school visitors, experts, and authors who represent a wide range of identities. Chapter 6, "Create with an Equitable Writer-in-Residence Model," centers this idea as a lens for equitable author visits.

AASL's Position Statement can also guide our professional learning networks (PLNs) in recognizing that multiple identities and intersectionalities should be evident in our PLNs—both in person and in the wide digital network of scholarship and resources that we access for the benefit of our practice. The resources here foreground learning from BIPOC scholars and authors and share learning from across the educational and library fields.

If you're looking for a list of follows to add to your digital PLN, the following scholars, authors, organizations, and practicing educators[1] consistently offer foundational learning that will help school librarians as we build our practices on the Shared Foundation of Include:

Abolitionist Teaching Network
Aeriale Johnson
Alex Shevrin Venet
Awo Okaikor Aryee-Price
Bettina Love
Britt Hawthorne
The Brown Bookshelf
Chad C. Everett
Christina Spears
Christine Tuttell
Christopher Emdin
Clint Smith
Cody Miller
Cornelius Minor
David Kirkland
Debbie Reese
Dena Simmons
Disability in Kidlit
Django Paris
Dulce-Marie Flecha
Ebony Elizabeth Thomas
Edith Campbell
#EduColor Movement
Erika Long
Gholdy Muhammad
Gloria Ladson-Billings
GLSEN
H. Samy Alim
Hasan Kwame Jeffries
IllumiNative
ISTE Digital Equity PLN
James E. Ford
Jess Lifshitz
Jesse Hagopian

Joel R. Garza
José Vilson
Julia E. Torres
Just Us Books
K. C. Boyd
Kelly Starling Lyons
Kelly Wickham Hurst
Kimberly Parker
Latinxs in KidLit
Laura Jimenez
Lauryn Mascareñaz
Learning for Justice
Lee & Low
Liz Kleinrock
Lorena Germán
Matthew Kay
NCTE
Paul Gorski
Pedro Noguera
Reading While White
Rethinking Schools
Rhonda Taylor Bullock
Robin DiAngelo
Sara K. Ahmed
Sarah Park Dahlen
Scott Bayer
Shana V. White
shea martin
Sheldon Eakins
Sonja Cherry-Paul
Teaching for Change
Teresa Bunner
Tiffany Jewell
Tricia Ebarvia
Val Brown
We Need Diverse Books
Yolanda Sealey Ruiz
Zaretta Hammond

This guide's amazing contributors—including Cicely Lewis, Kathryn Cole, and Ness Shortley—have included their social media handles in their bios. These sites are also "must follows" that will continue to enrich and inform our school library practice.

Foundational Visual Media, Sites, and Posts

"The Danger of a Single Story" by Chimamanda Ngozi Adichie
In this seminal TED Talk from 2009, Chimamanda Adichie describes the dangers inherent in a single story told about a people or community. Watch at https://www.ted.com/talks/chimamanda_adichie_the_danger_of_a_single_story.

***Defending Intellectual Freedom: LGBTQ+ Materials in School Libraries* (AASL)**
This guide, infographic, and applied framework use the AASL Standards Frameworks as scaffolding to support school librarians in addressing challenges related to censorship and in serving LGBTQ+ learners and families. Additional information on the use of this guide can be found in chapter 11, "Share through LGBTQ+-Inclusive School Libraries." Access at https://standards.aasl.org/project/lgbtq/.

***Developing Inclusive Learners and Citizens Activity Guide* (AASL)**

This helpful guide contains reflection activities and resources based on Include to help school librarians "nurture inclusive learning communities." Scenarios and activities are included to demonstrate how to foster balanced perspectives, global learning, empathy, tolerance, and equity in our school libraries. Access at https://standards.aasl.org/project/inclusive/.

"Don't Just Read about Racism—Read Stories about Black People Living" by Nic Stone

This powerful article unpacks the growing popularity of anti-racist titles in 2020 and why this approach is not enough. Nic Stone beautifully addresses the need for a wide range of books in our libraries that feature our teens' whole, joyful selves and that do not solely address trauma. Access at www.cosmopolitan.com/entertainment/books/a32770951/read-black-books-nic-stone/.

"An Equitable English Education Begins with Dignity" by Danielle Filipiak

This post, from the NCTE Standing Committee on Global Citizenship, highlights a dignity-centered practice whereby each child is seen as a valued member of a learning community. "If you say you love a young person but subscribe to beliefs or worldviews that position them as deficit, justify their mistreatment, or strip them of the ability to assert their full identities, then you are perpetuating violence, not love." Access at www2.ncte.org/blog/2019/04/an-equitable-english-education-begins-with-dignity/.

Gay, Lesbian and Straight Education Network (GLSEN)

GLSEN is a national organization supporting schools as they seek to build safe spaces for all youth and is a leading source of statistics on how LGBTQ+ youth are—or aren't—supported in schools. Visit the organization's site for free resources, including Educator Guides, Safe Space Kits, and curriculum ideas.

Learning for Justice (formerly Teaching Tolerance)

Learning for Justice, a project of the Southern Poverty Law Center, provides free resources for educators that are framed by social justice and antibias principles. The project's extensive resources include toolkits, lesson plans, webinars, and professional development guides. Learning for Justice resources are referenced multiple times throughout this guide and are featured in chapter 1, "Think with the Learning for Justice Social Justice Standards."

NCTE Committee Against Racism and Bias in the Teaching of English

The National Council of Teachers of English site explains that this committee's charge is "to investigate and make recommendations to counteract racism and racial bias in teaching materials, methods, and programs for language arts,

English, and humanities." In 2018 the committee released powerful resources that are available for download on the NCTE site: *What Anti-Racist Language Teachers Do* and *Qualities of Anti-Racist ELA Curricula.*

Opening Session Keynote from the 2019 ALA Annual Conference by Jason Reynolds

In his keynote address, Jason Reynolds spoke of libraries as "sacred spaces" where all are welcome and families can be built. "Maybe librarians are the architects of human libraries. . . . Imagine raising kids to be walking, talking libraries with their own reference desk in their head and heart, able to hold the stories of others who are different from them."

#OwnVoices Post by Corinne Duyvis

As a primary source of the #OwnVoices movement in youth literature—and to learn how and why she proposed the hashtag—read Corinne Duyvis's "#OwnVoices" post on her blog, *Corinne Duyvis—sci-fi & fantasy.* Access it at www.corinneduyvis.net/ownvoices/.

"Perceptions of Diversity in Book Reviews" by Malinda Lo

YA author and literature researcher Malinda Lo's powerful post on how diversity is treated in youth reviews is essential reading for anyone reading reviews and making book purchasing decisions. Find it on Diversity in YA at www.diversityinya.com/2015/02/perceptions-of-diversity-in-book-reviews/.

***The School Librarian's Role in Reading* (AASL)**

This position statement uses literacy research and the six Shared Foundations to examine the school librarian's responsibility in supporting learners' reading. Find it at www.ala.org/aasl/sites/ala.org.aasl/files/content/advocacy/statements/docs/AASL_Position_Statement_RoleinReading_2020-01-25.pdf.

We Are Kid Lit Collective founded by Edith Campbell

The website explains that the group "works to create materials and opportunities to recognize the humanity of Indigenous and People of Color (IPOC) in youth literature. . . . We look for ways to improve the literacies of IPOC children, promote books written by and about IPOC, and to encourage gatekeepers to bring a lens of critical literacy to their work." The collective's Summer Reading Lists are team curated and celebrate "diversity, inclusivity, and intersecting identities." The lists are a crucial resource, and school librarians can use them not only for titles to suggest to families over the summer but also for order lists and for read-alouds and class texts during the school year.

We Need Diverse Books

We're all aware of this amazing, necessary movement, but when is the last time you visited the organization's site at diversebooks.org? In addition to accessing their many programs and resources, you can download a Booktalking Kit designed to shed light on lesser-known books and to provide tips and tools for booktalking these titles with learners.

"Why Diverse Texts Are Not Enough" by Tricia Ebarvia
This powerful article details why including more diverse texts is only a preliminary step in creating equitable schools. Ebarvia includes specific steps and reflective questions for us as educators. The original article appeared in *Literacy Today* in 2019. Access a PDF version at triciaebarvia.org.

Essential Review Sites and Publishers

(Referenced in chapter 5, "Think with Read Woke")

- American Indians in Children's Literature
- Amistad Press
- Arte Público Press
- Booktoss
- The Brown Bookshelf
- CAKE Literary
- Cinco Puntos Press
- !Colorín Colorado!
- CrazyQuiltEdi
- Disability in Kidlit
- Diverse Book Finder (Picture Books)
- East West Discovery Press
- HighWater Press
- House of Anansi Press
- I'm Here, I'm Queer, What the Hell Do I Read?
- Interlude Press / Duet
- Just Us Books
- kiBooka
- KitaabWorld
- Lee & Low Books
- Latinxs in Kid Lit
- Make Me a World
- Oyate
- Reading While White
- Responsive Reads
- Rich in Color
- Social Justice Books (Teaching for Change)
- Versify
- We Need Diverse Books

Foundational Resources for School Librarians

Bishop, R. S. 1990. "Mirrors, Windows, and Sliding Glass Doors." *Perspectives: Choosing and Using Books for the Classroom* 6(3).

In this article, Dr. Rudine Sims Bishop introduces her seminal analogy for describing the importance of diverse youth literature. *Note:* Dr. Bishop should be cited whenever and wherever this analogy is used.

Dorr, C., and L. Deskins. 2018. *LGBTQAI+ Books for Children and Teens: Providing a Window for All.* Chicago, IL: ALA Editions.

This essential resource for school librarians curates recommended LGBTQAI+ titles and includes advice on starting discussions with youth and proactively dealing with censorship challenges, provides information about LGBTQAI+ terms, and details why LGBTQAI+ literature should be shared with all learners.

Dunbar-Ortiz, R., J. Mendoza, and D. Reese. 2019. *An Indigenous Peoples' History of the United States for Young People.* Boston, MA: Beacon Press.

The original book by Indigenous human rights advocate Roxanne Dunbar-Ortiz explored the roles that colonialism and genocidal policies played in forming the United States. This Young People's edition has been fully adapted by curriculum experts Drs. Mendoza and Reese for middle grade and YA readers and includes discussion topics and materials to help learners and school librarians think critically about history.

Hammond, Z. L. 2014. *Culturally Responsive Teaching and the Brain: Promoting Authentic Engagement and Rigor among Culturally and Linguistically Diverse Students.* Thousand Oaks, CA: Corwin Press.

In this innovative title, Zaretta Hammond marries neuroscience research with culturally responsive instruction to offer ten "key moves" to build engagement in schools and prepare our learners to become independent and empowered learners.

Hanley, M. S., and G. W. Noblit. 2009. *Cultural Responsiveness, Racial Identity, and Academic Success: A Review of Literature.* Prepared for the Heinz Endowments. Retrieved from www.heinz.org/UserFiles/Library/Culture-Report_FINAL.pdf.

This crucial paper discusses the connections between positive racial identity and learner achievement for youth of color.

Jewell, T. 2020. *This Book Is Anti-Racist: 20 Lessons on How to Wake Up, Take Action, and Do the Work.* Minneapolis, MN: Francis Lincoln Children's Books.

This engaging and interactive title for young people centers anti-racism work through honoring identities and learning history, framed in lessons and activities that empower, inform, and inspire the reader.

Kendi, I. X. 2017. *Stamped from the Beginning: The Definitive History of Racist Ideas in America*. London: The Bodley Head.

This National Book Award–winning title from Ibram Kendi, the founding director of the Anti-Racist Research and Policy Center at American University, illuminates a history of racist ideas in the United States and offers tools that can help expose—and transform—racist thinking.

Kendi, I. X. 2019. *How to Be an Antiracist*. New York, NY: One World.

In this memoir, Professor Ibram Kendi explains the structural nature of racism and lays out a key thesis: being not racist is not enough. We must be actively anti-racist and commit to disrupting all oppression, in all its intersectionalities, including oppression based in gender, identities, and body types.

Khailova, L. N. 2018. *The Stories We Share: A Guide to PreK–12 Books on the Experience of Immigrant Children and Teens in the United States*. Chicago, IL: ALA Editions.

To better support our learners who are first- and second-generation immigrants, this crucial resource identifies fiction and nonfiction titles that focus on the immigrant experience (organized by world region of birth), provides historical background, and offers identity-strengthening and empathy-building discussion starters. A review of literature on the need for all youth to experience diverse stories is included.

Kumasi, K. 2012. "Roses in the Concrete: A Critical Race Perspective on Urban Youth and School Libraries." *Knowledge Quest* 40 (5): 32–37.

Library Science Professor Kafi Kumasi applies Critical Race Theory to school library work, and the results are crucial for school librarians to understand. Includes learner impressions of school libraries.

Ladson-Billings, G. 2009. *The Dreamkeepers: Successful Teachers of African American Children*. 2d ed. San Francisco, CA: Jossey Bass Publishers.

In this second edition, Gloria Ladson-Billings—scholar of foundational concepts including *culturally relevant teaching* and the *opportunity gap*—highlights educators who are bringing the unique strengths of their learners into the classroom.

Manglik, G., and S. Siddique. 2019. *Muslims in Story: Expanding Multicultural Understanding through Children's and Young Adult Literature*. Chicago, IL: ALA Editions.

This beautiful title disrupts the ignorance that is often present in the portrayals of Muslims in media and popular culture by sharing curated titles that feature Muslim youth as heroes and by highlighting current and historical Islamic contributions and folktales. Hands-on activity ideas and discussion tools are included, as well as frequently asked questions on Islam, guidelines for evaluating Muslim children's literature, a timeline of Muslims in America, and a glossary of potentially unfamiliar words.

Minor, C. 2018. *We Got This. Equity, Access, and the Quest to Be Who Our Students Need Us to Be.* Portsmouth, NH: Heinemann.
In this engaging, empowering title, Cornelius Minor challenges teachers to confront "the scholastic manifestations of racism, sexism, ableism, and classism" by demonstrating how he plans lessons to ensure access and equity, offering suggestions on how to build classroom community, and sharing advocacy strategies for making changes to expand access for our learners.

Morris, M. W. 2016. *Pushout: The Criminalization of Black Girls in Schools.* New York, NY: The New Press.
Black girls represent 16 percent of female learners but almost 50 percent of female learners with a school-related arrest. In this powerful title, Morris highlights how the inequitable and institutionally racist policies and biased discipline practices in schools are pushing Black female learners out of school.

Morris, M. W. 2019. *Sing a Rhythm, Dance a Blues: Education for the Liberation of Black and Brown Girls.* New York, NY: The New Press.
This title continues the necessary conversation that Monique Morris introduced in *Pushout. Sing a Rhythm* includes solutions that are working in schools around the country to address the problems of biased discipline and inequitable policies that are pushing our Black female learners out of school.

Muhammad, G. 2020. *Cultivating Genius: An Equity Framework for Culturally and Historically Responsive Literacy.* New York, NY: Scholastic.
This guide presents a four-layered equity framework developed through the study of nineteenth-century Black literacy societies and is framed around four learning goals and pursuits: Identity Development, Skill Development, Intellectual Development, and Criticality. Includes practical approaches that are all grounded in recognizing the inherent genius in every learner.

Naidoo, J. C., and S. P. Dahlen. 2013. *Diversity in Youth Literature: Opening Doors through Reading.* Chicago, IL: ALA Editions.
This necessary resource includes contributions from a wide range of authors who share the historical trajectory of diverse youth literature, offer guidelines for evaluating and selecting titles, and suggest programs and strategies to promote diverse titles. In addition to presenting "traditional" categories, this title includes chapters on a wide range of categories of diverse literature, including incarceration, transnational adoption, and homelessness.

Oluo, I. 2018. *So You Want to Talk about Race.* Ashland, OR: Blackstone Publishing.
Being able to talk about race and racial inequities is necessary for school librarians seeking to build inclusive school spaces and meet Competencies related to Include. In this title, Oluo explains—in clear language—concepts that can bridge connections, broaden understandings, and disrupt inequities.

Paris, D., and H. S. Alim. 2017. *Culturally Sustaining Pedagogies: Teaching and Learning for Justice in a Changing World.* New York, NY: Teachers College Press.
This is the definitive resource on culturally sustaining pedagogies. This essential title includes examples of teaching that sustain the cultural practices, languages, and literacies of learners of color.

Reynolds, J., and I. X. Kendi. 2020. *Stamped: Racism, Antiracism, and You: A Remix of the National Book Award–Winning* Stamped from the Beginning. Boston, MA: Little, Brown.
This is a young adult version of Ibram X. Kendi's award-winning book, reimagined by Jason Reynolds and written to show that "while racist ideas have always been easy to fabricate and distribute, they can also be discredited. This book shines a light on the insidious forms of racist ideas—and on ways readers can identify and stamp out racist thoughts in their daily lives."

Singleton, G., and C. Linton. 2007. *Courageous Conversations about Race: A Field Guide for Achieving Equity in Schools.* Thousand Oaks, CA: Corwin Press.
This vital title offers strategies to disrupt inequities in schools by using "courageous conversations." Framed in Four Agreements, Six Conditions, and a Compass, the title explains these tools and guides educators in explorations of identity to create empowering and equitable learning communities in our schools.

Singleton, G., and J. P. Comer. 2013. *More Courageous Conversations about Race.* Thousand Oaks, CA: Corwin Press.
This companion title continues the work of the original, sharing success stories and challenges and providing clear strategies for "moving Courageous Conversations from racial equity theory to practice at every level."

Tatum, B. 2017. *"Why Are All the Black Kids Sitting Together in the Cafeteria?" and Other Conversations about Race.* Revised and updated. New York, NY: Basic Books.
This twentieth anniversary edition of the original 1997 classic on the psychology of racism is truly foundational reading for anyone seeking to understand

the dynamics of race in America—which should be every school librarian. "Straight talk about our racial identities is essential if we are serious about enabling communication across racial and ethnic divides."

NOTE

1. Thank you to Kathryn Cole who helped curate the digital PLN list.

APPENDIX B

Shelf Audits

The practice of conducting "diversity" audits on our school library collections—and additional school library elements including displays—is gaining traction. Any activity that requires us to assess the depth of our collections and reflect on what's missing or which communities are not represented can be beneficial for our learners. It can also be helpful to establish a baseline for your school library collection in terms of representation. Any diversity audit is only a piece of the puzzle, however.

Diversity audits are useful *only* if we are using the resulting data or process to change and improve our collecting. Our school libraries must represent "all members and their place in a global learning community by establishing and maintaining a collection of reading and information materials in formats that support the diverse developmental, cultural, social, and linguistic needs of the range of learners and their communities" (AASL 2018, School Library II.B.1.). If after we do a diversity audit, we are truly modifying *what* we are ordering and promoting and *how* we are ordering, then the audit is helping us represent our learners. If, however, we are only using an audit to tick off a box, that's not truly meeting a Competency. It's simply performative.

Meeting Competencies and Alignments through the AASL Standards is *active.* Audits of our collection must be part of an active collection management framework—and not be the only action. We cannot use them only as a stamp to show we've done something.

Auditing your collection is an activity that should be ongoing, not done just as a monumental, annual task. The check that I use in my collection is a "simple" shelf audit. It can be done quickly and consistently and gives me a snapshot for action I need. My shelf audit has flaws. It's assessing what is there on the shelf, so checked-out books aren't automatically captured. More problematically, it's also using white, cishet, and Christian as the norm and calculating what is *not*. I'll address both those flaws later in this appendix.

Some final thoughts about diversity audits for our collections. Collection purchasing and management systems, including Follett Titlewave and Mackin, have digital options for auditing our collections that can serve as another quick measurement to use as part of our ongoing assessments. However, no matter what audits we use—shelf, yearly, digital—there is no better check than ongoing, focused readers' advisory with our learners. Talking with learners and finding titles to match their interests inclusive of a wide range of identities are the best ways to find gaps in our collections. Those learner conversations are ultimately more important than any diversity audit we do of our titles.

Simple Shelf Audit

Step 1. Count the number of books on a randomly chosen shelf. This is our base or sample number.

N = ________

Step 2. Count the number of books that feature a main character from a marginalized community: race, disability, LGBTQ+, religion, language, country of origin. This is the set of books we'll be working with.

R = _______

If you know you have a book that would be here and it is checked out, go ahead and include it, but make sure to also add it to your N.

Step 3.

R / N = ______

This is your percentage of books that center characters from marginalized communities on this shelf.

Reflect for a moment on this percentage. What could be your school library goals for a number like this across your collection?

Keep in mind that this percentage is akin to the numbers in the infographic in appendix C. It is just a number—there is no measure for author or accuracy. So just like the publishing numbers in figure C.1, it can only get "worse" the more we dive in.

From here on out, we are looking only at our number from Step 2—our R number.

Step 4. Now let's see what percentage of our books centering characters from marginalized communities are #OwnVoices. First, count the number of #OwnVoices books.

OV = ________

How do we know if a book is #OwnVoices? This is where an always growing knowledge of authors across a range of identities is essential as we identify and order books. This is not us prying into our authors' lives—it is being aware of their self-stated identities that they've freely shared in articles, in interviews, or on social media. If you're unsure, do not include the book(s) in your OV number.

Step 5. Now let's get that percentage.

OV / R = _______

How high do we want this? *As high as possible.* This is a number we want to keep increasing. Absorb the number, and focus on growing it.

One of my favorite quotes from one of my favorite authors has become a defining framework for my collection. Malinda Lo wrote, "[B]ecause even though we need books that talk about race and racism, we also need books where characters of color can simply have the same kind of plot-driven adventures that white characters have all the time" (Lo 2015). We can adapt this idea across identities. Of course we need coming out stories, but we also need books in which LGBTQ+ characters are having plot-driven adventures. We need books in which disabled characters are having plot-driven adventures. *This is huge!* All our learners need to see wide representation of their whole selves. (This concept also connects to what Jaida referred to as "show the joy in our stories" in chapter 9.)

Step 6 (Optional). In an attempt to capture this wide collecting, I started checking my titles specifically for membership in either social issue or historical fiction categories. In looking at collecting habits of school librarians for a research project, I noticed that many titles featuring BIPOC characters were historical fiction as opposed to science fiction or fantasy. Are historical stories necessary? Of course, especially when they help us relearn erroneous history and center stories of marginalized people that have been erased. If the titles in your collection that feature BIPOC characters are *all* set in the past, however, that is highly problematic (particularly for Native/Indigenous stories). BIPOC characters need to be centered in the widest range of stories: past, present, future, alternate universes, speculative, stories in space, dystopian worldviews, fantasy worlds, and all.

If Your Collection Is Genrefied: Do Steps 1 through 4 on shelves that are *not* realistic fiction, focusing instead on fantasy, science fiction, romance, horror, and so on. Ensure that those genrefied shelves represent marginalized communities and foreground #OwnVoices titles.

If Your Collection Is Not Genrefied: On a "regular" shelf, after Step 5, count the number of R titles that are *not* social issue or historical fiction. This will be your P number. (Are there *amazing* #OwnVoices social issue and historical fiction titles in our school libraries? Of course. Of course! We need to keep purchasing and promoting those titles. We also need to be searching out contemporary and future "plot-driven adventures" to offer a wide and deep collection.)

P = _______

P / R = _______

This is your percentage of identified books that are outside the social issue and historical fiction categories. This is a number to reflect on—I cannot tell you what the "correct" percentage is. As we all know, effective collecting is extremely nuanced. This number should vary greatly by shelf. If your P numbers are extremely low, dedicate yourself to searching out more #OwnVoices titles across genres.

The Foundational Flaw in This Shelf Audit: This shelf audit uses white, cishet, Christian, and English-speaking as the norm and calculates what is not, perpetuating a problematic view of what is normal. While I am searching for, prioritizing, and celebrating all the titles that are not white, cishet, Christian, and English-speaking and attempting to raise that number to 85 percent or more for my school library, I am learning about the limitations in my audit and continue to modify it so that my foundational flaw is addressed.

APPENDIX C

Diversity in Publishing Infographic

The Key Commitment for the Shared Foundation of Include—"Demonstrate an understanding of and commitment to inclusiveness and respect for diversity in the learning community"—requires a school library collection that is flooded with books, displays, and instruction that reflect learners' lives. A school librarian who is casually collecting titles and expecting the publishing world to be offering a representative selection of books is enacting harm on their learners because the publishing world is far from representative of the learners in the United States today. The "casual" collector will be perpetuating the whiteness of children's literature.

In 2016 Dr. Sarah Park Dahlen, David Huyck, and Molly Beth Griffin published the infographic "Diversity in Children's Books 2015" (Dahlen, Huyck, and Griffin 2015) using publishing data from the Cooperative Children's Book Center (CCBC). It quickly went viral and was discussed on social media, published in articles, and included in conference presentations. It was an excellent, visual way for stakeholders to see the problems in publishing in the United States.

When my learners and I were preparing the #LibFive professional development (see chapter 9, "Think with the #LibFive"), we used the infographic on the 2015 data as a key talking piece in our discussion about how we can make school libraries more inclusive.

In June of 2019, Dr. Dahlen and David Huyck collaborated again on an updated infographic (figure C.1) using the 2018 data from the publishing statistics compiled by the librarians at the University of Wisconsin-Madison School of Education Cooperative Children's Book Center (Huyck and Dahlen 2019). This infographic indelibly portrays representation in youth books by revealing the low percentages of books published with BIPOC main characters. There are more youth books published with animal characters than there are the *combined* total numbers of books with American Indians/First Nations, Latinx, Asian Pacific Islander/Asian Pacific American, *and* African/African American characters. The presence of mirrors is an intentional nod to Dr. Bishop's mirrors and windows analogy. The white child in the infographic has an array of mirrors in which to see themselves reflected in a variety of realities, activities, dreams, and futures. All the other youth in the infographic have only one mirror—in some cases, ridiculously small—in which they are seeing only a single story or reflection of their experience.

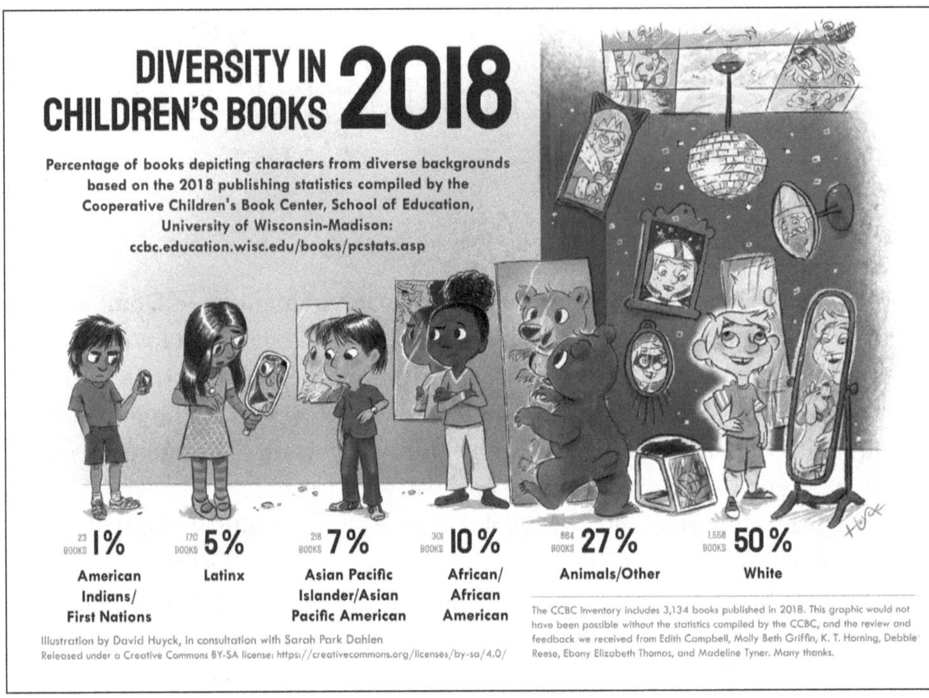

FIGURE C.1 / **Diversity in children's books 2018**

In her blog post[1] releasing the updated infographic, Dr. Dahlen highlighted a key element of the updated infographic:

> One important distinction between the 2015 and 2019 infographics is that we made a deliberate decision to crack a section of the children's mirrors [Bishop 1990] to indicate what Debbie Reese calls "funhouse mirrors" and Ebony Elizabeth Thomas calls "distorted funhouse mirrors of the self." Children's literature continues to misrepresent underrepresented communities, and we wanted this infographic to show not just the low quantity of existing literature, but also the inaccuracy and uneven quality of some of those books.

Dr. Dahlen suggests specific accompanying texts and resources to pair with the infographic to gain a full picture of the context surrounding these numbers, including Lee & Low's "Diversity Gap" blog posts, Debbie Reese's blog *American Indians in Children's Literature,* Edith Campbell's and Zetta Elliott's blogs, Maya Christina Gonzalez's "Children's Books as a Radical Act" blog posts, Malinda Lo's LGBTQ+ blog posts, We Need Diverse Books, Reading While White, and *Research on Diversity in Youth Literature.*

The power of this imagery showing the toxic disparities in U.S. publishing is undeniable. Also undeniable is school librarians' responsibility in shifting this reality. As school librarians, we should be prioritizing #OwnVoices literature from publishers and seeking out independent publishers that prioritize the work of BIPOC creators.

This infographic can clearly be used by school librarians to galvanize and demonstrate why we must disrupt the inequities and racism in publishing by intentionally and consistently foregrounding the active selection of #OwnVoices literature. Additionally, I have found it to be a helpful tool to share with school colleagues as they choose classroom texts and read-alouds and build classroom libraries. Remember, having an inclusive collection is never enough. We need to be displaying, reading, talking about, advocating for, and including reflective books in our school library spaces and instruction. If our learners don't see themselves represented in the texts privileged for use in the curriculum, how can they truly see themselves in the curriculum? Or feel empowered as valued members of our school community?

You can find a postcard edition of the infographic available for distribution that includes links to additional review sources at socialjusticebooks.org/diversity-graphic.

NOTE

1. https://readingspark.wordpress.com/2019/06/19/picture-this-diversity-in-childrens-books-2018-infographic/.

Resources and Works Cited

AASL American Association of School Librarians. 2018. "Defending Intellectual Freedom: LGBTQ+ Materials in School Libraries." https://standards.aasl.org/project/lgbtq.

———. 2019. "Developing Inclusive Learners and Citizens." https://standards.aasl.org/project/inclusive.

———. 2018. *National School Library Standards for Learners, School Librarians, and School Libraries*. ALA: Chicago.

———. 2011. "Position Statement on Diversity in the Organization." www.ala.org/aasl/advocacy/resources/statements/diversity.Acevedo, E. 2018. *The Poet X.* New York, NY: HarperCollins.

Acevedo, E. 2018. *The Poet X.* New York, NY: HarperCollins.

———. 2019. *With the Fire on High*. New York, NY: HarperCollins.

———. 2020. *Clap When You Land*. New York, NY: HarperCollins.

Adichie, C. 2009. "The Danger of a Single Story." Filmed July 2009 in Oxford, England. TED video, 18:34. www.ted.com/talks/chimamanda_adichie_the_danger_of_a_single_story.

ALA American Library Association. 2017. "Interpretations of the Library Bill of Rights." www.ala.org/advocacy/intfreedom/librarybill/interpretations.

Barack, Lauren. 2014. "LGBTQ and You: How to Support Your Learners." *School Library Journal*. www.slj.com/2014/05/diversity/lgbtq-you-how-to-support-your-learners/#.

Bintliff, A. 2014. "Talking Circles: For Restorative Justice and Beyond." Learning for Justice. July 22, 2014. www.learningforjustice.org/magazine/talking-circles-for-restorative-justice-and-beyond.

Bishop, R. S. 1990. "Mirrors, Windows, and Sliding Glass Doors." *Perspectives: Choosing and Using Books for the Classroom* 6(3).

Brault, M. M. 2011. *School-Aged Children with Disabilities in U.S. Metropolitan Statistical Areas: 2010*. U.S. Census Bureau. www.census.gov/prod/2011pubs/acsbr10-12.pdf.

Brown, L. X. Z. 2011. "The Significance of Semantics: Person-First Language; Why It Matters." *Autistic Hoya* (blog). August 4, 2011. www.autistichoya.com/2011/08/significance-of-semantics-person-first.html.

Bruce, A. J. 2015. "Allie's Reflections (Loudness in the Library Year Three, Part 4)." *The Bank Street Center for Children's Literature* (blog). August 13, 2015. https://bankstreetcollegeccl.wordpress.com/2015/08/13/allies-reflections-loudness-in-the-library-year-three-part-4/

———. 2013. "Part I: Are All Covers Created Equal? Bank Street 6th-Graders Weigh In on RACE." *The Bank Street Center for Children's Literature* (blog). March 18, 2013. https://bankstreetcollegeccl.wordpress.com/2013/03/18/part-i-are-all-covers-created-equal-bank-street-6th-graders-weigh-in-on-race/.

———. 2015. "Rewriting History: American Indians, Europeans, and an Oak Tree (Loudness in the Library Year Three, Part 3)." *The Bank Street Center for Children's Literature* (blog). August 12, 2015. https://bankstreetcollegeccl.wordpress.com/2015/08/12/rewriting-history-american-indians-europeans-and-an-oak-tree-loudness-in-the-library-year-three-part-3/.

Bruchac, J., and G. Ross. 1995. *The Story of the Milky Way: A Cherokee Tale* (V. A. Stroud, Illus.). New York, NY: Dial Books.

CDC Centers for Disease Control and Prevention. 2017. *Lesbian, Gay, Bisexual, and Transgender Health*. www.cdc.gov/lgbthealth/youth.htm.

Cisneros, S. 1989. *The House on Mango Street*. New York, NY: Vintage Books.

Confederated Salish and Kootenai Tribes. 2005. *Beaver Steals Fire: A Salish Coyote Story* (S. Sandoval, Illus.). Lincoln, NE: University of Nebraska Press.

Crenshaw, K. 1989. "Demarginalizing the Intersection of Race and Sex: A Black Feminist Critique of Antidiscrimination Doctrine, Feminist Theory and Antiracist Politics." *University of Chicago Legal Forum* 1989 (1): 139–167.

Curwood, J. S. 2013. "Redefining Normal: A Critical Analysis of (Dis)ability in Young Adult Literature." *Children's Literature in Education* 44:15–28.

DO-IT Center. n.d. "Universal Access: Making Library Resources Accessible to People with Disabilities." www.washington.edu/doit/universal-access-making-library-resources-accessible-people-disabilities#L1.

Dunn, P. 2015. *Disabling Characters: Representations of Disability in Young Adult Literature*. New York: Peter Lang Publishing.

Facing History and Ourselves. 2020. "Socratic Seminar: Rationale." www.facinghistory.org/resource-library/teaching-strategies/socratic-seminar.

Gansworth, E. 2013. *If I Ever Get Out of Here*. New York, NY: Arthur A. Levine Books.

Gorski, P. 2019. "Avoiding Racial Equity Detours." *Educational Leadership* 76 (7): 56–61.

Grandmont, M. 2017. "Crafting and Conducting a Successful Socratic Seminar." *NCTE Blog*. December 9, 2017. www2.ncte.org/blog/2017/12/crafting-conducting-successful-socratic-seminar/.

Guerrero, Diane. 2016. *In the Country We Love: My Family Divided*. With Michelle Burford. New York: St. Martin's Griffin.

Hale, N. 2014. *Treaties, Trenches, Mud, and Blood*. New York, NY: Abrams.

Hanley, M. S., and G. W. Noblit. 2009. *Cultural Responsiveness, Racial Identity and Academic Success: A Review of Literature*. Prepared for The Heinz Endowments. www.heinz.org/UserFiles/Library/Culture-Report_FINAL.pdf.

Harrington, L. 2011. *Alice Bliss*. New York, NY: Pamela Dorman Books.

Henken, V. J., and S. Krashen. 2015. "The Naruto Breakthrough: The Home Run Book Experience and English Language Development." *Language Magazine* 15 (1): 32–35.

Hollingsworth, L., M. Didelot, and J. Smith. 2003. "REACH Beyond Tolerance: A Framework for Teaching Children Empathy and Responsibility." *Journal of Humanistic Counseling, Education and Development* 42 (2): 139–151.

Hughes-Hassell, Sandra, Pauletta Brown Bracy, and Casey H. Rawson, eds. 2016. *Libraries, Literacy, and African American Youth*. Santa Barbara, CA: Libraries Unlimited.

Huyck, D., and S. P. Dahlen. 2019. "Diversity in Children's Books 2018" (infographic). *sarahpark.com* (blog). June 19, 2019. Created in consultation with Edith Campbell, Molly Beth Griffin, K. T. Horning, Debbie Reese, Ebony Elizabeth Thomas, and Madeline Tyner, with statistics compiled by the Cooperative Children's Book Center, School of Education, University of Wisconsin–Madison, http://ccbc.education.wisc.edu/books/pcstats.asp; https://readingspark.wordpress.com/2019/06/19/picture-this-diversity-in-childrens-books-2018-infographic/.

Huyck, D., S. P. Dahlen, and M. B. Griffin. 2016. "Diversity in Children's Books 2015" (infographic). *sarahpark.com* (blog). September 14, 2016. Statistics compiled by the Cooperative Children's Book Center, School of Education, University of Wisconsin–Madison, https://ccbc.education.wisc.edu/books/

pcstats.asp; https://readingspark.wordpress.com/2016/09/14/picture-this-reflecting-diversity-in-childrens-book-publishing/.

International Institute for Restorative Practices. n.d. "What Is Restorative Practices?" www.iirp.edu/index.php?option=com_content&view=article&id=8&Itemid=167.

Iturbe, Antonio. 2017. *The Librarian of Auschwitz.* Translated by Lilit Thwaites. New York: Henry Holt.

Kosciw, J. G., C. M. Clark, N. L. Truong, and A. D. Zongrone. 2020. *The 2019 National School Climate Survey: The Experiences of Lesbian, Gay, Bisexual, Transgender, and Queer Youth in Our Nation's Schools.* New York: GLSEN.

Kuhlthau, C., L. Maniotes, and A. Caspari. 2015. *Guided Inquiry Learning in the 21st Century.* Santa Barbara, CA: Libraries Unlimited.

Kumasi, K. 2012. "Roses in the Concrete: A Critical Race Perspective on Urban Youth and School Libraries." *Knowledge Quest* 40 (5): 32–37.

Kunai, I., and C. Ryan. 2007. *Manga as a Teaching Tool: Comic Books without Borders.* California Teachers of English to Speakers of Other Languages Conference.

Ladson-Billings, G. 2006. "From the Achievement Gap to the Education Debt: Understanding Achievement in U.S. Schools." *Educational Researcher* 35 (7): 3–12.

Lance, K. C., and D. E. Kachel. 2018. *Why School Librarians Matter: What Years of Research Tell Us.* www.kappanonline.org/lance-kachel-school-librarians-matter-years-research/.

Lo, M. 2015. "Recommended Read: 'The Third Twin' by CJ Omololu." *Malinda Lo* (blog). February 24, 2015. www.malindalo.com/blog/tag/The+Third+Twin.

Maiers, A. 2012. *Classroom Habitudes: Teaching Habits and Attitudes for 21st Century Learning.* Bloomington, IN: Solution Tree.

Mairs, N. 2008. "Sex and Death and the Crippled Body: A Meditation." In *Disability and the Teaching of Writing: A Critical Sourcebook,* edited by C. Lewiecki-Wilson and B. J. Brueggemann, 234–237). Boston, MA, and New York: Bedford/St. Martin's.

Manassah, T. 2019. "A New Vision of School." *Morningside Center for Teaching Social Responsibility* (blog). May 9, 2019. www.morningsidecenter.org/news/new-vision-school.

Matam, P., E. Acevedo, and G. Yamazawa. 2014. *Unforgettable.* Performed at the 2014 National Poetry Slam. www.youtube.com/watch?v=Xvah3E1fP20.

Myers, C., and H. Bersani Jr. 2008. "Ten Quick Ways to Analyze Children's Books for Ableism." *Rethinking Schools* 23(2).

NAMI National Alliance on Mental Illness. 2016. "Mental Health by the Numbers." www.nami.org/learn-more/mental-health-by-the-numbers.

National Paideia Center. n.d. "Paideia Socratic Seminar." www.paideia.org/our-approach/paideia-seminar/index.

NCTE Committee Against Racism and Bias in the Teaching of English. 2018. "First-Day Actions for a Culturally Sustaining Classroom Environment." *NCTE Blog.* August 23, 2018. www2.ncte.org/blog/2018/08/first-day-actions-for-a-culturally-sustaining-classroom-environment/.

Noguera, P. 2003. "The Trouble with Black Boys: The Role and Influence of Environmental and Cultural Factors on the Academic Performance of African American Males." *Urban Education* 38 (4): 431–549.

Older, D. J. (2015, August 24). Diversity = Honesty (with image, tweets) · djolder. Retrieved October 21, 2016, from https://storify.com/djolder/we-need-honest-books.

Paris, D., and H. S. Alim. 2017. *Culturally Sustaining Pedagogies: Teaching and Learning for Justice in a Changing World.* New York, NY: Teacher's College Press.

PEN America. 2017. *The PEN Ten: Banned Books Edition with Meg Medina.* September 24, 2017. https://pen.org/the-pen-ten-with-meg-medina/.

Quayson, A. 2007. *Aesthetic Nervousness: Disability and the Crisis of Representation.* New York: Columbia University Press.

Reese, D. 2013. "Critical Indigenous Literacies." In *The SAGE Handbook of Early Childhood Literacy,* edited by J. Larson and J. Marsh, 251–263. Thousand Oaks, CA: SAGE.

———. 2018. "Critical Indigenous Literacies: Selecting and Using Children's Books about Indigenous Peoples." *Language Arts* 95 (6): 389–393.

Retief, M., and R. Letšosa. 2018. "Models of Disability: A Brief Overview." *HTS Teologiese Studies / Theological Studies* 74 (1).

Rodanas, K. 1995. *Dragonfly's Tale.* New York, NY: Clarion Books.

Schott Foundation. 2014. *Restorative Practices: Fostering Healthy Relationships and Promoting Positive Discipline in Schools.* http://schottfoundation.org/sites/default/files/restorative-practices-guide.pdf.

Smith, C. L. 2000. *Jingle Dancer.* Illustrated by C. Van Wright and Y. Hu. New York, NY: Morrow Junior Books.

Smith, D., D. Fisher, and N. Frey. 2015. *Better Than Carrots or Sticks: Restorative Practices for Positive Classroom Management.* Alexandria, VA: ASCD.

Sparks, S., and A. Harwin. 2018. "Schools See Steep Drop in Librarians, New Analysis Finds." *Education Week.* www.edweek.org/ew/articles/2018/05/16/schools-see-steep-drop-in-librarians-new.html.

Spier, P. 1992. *Noah's Ark.* New York, NY: Doubleday.

Tatum, B. D. 2017. *"Why Are All the Black Kids Sitting Together in the Cafeteria?" and Other Conversations about Race.* Revised and updated. New York: Basic Books.

Teaching Tolerance. n.d. "About Teaching Tolerance." Accessed August 10, 2019. www.tolerance.org/about (site discontinued).

Teaching Tolerance. 2018. *Social Justice Standards: The Teaching Tolerance Anti-Bias Framework.* Southern Poverty Law Center. www.learningforjustice.org/sites/default/files/2020-09/TT-Social-Justice-Standards-Anti-bias-framework-2020.pdf.

Torres, J. E. 2018a. "Be the Lighthouse." *juliaetorres.blog* (blog). September 17, 2018. https://juliaetorres.blog/2018/09/17/be-the-lighthouse/.

———. 2018b. "Hold Fast to Dreams." *juliaetorres.blog* (blog). June 23, 2018. https://juliaetorres.blog/2018/06/23/hold-fast-to-dreams/.

Toure, C. 2019. "Poetic Expressions: Slamming in the Library." *Knowledge Quest* (blog). April 18, 2019. https://knowledgequest.aasl.org/poetic-expressions-slamming-in-the-library/.

Valenza, J. 2008. "Library as Domestic Metaphor." *Neverending Search* (blog). August 25, 2008. http://blogs.slj.com/neverendingsearch/2008/08/25/library-as-domestic-metaphor/.

Vasquez, V. 2014. *Negotiating Critical Literacies with Young Children.* New York, NY: Routledge.

Wellman, David. 1977. *Portraits of White Racism.* Cambridge: Cambridge University Press.

Winkler, E. N. 2009. "Children Are Not Colorblind: How Young Children Learn Race." *PACE: Practical Approaches for Continuing Education* 3, no. 3 (August): 1–8.

Wright, T. M. 2015. "Why Do We Need Diverse Books in Non-Diverse Schools?" *The Open Book Blog.* March 25, 2015. http://blog.leeandlow.com/2015/03/25/why-do-we-need-diverse-books-in-non-diverse-schools.

Yorio, K. 2019. "Denver Teacher Librarian Brings Students Back to Library." *School Library Journal* (blog). April 25, 2019. www.slj.com/?detailStory=denver-teacher-librarian-brings-students-back-to-library.

About the Author

Julie Stivers is the librarian at Mount Vernon Middle School, an alternative public school in Raleigh, North Carolina. Her work has been published in *Knowledge Quest, School Libraries Worldwide, School Library Journal,* and *YALS,* and she was named a 2019 *Library Journal* Mover and Shaker. She worked alongside her ALA Emerging Leaders group to create *Defending Intellectual Freedom: LGBTQ+ Materials in School Libraries.* Her research and practical interests include culturally sustaining pedagogy, building inclusive library spaces, and exploring the power of manga and anime with her students. Find her on Twitter: @BespokeLib.

Contributors

Rachel Altobelli is the director of library services and instructional materials for Albuquerque Public Schools. Her work has appeared in *Knowledge Quest,* in *American Libraries,* on the *KQ* website, and on the *School Library Journal* website. Rachel served on the 2019–2020 AASL Presidential Initiative Task Force, focusing on issues of equity, diversity, and inclusion. She was privileged to be the AASL member guide for the group of ALA Emerging Leaders who created *Defending Intellectual Freedom: LGBTQ+ Materials in School Libraries.* She is passionate about advocating for the representation of all learners in school library collections.

Allie Jane Bruce is an adventurer, traveler, critical thinker, and lifelong learner. She entered the field of children's literature via a straight-out-of-college job at Politics and Prose bookstore in Washington, D.C., and went on to gain her master's degree in library science and education from the Pratt Institute in New York City. She cofounded ReadingWhileWhite.com, worked as children's librarian at the Bank Street College of Education for six years, and served on the 2016 Newbery Committee.

Anita Cellucci is the school librarian and K–12 Library Department head at Westborough (Massachusetts) High School and a teaching lecturer for Plymouth State University (New Hampshire). She is the author of "Using Inquiry Tools to Activate Reflection and Assess Student Learning" in the book *Guided Inquiry Design in Action: High School* (Libraries Unlimited, 2017). Anita has also published articles in publications such as *School Library Journal* and *Teacher Librarian* and is a monthly columnist for *School Library Connection*'s "Full Voice." For her work in relation to mental health and social-emotional learning, she was named a 2019 *Library Journal* Mover and Shaker and received the School Librarian of the Year 2016 Finalist Award.

Kathryn Cole is a librarian at Northside Elementary in Chapel Hill, North Carolina. In 2016 she was recognized with ALA's *I Love My Librarian* award for community service. As an active leader in her school's equity team, Kathryn has shared equity practices through library service at North Carolina's "Let's Talk Race" conference and other state and national conferences. Most recently, she was presented with the Mary U. Andrews Chair for Excellence in Teaching Literacy. She encourages all school librarians to reimagine how school libraries can serve as joyful community spaces that center and engage the families they serve. Find her on Twitter: @KatColeReads.

Cesar Falcon is a student at Athens Drive High School in Raleigh, North Carolina. He co-wrote and co-presented professional development on the *#LibFive: Five Key Foundations for Building Inclusive Libraries* at the Wake County Public School System (WCPSS) Convergence Conference and at the North Carolina School Library Media Association Conference. He participated in the WCPSS Summer Writing Institute for three summers where he wrote and performed original poetry.

Jose Gomez is a student at North Wake College and Career Academy in Wake Forest, North Carolina. He co-wrote and co-presented professional development on the *#LibFive: Five Key Foundations for Building Inclusive Libraries* at the Wake County Public School System (WCPSS) Convergence Conference and at the North Carolina School Library Media Association Conference.

Kimberly Hirsh, PhD, is a researcher and consultant whose research interests include fan studies, making, connected learning, information literacy, school librarianship, and youth services in libraries. Before beginning her doctoral program, Kimberly worked as public communications specialist and managing editor for LEARN NC, a university outreach program that shared innovative teaching techniques with K-20 educators. She has also been a high school Latin teacher and middle school librarian. She shares her research at kimberlyhirsh.com.

Sandra Hughes-Hassell, PhD, is a professor in the School of Information and Library Science at the University of North Carolina at Chapel Hill. In her current research, she focuses on social justice issues in youth library services. She has written and presented extensively on culturally relevant pedagogy, critical race theory, and the role of libraries in serving youth of color. Her most recent project is the development of a research-based professional development curriculum that includes a suite of blended professional development experiences focused on cultural competence, culturally relevant pedagogy, and equity literacy. Project READY: Reimagining Equity and Access for Diverse Youth is funded by a grant from the Institute of Museum and Library Services (http://projectready.web.unc.edu/).

Cicely Lewis, the 2020 SLJ Librarian of the Year, is a school librarian with a passion for creating lovers of reading. In 2019 she was named a *Library Journal* Mover and Shaker and Georgia Library Media Specialist of the Year. In 2017 she started the Read Woke challenge, requiring her students to read books that challenge the social norm and amplify voice. Using this platform, she has inspired the nation to Read

Woke, with educators across the world joining in and sharing the movement with their students. Cicely shares her book recommendations in her bimonthly column in *School Library Journal* and is currently working on her own "woke" young adult novel. Follow her on Twitter @cicelythegreat or check out her blog *cicelythegreat.*

Jaida Morris is a student at Enloe High School in Raleigh, North Carolina. She co-wrote and co-presented professional development on the *#LibFive: Five Key Foundations for Building Inclusive Libraries* at the Wake County Public School System (WCPSS) Convergence Conference and at the North Carolina School Library Media Association Conference. She also co-presented on *Books You'll WANT to Read* at the WCPSS Young Women's Summit. She is a member of her high school track team, a JROTC student, and a former football manager. She is passionate about helping her community and bettering herself and the world around her. Her future goals include obtaining a degree in sports medicine, becoming an author, presenting at conferences, and becoming an activist.

Liz Porter is the school librarian at Menchaca Elementary School in Austin, Texas. She received her BA in French from Oberlin College in Ohio, and her love of languages is evident in her library's collection of Spanish-language and bilingual texts. After working as a teacher assistant at a local elementary school, she enrolled in the University of North Carolina at Chapel Hill's Graduate School of Information and Library Science. There she was able to channel her passion for social justice into a master's paper annotating children's and young adult texts that feature social action. She is continually inspired by fellow librarians and educators who work to encourage kids' love of reading, inquiry, and participation in this information-rich world!

Casey H. Rawson teaches research methods and youth services at the School of Information and Library Science at the University of North Carolina at Chapel Hill. She also works with Project READY (ready.web.unc.edu) to create racial equity-focused online and face-to-face professional development for school librarians and other educators. Her research interests include equity and inclusion in youth services librarianship, instruction in school and public libraries, and education of LIS professionals. She has written, taught, and presented widely in these areas. Dr. Rawson holds a PhD and an MSLS in information and library science, an MAT in middle grades education, and a BS in biology.

Dr. Debbie Reese, tribally enrolled at Nambé Pueblo, was an assistant professor in American Indian Studies at the University of Illinois at Urbana-Champaign (UIUC). Prior to that, she taught in UIUC's College of Education and its School of Information Sciences (now an iSchool). Her book chapters and articles in professional and academic journals are used in LIS, English, and education courses in the United States and Canada. Her website, American Indians in Children's Literature, is widely recognized as an authoritative source of information. In 2018 the American Library Association's ALSC selected her to deliver the prestigious 2019 May Hill Arbuthnot Lecture.

Juan Rivera is the school librarian at A. Philip Randolph High School in West Harlem. As a 2018 ALA Emerging Leader, Juan worked alongside a team of public and school librarians to create *Defending Intellectual Freedom: LGBTQ+ Materials for School Libraries,* a resource guide from AASL. He is a member of the New York State Education Department's Regents Advisory Council on Libraries and a board member of the New York City School Librarians' Association. He has presented at the New York Comic Con on "Building a Culture of Reading: Comics, Graphic Novels and Manga in Schools." Follow him on Twitter: @libraryjuan.

Ness Shortley is the librarian and digital learning co-lead at Horton Middle School in Pittsboro, North Carolina, where she works with each student and teacher to make Horton a learning community that includes everyone. She received a 2019 AASL Inspire Grant and a YALSA and Dollar General Digital Equipment Grant. She is a 2020 Cybils Awards round 1 panelist for middle grade fiction and was previously a member of the 2020 blogging team for YALSA's Best Fiction for Young Adults and the 2019 Odyssey Award committee. She is committed to making the library a loving, equitable, and inclusive space for all students. She tweets @sewbrarian.

Jennifer Sturge is the teacher specialist for school libraries and digital learning for Calvert County (Maryland) Public Schools. Jennifer believes that a strong school library can be the catalyst for lifelong learning and can make an enduring impact on the life of every child. Jennifer was a 2017–2018 Lilead Fellow for School Library Leaders. She blogs for Programming Librarian, coauthoring posts with librarian Donna Mignardi. She also blogs for *Knowledge Quest* and has been published by *School Library Journal.* Jennifer is an adjunct professor and is currently pursuing her doctorate in educational leadership from Point Park University.

Julia E. Torres is a teacher-librarian for the Montbello Campus serving five schools within the Far Northeast region of Denver Public Schools. Formerly a teacher of AP English language/literature, Julia has served Colorado language arts teachers as vice-president and president of the regional National Council of Teachers of English (NCTE) affiliate—the Colorado Language Arts Society. As a teacher and activist committed to education as a practice of freedom, Julia grounds her practice in the work of empowering students to use language arts to fuel resistance and positive social transformation. In cooperation with The Educator Collaborative, Julia facilitates workshops about antibias and anti-racist education and social justice. Julia also serves on several local and national boards and committees promoting educational equity and progressivism.

Chiquita Toure is a school librarian at Eastmoor Academy in Columbus, Ohio. She is the advisor for the Warrior Words Writing Club and a blogger for *Knowledge Quest*. She is also a virtual coach for early career educators for the National Education Association. She was selected to serve as a member of the 2019–2020 AASL Presidential Task Force on Diversity and Inclusion.

Index

An italicized page number indicates an illustration or table.